35.00
80E

30

Critical Essays on Joseph Conrad

Critical Essays on Joseph Conrad

Ted Billy

G. K. Hall & Co. • Boston, Massachusetts

Library of Congress Cataloging in Publication Data

Critical essays on Joseph Conrad.

(Critical essays on modern British literature)
Includes index.
1. Conrad, Joseph, 1857–1924 — Criticism and interpretation.   I.
Billy, Theodore.   II. Series.
PR6005.04Z594   1987   823'.912   86-29494
ISBN 0-8161-8763-0

This publication is printed on permanent/durable acid-free paper
MANUFACTURED IN THE UNITED STATES OF AMERICA

CRITICAL ESSAYS ON BRITISH LITERATURE

Ted Billy's informative introduction begins with biographical material relevant to Conrad's fiction and proceeds to a discussion of his letters and personality before presenting a comprehensive overview of the major critical questions associated with Conrad's work. These include questions of Conrad's place in literature, especially his modernity, his technical experimentation, his language, and his association with Ford and impressionism. The bibliography of works Billy cites in his discussion will be especially helpful to students of Conrad's novels.

In his comprehensive selection of essays, Billy chooses five which provide overviews of different critical aspects of Conrad's work: historical perspective, narrative structure, plot, and language. Each of the remaining six essays concentrates on a major novel: *Lord Jim*, *Heart of Darkness*, *Nostromo*, *Victory*, *Under Western Eyes*, and *The Secret Agent*. The range of critical stances covers the whole critical spectrum from traditional New Criticism to postmodern approaches.

Zack Bowen, GENERAL EDITOR

University of Delaware

*To my mother and father
and
to the students of
the University of Delaware*

CONTENTS

ACKNOWLEDGMENTS

First and most importantly, I wish to express my gratitude to Zack Bowen for his guidance and support throughout this endeavor. I am also indebted to the editors who responded so promptly and positively to my requests to reprint articles from their scholarly journals. From among these, I must single out for special mention David Leon Higdon, editor of *Conradiana*, who provided valuable information and timely counsel. Finally, I want to thank Milena and Richard Davison for their thoughtful suggestions and constant encouragement.

INTRODUCTION

No other novelist (excepting, perhaps, James Joyce) has had a more profound and pervasive influence on twentieth-century fiction than Joseph Conrad. In a relatively brief literary career, he produced a distinctive body of work that remains unique in British literary history. The authors who inspired Conrad are as diverse as his modern and contemporary successors. Cooper, Marryat, Balzac, Daudet, Maupassant, Flaubert, James, and Turgenev shaped Conrad's artistic sensibility; patently Conradian themes and narrative techniques are apparent in the work of authors as varied as Fitzgerald, Hemingway, Eliot, Faulkner, Gide, Greene, Bellow, Fowles, and Kosinski. From the outset of his literary career, however, Conrad's fiction has been subject to reductive criticism that attempts to place his work in a convenient tradition or else to associate him with writers of his generation. Thus, early reviewers and modern critics have stereotyped Conrad variously as a romantic, a realist, an impressionist, a symbolist, a modernist, an existentialist, a nihilist, and even a romantic realist. He has been called another Kipling, a second Melville, a Polish Dostoevsky, a lesser James, and a precursor of Camus and Sartre. Such labels provoked amusement from Conrad rather than rage (except when he was termed a spinner of sea yarns). But even Conrad's most recent commentators continue to dispute his consecration as either the last Victorian or the first modernist. Cedric Watts acknowledges the futility of trying to simplify Conrad's complex nature: "In Conrad's writing we see a combination of nineteenth-century and twentieth-century preoccupations; he stands at the intersection of the late Victorian and the early modernist cultural phases; he is both romantic and anti-romantic, both conservative and subversive" (*A Preface* 46). To understand Conrad, one must consider his different faces and divergent phases.

I

Chronologically, of course, Conrad belongs to the Victorian Era. Born 3 December 1857 as Jósef Teodor Konrad Korzeniowski (at Berdyczów, in the Ukraine), he was the only child of Apollo and Ewa (Eva)

1

Korzeniowski, both of whom belonged to the Polish gentry. His father, a translator as well as a revolutionist, was arrested by Russian police in 1861 and charged with participation in an unsuccessful political insurrection. In 1862 both Apollo and Ewa were sentenced to exile in Vologda (in Northern Russia) after being convicted of subversive actions. Conrad accompanied his parents into exile and became the sole companion of his father after the death of Ewa in 1865. For the next four years he remained under the influence of his father, whose bereavement, failing health, and political pessimism made a lasting impression on young Conrad.[1] After the death of Apollo in 1869, Conrad was cared for by his maternal uncle, Tadeusz Bobrowski, whose cautious conservatism sharply contrasted with his father's passionate radicalism. Zdzisław Najder describes these authority figures as polarized personalities; "Apollo was the very opposite of Tadeusz: emotional and impulsive, he made close friends easily, whereas Tadeusz had none; deeply religious but at the same time a radical 'Red': a rebel and conspirator while Bobrowski was a rationalist, skeptic, and political conformist" (*Joseph Conrad: A Chronicle* 165). As early as 1872, Conrad conceived the idea of going to sea, perhaps inspired by his enthusiastic reading of Marryat and Cooper. Two years later his uncle granted him permission to leave landlocked Poland for Marseilles and maritime service. Conrad's decision to leave his homeland has provoked extensive commentary among his biographers. Jocelyn Baines attributes this momentous decision to young Conrad's intense dislike for "the conventional, disciplined school life to which he had been forced to submit and . . . he therefore longed primarily to escape to freedom and adventure, a form of psychological, rather than political claustrophobia" (31). Frederick Karl agrees that Conrad desired to escape from a restrictive environment and to free himself from the legalities that made him subject to Russian military service (*Joseph Conrad* 120). Many critics, particularly Gustave Morf, have speculated on the psycho-literary consequences of what they perceive as Conrad's abandonment of Poland. (Betrayal, after all, is a prominent motif in his fiction.) But it remains an open question to what degree Conrad felt guilty about his departure from Poland. (Guilt did not prevent him from taking his whole family on an extended visit to his homeland just before the outbreak of World War I.)

Conrad climaxed his obscure four-year career in the French merchant marine with an unsuccessful suicide attempt in 1878. For many years, biographers accepted the romantic duel described in *The Arrow of Gold* as a thinly disguised version of the author's own experience. But the publication of a letter from Bobrowski clarified the situation: the story of Conrad's "duel" was designed to conceal a more embarrassing deed (Baines 44–45). Romance may have played a role in his flirtation with self-destruction, but gambling debts apparently precipitated Conrad's desperate decision. Once rescued from his physical and financial maladies by his uncle, Conrad signed on to his first British ship, the *Skimmer of the Sea*, embarking on sixteen years of service under "the red ensign."[2] In 1886 Conrad became a naturalized British subject and passed his examination for the Master's Certificate. But he found commands difficult to obtain, and he served as captain only once, in 1888, aboard the *Otago*. By the next year, he had already begun his first novel (*Almayer's Folly*) and carried it to the Belgian Congo, where his appointment as a steamboat captain led to the undermining of his health. He spent much of 1891 convalescing, and (though he continued to inquire about the possibility of a command years after his first novel) he left the merchant marine in 1894, the year of his uncle's death and of the completion of *Almayer's Folly* (published in 1895 and dedicated to Bobrowski).

Why did Conrad choose to write fiction in English rather than in his native Polish or French, his second language? Baines argues that Conrad had been exposed to English and Englishmen for more than ten years prior to taking pen in hand. He also notes that the Congo diary is written in English, though Conrad was among French-speaking people while he kept the diary. Baines affirms that English was a natural choice because Conrad "had absorbed much of the idiom of the language" (153). Najder cites Conrad's need to gain command of English to pass his Master's examination as a contributing factor, and he notes that Conrad wrote several letters in English long before the composition of *Almayer's Folly*. However, Najder qualifies Conrad's public stance on his choice of language:

> It is true that his English was not a matter of "adoption" but simply a result of partly accidental turns his life had taken. Nevertheless, Conrad wished to infuse his life, and particularly the public aspect of it that he regarded as most precious — his works of fiction — with the sense of overriding purposefulness; he did not want the tricky problem . . . to appear to have been determined by external circumstances.
>
> And yet this is exactly what happened: making a start on *Almayer's Folly* Korzeniowski did not "choose" the language. For eleven years he had been in daily contact with English-speaking people, he spoke English, read English books, he even gradually accepted the English point of view on political matters. (*Joseph Conrad: A Chronicle* 115–16)

One must also consider England's prestigious position as a sea power and the large English-reading public on both sides of the Atlantic as factors in Conrad's affirmation of English as his literary language.

In 1896 Conrad published *An Outcast of the Islands* and married Jessie George shortly thereafter. (Their marriage produced two sons, Borys and John.) Conrad hit his stride as an artist with *The Nigger of the "Narcissus"* (1897) and for the next fourteen years created a series of major works of unquestionable merit: *Lord Jim* (1900), *Heart of Darkness* (1902), *Typhoon* (1903), *Nostromo* (1904), *The Secret Agent* (1907) and *Under Western Eyes* (1911). The completion of the latter work, Conrad's Russian novel, resulted in the author's nervous breakdown in 1910. Bernard Meyer argues that Conrad's anxiety was compounded by his estrangement from Ford Madox Ford (Hueffer), his former collaborator (207–10). After recovering from this breakdown, Conrad produced more fiction, but his best work was already behind him. In 1923 an astonished Conrad was lionized on a tour of the United States. He declined the offer of a knighthood in 1924 and died of a heart attack on August 3rd of that year.

When Conrad achieved commercial success after the publications of *Chance* and *Victory*, he gained a small measure of financial security. But he had resolved one problem only to encounter another, as Conrad's chronic complaints of creative paralysis gave way to symptoms of artistic sterility. His letters after 1914 document his sense of eclipsing imaginative power as he labored at flawed novels such as *The Arrow of Gold, The Rescue, The Rover*, and the incomplete *Suspense*. (Only *The Shadow Line* merits distinction among the books published during Conrad's last eight years.) The critical controversy over his decline did not develop, however, until the 1950s, when Douglas Hewitt, Thomas Moser, and Albert J. Guerard published important studies of Conrad's artistry. Hewitt maintains that most of Conrad's great work came comparatively early; he marks the start of the decline after the composition of "The Secret Sharer" (roughly 1909). From this point on, Hewitt argues, Conrad actually suppressed his unique sensibility to write fiction appealing to a larger audience (4). Moser views the publication of *Chance* (1913) as the beginning of Conrad's decline and designates romantic love, "the uncongenial subject," as the common denominator of the lackluster later fiction. Calling attention to Conrad's trouble with two early, fragmentary works (*The Sisters* and "The Rescuer"), both dealing with a strong love interest, Moser affirms the novelist's ambivalence about sex as a major cause of his decline (8). Along similar lines, Guerard traces Conrad's imaginative deterioration to his abandonment of pessimism and psychological complexity in favor of an affirmative sentimentality. Disparaging *Victory* (yet commending *Chance* and *The Shadow Line*), Guerard blames Conrad's decline on three factors: a "sentimental ethic," dull narrators, and a failure of imagination (257–61).

From his Freudian vantage point, Meyer sees the decline as a consequence of Conrad's nervous breakdown in 1910. After his collapse, Conrad no longer dared to descend within himself, and he ultimately deteriorated as an artist. Meyer concludes that the novelist was reluctant to make "introspective journeys into the self" and limited his art to merely "the surface of life" thereafter (243). Meyer's psychoanalytical assessment has merit (as do the critiques of Hewitt, Moser, and Guerard), but perhaps there has been too much speculation on this topic.[3] After all, consider the circumstances. Conrad did not publish his first novel until he was thirty-eight. For the next fifteen years he was extremely productive (while writing in his third language), intermittently plagued by gout, neuralgia, nervous exhaustion, and financial duress. It is small wonder he depleted his creative potential in his mid-fifties. It would have been a remarkable accomplishment had he managed to sustain his intense vision throughout the thirty years of his career as a novelist.

Nevertheless, critics have come to the defense of the later fiction. Among recent voices calling for a revaluation of these works, Gary Geddes argues that Conrad's technique continued to evolve during his final years. Rejecting the idea that the novelist's talent atrophied after *Under Western Eyes*, Geddes asserts that the later works show Conrad extending his psychological themes into the broader context of the individual in society (3). Geddes also opposes Moser's contention that "the uncongenial subject" of love pervades Conrad's later work, affirming the theme of solidarity as the common element (5). According to Geddes, Conrad's attitude toward technique was fundamentally dynamic, and there is a greater complexity and scope in the later works than customarily believed. By making use of mythic patterns and "ironic romances," Conrad went beyond his usual preoccupation with psychological realism in the later novels without totally abandoning his earlier artistic concerns (Geddes 199–200). Also taking issue with the "achievement and decline" approach, Daniel R. Schwarz views the later fiction as part of the natural evolution of Conrad's art (*Conrad: The Later Fiction*). Schwarz maintains that these works "continue to test and explore ways of feeling and ways of knowing. To the last, Conrad was interested in dramatizing states of consciousness, and the later Conrad novels, like his prior work, explore how men cope in an amoral cosmos more than they argue for a system of values. Conrad still shows that each person sees reality according to his own needs" (*Conrad: The Later Fiction* 33).

Taking a middle road in the "achievement and decline" controversy, Karl sees a definite deterioration in the later works but also underscores the value of *Victory* and *The Shadow Line* as conspicuous exceptions.[4] Karl fixes the beginning of the decline in 1915 (after the exhausting trip to Poland): "The chronicle of illness becomes Conrad's history: lumbago, gout, depression, irritability, an intellectual and moral enervation" (*Joseph Conrad* 772). He observes in the later works an attempt to reproduce the memories of Conrad's own experience and a tendency to reshape old material into new artistic forms (Karl, *A Reader's Guide* 269). Karl views *The Rescue* and *The Rover* as symptomatic of Conrad's compromise with conventionality, as the exhausted novelist accepted traditional methods of narration as a necessary expediency (*A Reader's Guide* 293). In summary, Conrad's later works may have been unduly slighted, but they certainly do not compare favorably to the masterpieces of his peak years of artistic creativity (1897–1910).

What does compare favorably to Conrad's best fiction is his impressive and extensive correspondence. Shortly after Conrad's death, his French admirer Gerard Jean-Aubry began selecting material from among 2,000 of Conrad's letters for his two-volume study, *Joseph Conrad: Life and Letters.* In 1928, Edward Garnett and Richard Curle each published a volume of letters from Conrad. A year later, Jean-Aubry published another collection consisting of Conrad's letters in French (*Lettres françaises*). But this edition (like his previous collection) was marred by poor editing and prejudicial omissions. In 1940, Conrad's 110 letters to his "Aunt" (actually a distant cousin's wife) Marguerite Poradowska were published in an English translation from the original French (Gee and Sturm). Oddly enough, the French version did not appear until twenty-six years later (Rapin). In 1958, William Blackburn edited an extensive collection of Conrad's letters to his *Blackwood's* publisher, William Blackwood, and Blackwood's assistant, David S. Meldrum. This collection of nearly 150 letters covers the early years of Conrad's major phase, 1897–1903. In 1964, Najder contributed another bundle of letters addressed to Conrad's Polish friends and relatives (*Conrad's Polish Background*). Five years later, Cedric Watts published perhaps the most revealing collection of Conrad's correspondence, consisting of eighty-one letters to R. B. Cunninghame Graham.

Despite all these collections, more than 1,500 of Conrad's letters remained unpublished. However, the first volume of a projected eight-volume Cambridge edition of *The Collected Letters of Joseph Conrad* appeared in 1983 (Karl and Davies). When completed, the Cambridge edition will supercede all other collections of Conrad's letters, reprinting 2,000 items and publishing 1,500 items for the first time. And, as the bulk of Conrad's correspondence is displayed in its totality, it might not be surprising if his fame as a letter writer eventually rivals his reputation as a novelist. For Conrad's letters, like his fiction, reveal not only his fascinating development as an artist but also the contradictions and inconsistences, ambiguities and ambivalences that made Conrad such a complex personality (Karl and Davies xxvii). Conrad maintained a lively correspondence with many of the prominent writers of his day (e.g., James, Crane, Wells, Ford, Galsworthy, Gide, Bennett, Gissing, Gosse, Bertrand Russell, and Norman Douglas). Spanning thirty-five years of his mature life, Conrad's letters — written in three languages to a wide assortment of authors, publishers, agents, friends, and relatives — demonstrate that (like Poe) the private Conrad assumed many masks and spoke in many different voices. Edward Garnett was among the first to detect "a wonderful chameleon-like quality" in Conrad's letters (xxv). Writing more than fifty years later, Laurence Davies, in his "Introduction to Volume One" of *The Collected Letters*, amplifies Garnett's original insight: "Reading such an edition, one is conscious, above all, of the range of personalities at Conrad's disposal. While remaining essentially Conrad, he seems to reshape himself for each correspondent: subversively cynical for Garnett; sympathetic, encouraging, upright, rather respectable for Ted Sanderson and Helen Watson; soulful for the Briquels; Byronic for Marguerite Poradowska; provocatively nihilistic for Cunninghame Graham; fussily professional for Unwin; good natured for the Polish cousins; frank for Janina de Brunnow. In these letters, often so personal, yet so much of a performance, we hear not one but many voices" (Karl and Davies lviii). Conrad's letters manifest the enigmatic quality that pervades his fiction — a perplexing combination of revelation and mystification. They also document the self-doubts that haunted his early years as a writer, the struggle to master the prose style of a foreign language, and the pathos of creative sterility in his declining years.

Although Conrad's fiction generally earned praise from reviewers throughout his career, he was frequently associated with other writers in the attempt to reduce to comprehensible terms what was perceived as a foreign phenomenon.[5] Thus, it is not surprising that, especially early in his career, Conrad was most often compared to Kipling and Stevenson. When an anonymous reviewer dubbed him, "the Kipling of the Malay Archipelago" (Sherry, *Conrad: The Critical Heritage* 61), the label stuck with Conrad until his later years, when his superiority finally was recognized. Likewise, the comparisons with Stevenson were slanted against Conrad early on, but they also turned in his favor once Conrad gained his reputation. Reviewers also stereotyped Conrad as "a writer of sea stories," linking him to Marryat, Dana, and William Clark Russell. Conrad chafed at this sobriquet, particularly when he was associated with Melville. Yet reviewers persisted in seeing affinities in both authors (Sherry, *Conrad: The Critical Heritage* 63–64). *Under Western Eyes* naturally prompted comparisons with Dostoevsky, once again much to Conrad's chagrin. (He often vented his disgust at the Russian novelist, at least in his public voice.) The influence of James was a popular topic of discussion, often ending in the lament that Conrad's style was becoming too Jamesian.[6] (Elsa Nettels, in a recent comparative study of the two literary giants, examines them as expatriate writers dealing with the international theme. In her view, both novelists celebrate the power of imagination — James stressing the positive aspects and Conrad emphasizing the negative.)

If the scope of Conrad's achievement exceeds the accomplishments of his British contemporaries (Kipling, Stevenson, Ford, Wells, and Galsworthy),[7] is it then proper to include him in the company of the modernist innovators who radically altered the conception of literature in the twentieth century? The case against Conrad's modernity has been stated in its most extreme form by Charles Burkhart, who views Conrad's moral outlook and characterization as distinctly Victorian. Burkhart maintains that Conrad has been placed among modernists like Joyce, Lawrence, and Virginia Woolf "simply on the basis of chronology, and not on the actual intent and execution of his work" (1). Instead, Burkhart puts him in the context of mid-Victorian authors such as Dickens, Thackeray, and Charlotte Bronte. Conrad is Victorian, Burkhart argues, in his bombastic rhetorical style and excessive use of melodrama and coincidence. Conrad also displays the Victorian tendency to allegorize characters (as in Thackeray's novels), often classifying characters too simply in terms of a black / white moral polarity. Unlike modern writers, Burkhart asserts, Conrad views his characters chiefly in moral terms, and, consequently, presents little character development (3). The weakness of such rigid characterization is magnified by Conrad's "omnipresent" moralizing (particularly in Marlow's narratives). Conrad's moralizing tendencies show that he "seldom attained" the "authorial aloofness" that he admired in Flaubert (Burkhart 5). Conceding that some of Conrad's techniques were innovative, Burkhart argues that their function has been exaggerated. For example, Conrad's management of time is essentially a device to create suspense and does not compare to Proust's truly modern manipulation of chronology (Burkhart 6). He also downgrades Conrad's experimentation with point of view, which fails due to a heavy burden of irony. In Burkhart's estimation, point of view in Conrad's fiction is a contrivance; the narrators serve as a mouthpiece for the author, not as a filtering agent (7). Ultimately, however, Burkhart admits that Conrad does not belong exclusively to a Victorian context: "Conrad, if anyone, should be called a transitional novelist. He was a novelist who embodied an older concept of character and morality in an art whose techniques, if only at times, and if only faintly, foreshadowed the modern. He was indeed between two worlds" (7).

In contrast to Burkhart's attempt to drag Conrad back into the nineteenth century, John Batchelor takes a more positive approach, endeavoring to determine how much Conrad had in common with his Edwardian contemporaries: Ford, Wells, Bennett, Galsworthy, and Forster. Edwardian writers confronted a world in which traditional moral values began to lose their meaning. Batchelor relates this situation to the steady decline of Christianity and what Ian Watt termed the "epistemological crisis" (Batchelor 6). They felt a need to affirm values in a world of disintegrating certainties. Conrad's best fiction dramatizes the Edwardian preoccupation with dissolving absolutes: "Nothing is fixed or certain for Conrad. . . . Life is a *process*, not a fixed fact, and no formulation which treats it as a fixed fact can encompass it" (Batchelor 51). Conrad dramatizes the individual's loss of moral direction, at times approaching a futilitarian position diametrically opposed to Victorian optimism. Batchelor admits that Conrad's use of caricatures shows an affinity with Dickens, but in Conrad's world there is no consensus of values as one finds in the fiction of Dickens (70). Like Galsworthy, Conrad is a curious blend of pessimism and idealism, faith and skepticism (Batchelor 184). Like Bennett, he has a vision of the modern individual trapped within the isolation of consciousness and deprived of the "moral values by which the Victorians lived" (Batchelor 179). But, unlike Galsworthy and Bennett, Conrad sensed the epistemological wilderness into which the twentieth century was racing. *Lord Jim* is modern in its defiance of the reader's customary anticipations of the experience of reading a novel. This is even more apparent in another inconclusive narrative, *Heart of Darkness*:

> The reader himself is forced into the epistemological wilderness in this wrestle with the text; the normal premises, the normal contractual relationship between writer and reader have been discarded. . . .
>
> *Heart of Darkness* can be read as a modernist fiction, perhaps the first consistently self-referential fiction in English. Its surface can be taken as a system of signs and secrets, mysteries leading to other mysteries none of which are explained. (Batchelor 37)

Batchelor concludes that, although Conrad had much in common with his contemporaries, he still stands significantly apart from the other Edwardian writers.

Politically, also, Conrad stands apart from his contemporaries, for he never shared in the turn of the century exaltation of progress, and he never forgot the legacy of his father's revolutionary idealism and the tragic partitioning of his homeland. Except for a brief time following his visit to Poland in 1914, Conrad steadfastly refused to become a political activist, preferring to deal with sociopolitical issues in the crucible of his art. Eloise Knapp Hay, depicting Conrad as a man divided by loyalty to the memories of his radical father and accommodating uncle, emphasizes Conrad's Polish background as the seedbed for the "political imperative" that informs much of his fiction in addition to the more overtly political novels (*Nostromo, The Secret Agent,* and *Under Western Eyes*).[8] Approaching the political works from a Jungian perspective, Claire Rosenfield sees Conrad employing archetypal patterns to create variations on the motif of the "night-sea journey" (42). She contends that Conrad's political imagination readily explored the possibilities of archetypal mythmaking, as in the fabrication of a totally fictive country in *Nostromo* and in "the alchemical process of transmuting objective data into an imaginative construct, of turning history and political theory into story" in *The Secret Agent* (Rosenfield 79).

In contrast to these viewpoints, Avrom Fleishman presents Conrad's political outlook in a different context, challenging Morf's emphasis on the Polish background as essential to understanding Conrad. Viewing the novelist in the tradition of Burke and Mill, Fleishman reads the political novels as "dramatic expressions of a complex political imagination" and not as theoretical tracts (ix). Objecting to the "Polish Myth" espoused by Morf, Megroz, and Najder (among others), he disputes the notion of Conrad's divided loyalties, arguing that Bobrowski exercised a moderating influence on young Conrad's political conscience, which had been exposed to Apollo's revolutionary extremism. Fleishman also credits Bobrowski with instilling in Conrad "the Western, democratic-nationalist tradition" (7). Affirming Conrad's faith in the "organicism" of the wider, sociopolitical community, Fleishman analyzes the novels as dramatizations of the failure of individualism outside the community (99). Thus, the individualistic tendencies of the outsider stand opposed to the balancing solidarity of society.

In opposition to Fleishman's emphasis on community-oriented values, Daniel R. Schwarz suggests a different scale of values pervading Conrad's political fiction: "The novels affirm the primacy of family, the sanctity of the individual, the value of love, and the importance of sympathy and understanding in human relations" (*Conrad:* Almayer's Folly *to* Under Western Eyes 133). Schwarz argues that Conrad thought of social institutions as a necessary evil in the modern world. He also suggests that Conrad's political novels are responses to the burden of the novelist's melancholy past, a kind of atonement for his lack of political involvement: "The means of his palliation are his political novels. *Nostromo* justifies the choice of personal fulfillment over political involvement because it shows politics as a maelstrom that destroys those it touches and shows, more importantly, that one inevitably surrenders a crucial part of one's personality when one commits oneself to ideology" (Schwarz, *Conrad*: Almayer's Folly *to* Under Western Eyes 153–54).

II

If Conrad's politics harkened back to a troubled past, the psychology of his fiction foreshadowed the modernist preoccupation with consciousness (especially in Joyce and Woolf). Conrad shared the late Victorian fascination with "the true self," "the other self," and "the higher self" that informs so much of nineteenth-century literature. He also explored the *doppelgänger* motif in the tradition of Hoffmann, Poe, Dostoevsky, Stevenson, and Wilde.[9] But in addition to his intuitive awareness of the divided psyche, Conrad also probed more deeply into the duplicities of personality and dramatized the complexities of selfhood in a way that anticipated radical developments in twentieth-century psychoanalytical theories, not only in his depiction of fragmented or multiple personalities, but also in his presentation of the vacuous self.

Among the first critics to discuss the psychological dimensions of Conrad's fiction, Guerard examines the psycho-moral ambiguity of the major works from Freudian and Jungian perspectives. Identifying "The Journey Within" as the key to Conrad's art, Guerard views the descent into the self as an archetypal "night-sea journey" (1–59). He sees Conrad's best fiction as "dark meditations" on the modern ego and its illusions of dominion. Blending the realms of psychology and global politics, Karl views Conrad as a prophet of twentieth-century cultural trauma: "Conrad and Freud were pioneers in stressing the irrational elements in man's behavior which resisted orthodox interpretation" (*A Reader's Guide* 137). In a similar vein, Meyer probes the intricacies of Conrad's psyche to understand his creative process. Meyer's Freudian analysis offers speculations on Conrad's proclivities toward mother worship, fetishes, and psycho-somatic illnesses, but it also provides insight into the novelist's apprehension of self-consciousness, both before and after his nervous breakdown.[10] In contrast to the views mentioned above, Edward Said approaches Conrad from a phenomenological perspective, arguing that his creativity was part of a lifelong quest for identity (3–28). Employing the letters and tales as raw material for his psychological / philosophical analysis, Said finds Conrad dredging up his past experiences to reshape a new self-image in his fiction (95).

Rejecting overtly Freudian interpretations, Paul Kirschner places Conrad in the European tradition of psychological novelists (284). In Kirschner's view, Conrad ultimately deals with ego-assertion and the unrealized ideal in his psychological fiction: "Conrad began by studying the self in conditions of isolation, defending its idea against chaotic natural forces or unconscious impulses. He expanded his interests to show how the self is led into betraying a moral identity by seeking to realise it in society" (286). "The Psychology of Self-Image" also lies at the heart of Bruce Johnson's analysis of Conrad's mind, which traces the novelist's movement toward a "new psychology" emphasizing the self-image (*Conrad's Models* 5). In Conrad's fiction, the question of identity subsumes all other impulses and motivations, including political ideals serving as masks for characters torn between egoism and solidarity, self and community. Conrad turns from the late Victorian fascination with Schopenhauer's dominant will to a modern sense of self-responsibility (Johnson, *Conrad's Models* 206–08). Describing the novelist as an existential forerunner of Camus and Sartre, Johnson cites Conrad's presentation of the self as multiple and elusive as a testament to the instability of personal identity (*Conrad's Models* 213–14). If the traditional concept of the self is the grand illusion in Conrad's fictive house of mirrors, then he may well have pioneered the modern notion of a vacuous psyche requiring masks and disguises to assume its illusive repertoire of roles in order to validate its own existence. And if Conrad attempted to reveal the "inner truth" about his characters, as Norman Sherry affirms (*Conrad's Western World* 339–72), then the shadowy personalities of Jim, Kurtz, Marlow, Nostromo, and Leggatt represent the enigmatic abyss within all individuals.

Although Conrad was not recognized as a great modern writer at the time of his death, Ford Madox Ford, his early collaborator and confidant, championed his modernity enthusiastically, until critics such as M. C. Bradbrook, F. R. Leavis, and Morton Dauwen Zabel initiated the Conrad revival after World War II. Ford's promotion of Conrad's innovative techniques began with *Joseph Conrad: A Personal Remembrance*, published in the year of Conrad's death. In this volume, as in later reminiscences and miscellaneous critical pieces, Ford elaborated on the impressionistic method he claimed to share with Conrad.[11] Although the

Ford / Conrad collaborations produced inferior fiction, their imaginative interaction generated a radically new understanding of the novel as an art form.[12] And, though Conrad once claimed that Stephen Crane was *"the only* impressionist and *only* an impressionist" (Garnett 107), Ford readily accepted the "stigma" of impressionism and detailed the phases by which Conrad and he created the impressionistic prototype of the modern novel (*Critical Writings* 34).

Ford's recollections (though never completely reliable) offer an intriguing portrait of Conrad the experimental artist—the architect of the "New Form" of the novel. The starting point, according to Ford, was a dissatisfaction with the straightforward chronology of the traditional novel; the theoretical solution was to begin *in medias res* "with a strong impression [of the protagonist] and then work backwards and forwards over his past" (*Joseph Conrad* 136–37). They agreed that a novel should not be a narrative or report of experiences but a rendering or artistic presentation of the events: "we saw that Life did not narrate, but made impressions on our brains. We in turn, if we wished to produce . . . an effect of life, must not narrate but render impressions" (Ford, *Joseph Conrad* 194–95). By means of selection and surprise, impersonality and indirect speech, they hoped to create the illusion of reality for the reader, who was always the focus of their artistic strategies.

Ford describes Conrad's technical experimentation as an artistic revolution against the "tyranny" of fixed forms of narrative (*Return to Yesterday* 203). To facilitate the reader's willing suspension of disbelief, Conrad devised the persona of Marlow as the oracle for the new form of the novel, so that the development of the scenario has the freedom to shift backward and forward through time and avoid the stultification of the Victorian novel: "a rattling narrative beginning at a hero's birth and progressing to his not very carefully machined yet predestined glory" (Ford, *Return to Yesterday* 218). Conrad's impressionistic method also aimed for prismatic simultaneity of events (Ford, *Critical Writings* 41). For every recollection is a record of impressions, not a linear narration. Thus, presentation—showing, not telling—is crucial to producing the illusion of reality that enchants the reader (Ford, *Critical Writings* 43). Experimentation with point of view and ironic distancing play a vital role in the reader-oriented approach of Conrad and Ford: "our eyes were forever on the reader" (Ford, *Critical Writings* 69). Ford defines impressionism as an impulse toward greater narrative complexity to mirror the variety and ambiguities of modern life. For Ford, the distinction between a traditional (Victorian) writer and an impressionist (modernist) is largely a matter of technique: "The one makes statements; the other builds suggestions of happenings on suggestions of happenings" (*Critical Writings* 59).

Although early critics, such as Joseph Warren Beach and Edward Crankshaw, followed Ford's lead in labeling Conrad as a literary impressionist, scholars have generally discussed his impressionistic techniques in the broader context of modernism. Eloise Knapp Hay, in "Impressionism Limited," cites Conrad's ambivalent attitude toward impressionistic painting and literature as evidence that the novelist (who sought "the inner truth" of life) did not wholeheartedly accept the art of "surface effects" (59). Ian Watt sees impressionism and symbolism as inextricably united in Conrad's method. He most convincingly describes these impressionistic techniques in defining what he calls "delayed decoding":

> One of the devices . . . was to present a sense impression and to withhold naming it or explaining its meaning until later; as readers we witness every step by which the gap between the individual perception and its cause is belatedly closed within the consciousness of the protagonist. . . .
>
> This narrative device may be termed delayed decoding, since it combines the forward temporal progression of the mind, as it receives messages from the outside world, with the much slower reflexive process of making out their meaning. (Watt 175)

Although Watt refers to Conrad's "delayed decoding" as "one of the minor innovations of his narrative technique" (174), other critics find greater significance in the concept. For example, Cedric Watts views the intentional "delay of logical connections" as one of Conrad's major preoccupations (*The Deceptive Text* 43–46). In Watts's view, Conrad employs this technique to present the effect of a sense impression, while delaying knowledge of its cause, to make the sensation more vivid to the reader, yet also shrouding the scene with strangeness (*The Deceptive Text* 43–44). Thus, "delayed decoding" functions as a defamiliarizing device, forcing the reader to share "the misleadingly incomplete vision of the central observer" (Watts, *The Deceptive Text* 44, 46). Relating the defamiliarization of mundane events to David Hume's sensationalist psychology and Zola's literary naturalism, Todd K. Bender maintains that Conrad employs impressionistic techniques to create a more sophisticated realism (220). Similarly, Bruce Johnson views Conrad's strategy of "delayed decoding" as "one of the original purposes of impressionism: to return to the most aboriginal sensation before concepts and rational categories are brought to bear" ("Conrad's Impressionism" 53).

Applying the principles of impressionism to Conrad's rhetorical strategies, Owen Knowles finds that the novelist's commentary serves as a constantly shifting perspective, composed of varied tones and conflicting attitudes (7). Conrad's philosophical and psychological speculations conceal as much as they reveal, allowing no final judgment for easy compartmentalization (Knowles 9). Employing a verbal irony based on shifting distances between author and characters, the novelist opposes all formulaic generalizations that simplify the manifold complexities of life (Knowles 14–15). According to Knowles, Conrad never loses his awareness of the irreconcilable contradictions of existence, and his narrative voices convey this recognition: "the voice of the detached analyst, the tones of the ironist, the intimate address, the voices of the interpreter who regards man in the light of his own values" (22).

In a discussion of "The Working Aesthetic," Karl identifies Conrad with the assumption that fiction is the art of suggestions rather than "final meanings"; the novelist also recognized that words cannot adequately convey subtle nuances concerning a perpetually changing world: "Conrad placed himself in a general position we may consider 'modern.' He saw fictional art as the manifestation of a fluid and ever shifting world responsive to immediate intuition but inaccessible to the intellect" (*A Reader's Guide* 33). Conrad also displayed his modernity in his strategic scrambling of chronological sequences (labeled "time shifts" by Ford, "chronological looping" by Beach, and *anachrony* by Watt). Reacting against the linear narrative and its predictable *denouement*, Conrad toppled the traditional architecture of the house of fiction. (Karl, *A Reader's Guide* 45). Conrad's employment of elaborate framing devices was another offshoot of his dissatisfaction with conventional novelistic structure, resulting in what Karl terms "Chinese-box-like" narrations (*A Reader's Guide* 56). These framing devices facilitated Conrad's experimentation with point of view. His radical temporal involutions put him in the forefront (with Joyce, Woolf, and Faulkner) of the modernist fascination with the specious certitudes of conventional time (Karl, *A Reader's Guide* 62, 72). Karl also finds in Conrad's fiction an embryonic form of stream-of-consciousness stemming from an "attempt to integrate past and present in the narrative" that the Victorian novel would not allow (*A Reader's Guide* 77).

In a consideration of Conrad's innovative techniques, Guerard discerns a unifying purpose: the deliberate manipulation of the reader's responses, which distinguishes him from prior British novelists (59). The key word in Guerard's scrutiny of Conradian art is "evasiveness," which he views as essentially temperamental and deeply ingrained in the novelist's life as well as in his works. Calling attention to the twentieth-century preoccupation with the nature of time, Watt sees Conrad attempting to "portray the multiplicity and randomness of the individual's immediate experience" (287). Watt clarifies some of the misconceptions about Conrad's chronological manipulation, discounting terms like *flashback* and *time shift* as misleading approximations of the novelist's actual procedure. Instead, Watt discusses Conrad's handling of time in terms of "a series of minute movements forwards and backwards in time" (300). It functions as "a means of representing a progression of moral understanding" (Watt 300). Conrad's fracturing and rearrangement of chronological order in fiction serve the dual purpose of prefiguring and concentrating the main events of the narrative (Watt 292–93). Watt finds these structural principles in *Heart of Darkness* and *Lord Jim*, fictions that fuse symbolist and impressionist techniques and herald the dawn of modernist literature.

Given his radical departure from the conventions of Victorian fiction, Conrad was certainly justified in affirming his innovativeness, as he stated boldly in a letter to Blackwood (31 May 1902):

> I am *modern*, and I would rather recall Wagner the musician and Rodin the sculptor who both had to starve a little in their day—and Whistler the painter who made Ruskin the critic foam at the mouth with scorn and indignation. They too have arrived. They had to suffer for being "new." And I too hope to find my place in the rear of my betters. But still—my place. My work shall not be an utter failure because it has the solid basis of a definite intention—first: and next because it is not an endless analysis of affected sentiments but in its essence it is action . . . nothing but action—action observed, felt and interpreted with absolute truth to my sensations (which are the basis for art in literature)—action of human beings that will bleed to a prick, and are moving in a visible world.
>
> This is my creed. Time will show. (Blackburn, 155–56)

Conrad's "creed' demonstrates that behind the chronological manipulations, framing devices, interior monologues, indirect dialogues, and multiple points of view, there was an active imagination that refused to be bound by preconceptions and conventions. In Conrad's work, one can find early examples of self-reflexive strategies and a skepticism toward language that seem to prefigure the main concerns of what has been termed postmodern fiction.[13] The proof of a great artist is his pertinence to all ages. In his determination to make the reader *see*, Conrad will always be our contemporary.

TED BILLY

University of Delaware

Notes

1. Much of what is known about Conrad's early years has been provided by scholars who have had access to Polish records unavailable to British and American critics. See Mégroz, Morf, and especially Najder.

2. Thanks in large part to the meticulous scholarship of Norman Sherry (*Conrad's Eastern World*, *Conrad's Western World*, *Conrad and His World*), Conrad's numerous voyages have been charted in considerable detail.

3. For a more elaborate summary of these early proponents of the "achievement and decline" approach, see the "Bibliographical Note" in Palmer 260–68.

4. See *Joseph Conrad* 683–87, 770–72, 797–800, and *A Reader's Guide* 245–98. Karl also makes a strong case for the value of parts of *Chance*, *The Rescue*, *The Rover*, and "The Planter of Malata."

5. See Sherry, ed., *Conrad: The Critical Heritage*, for a broad cross-section of contemporary reviews of Conrad's works. Sherry's "Introduction" (1–44) provides an excellent overview.

6. Even James complained about the narrative involutions of Conrad's most Jamesian novel, *Chance* (Sherry, *Conrad: The Critical Heritage* 263–70).

7. See Saveson for a detailed commentary on Conrad's relations with these writers.

8. For a summary of Conrad's Polish background, his sense of political desertion, and the dramatization of betrayal in *Lord Jim*, see Hay, *The Political Novels* 31–80.

9. "The Secret Sharer," provisionally entitled "The Secret Self" and "The Other Self," is the most overt example of psychological doubling in Conrad's fiction. Karl sees Conrad working in the tradition of the German romanticists and Dostoevsky to create the modern split-personality in fiction (*A Reader's Guide* 124).

10. According to Meyer, after 1910 Conrad "turned from a faithful depiction of sentient human beings to the creation of a gallery of puppets representing the good man, the bad man, the monumental goddess, and the cat-like woman. . . . [H]is fictional characters were transformed from complex personalities into cardboard figures of two-dimensional simplicity" (240).

11. See, in particular, *Return to Yesterday* 31–35, 58–61, 186–201, 215–18, 282–95, and *Critical Writings* 33–88.

12. For a recent overview of the Ford / Conrad relationship, see Delbanco 85–133.

13. For a metafictional critique of *Chance* as a reflexive novel, see Boyd 43–65. For commentary on Conrad's ambivalent attitude toward language, see especially Guetti (46–68), Hawthorn, Senn, and Ray.

Works Cited

Baines, Jocelyn. *Joseph Conrad: A Critical Biography*. New York: McGraw-Hill, 1960.

Batchelor, John. *The Edwardian Novelists*. London: Duckworth, 1982.

Beach, Joseph Warren. "Impressionism: Conrad." *The Twentieth Century Novel: Studies in Technique*. New York: Appleton-Century, 1932. 337–65.

Bender, Todd K. "Conrad and Literary Impressionism." *Conradiana* 10 (1978):211–24.

Blackburn, William, ed. *Joseph Conrad: Letters to William Blackwood and David S. Meldrum*. Durham: Duke Univ. Press, 1958.

Boyd, Michael. *The Reflexive Novel: Fiction as Critique*. Lewisburg: Bucknell Univ. Press, 1983.

Bradbrook, M. C. *Joseph Conrad: Poland's English Genius*. Cambridge: Cambridge Univ. Press, 1941.

Burkhart, Charles. "Conrad the Victorian." *English Literature in Transition 1880–1920* 6 (1963): 1–8.

Crankshaw, Edward. *Joseph Conrad: Some Aspects of the Art of the Novel*. London: Lane, 1936.

Curle, Richard, ed. *Conrad to a Friend: 150 Selected Letters from Joseph Conrad to Richard Curle*. New York: Crosby Gaige, 1928.

Delbanco, Nicholas. *Group Portrait*. New York: Quill, 1984.

Fleishman, Avrom. *Conrad's Politics: Community and Anarchy in the Fiction of Joseph Conrad*. Baltimore: Johns Hopkins Press, 1967.

Ford, Ford Madox. *Critical Writings of Ford Madox Ford*. Ed. Frank MacShane. Lincoln: Univ. of Nebraska, Press, 1964.

————. *Joseph Conrad: A Personal Remembrance*. Boston: Little, Brown, 1925.

_____. *Return to Yesterday.* New York: Liveright, 1932.

Garnett, Edward, ed. *Letters from Joseph Conrad 1895–1924.* London: Nonesuch Press, 1928.

Geddes, Gary. *Conrad's Later Novels.* Montreal: McGill-Queen's Univ. Press, 1980.

Gee, John A. and Paul J. Sturm, eds. *Letters of Joseph Conrad to Marguerite Poradowska, 1890–1920.* New Haven: Yale Univ. Press, 1940.

Guerard, Albert J. *Conrad the Novelist.* New York: Atheneum, 1967. Cambridge: Harvard Univ. Press, 1958.

Guetti, James. *The Limits of Metaphor: A Study of Melville, Conrad, and Faulkner.* Ithaca: Cornell Univ. Press, 1967.

Hawthorn, Jeremy. *Joseph Conrad: Language and Fictional Self-Consciousness.* Lincoln: Univ. of Nebraska Press, 1979.

Hay, Eloise Knapp. "Impressionism Limited." *Joseph Conrad: A Commemoration.* Ed. Norman Sherry. London: Macmillan, 1976. 54–64.

_____. *The Political Novels of Joseph Conrad.* Chicago: Univ. of Chicago Press, 1963.

Hewitt, Douglas. *Conrad: A Reassessment.* London: Bowes & Bowes, 1975. 3rd ed.

Jean-Aubry, Gerard. *Joseph Conrad: Life and Letters.* 2 vols. Garden City: Doubleday, Page, 1927.

_____. *Lettres françaises.* Paris: Gallimard, 1929.

Johnson, Bruce. "Conrad's Impressionism and Watt's 'Delayed Decoding.' " *Conrad Revisited: Essays for the Eighties.* Ed. Ross C. Murfin. University, Alabama: Univ. of Alabama Press, 1985. 51–70.

_____. *Conrad's Models of Mind.* Minneapolis: Univ. of Minnesota Press, 1971.

Karl, Frederick R. *Joseph Conrad: The Three Lives.* New York: Farrar, Straus, Giroux, 1979.

_____. *A Reader's Guide to Joseph Conrad.* New York: Farrar, Straus and Giroux, 1960. 1969 ed.

Karl, Frederick R. and Laurence Davies. *The Collected Letters of Joseph Conrad: Volume I: 1861–1897.* Cambridge: Cambridge Univ. Press, 1983.

Kirschner, Paul. *Conrad: The Psychologist as Artist.* Edinburgh: Oliver and Boyd, 1968.

Knowles, Owen. "Commentary as Rhetoric: An Aspect of Conrad's Technique." *Conradiana* 5 (1973:5–27.

Leavis, F. R. *The Great Tradition.* London: Chatto and Windus, 1948.

Mégroz, R. L. *Joseph Conrad's Mind and Method: A Study of Personality in Art.* London: Faber and Faber, 1931.

Meyer, Bernard C. *Joseph Conrad: A Psychoanalytical Biography.* Princeton: Princeton Univ. Press, 1967.

Morf, Gustave. *The Polish Heritage of Joseph Conrad.* London: Samson, Lowe, Marston, 1930.

_____. *The Polish Shades and Ghosts of Joseph Conrad.* New York: Astra Books, 1976.

Moser, Thomas C. *Joseph Conrad: Achievement and Decline.* Cambridge: Harvard Univ. Press, 1957.

Najder, Zdzislaw. *Conrad's Polish Background: Letters to and from Polish Friends.* Trans. Halina Carroll. London: Oxford Univ. Press, 1964.

_____. *Conrad Under Familial Eyes.* Trans. Halina Carroll-Najder. Cambridge: Cambridge Univ. Press, 1983.

_____. *Joseph Conrad: A Chronicle.* Trans. Halina Carroll-Najder. New Brunswick, Rutgers Univ. Press, 1983.

Nettels, Elsa. *James and Conrad.* Athens: Univ. of Georgia Press, 1977.

Palmer, John A. *Joseph Conrad's Fiction: A Study in Literary Growth.* Ithaca: Cornell Univ. Press, 1968.

Rapin, René, ed. *Lettres de Joseph Conrad à Marguerite Poradowska*. Geneva: Droz, 1966.

Ray, Martin S. "The Gift of Tongues: The Languages of Joseph Conrad." *Conradiana* 15 (1983):83–109.

Rosenfield, Claire. *Paradise of Snakes: An Archetypal Analysis of Conrad's Political Novels*. Chicago: Univ. of Chicago Press, 1967.

Said, Edward W. *Joseph Conrad and the Fiction of Autobiography*. Cambridge: Harvard Univ. Press, 1966.

Saveson, J. E. *Conrad, The Later Moralist*. Amsterdam: Editions Rodopi, 1975.

Schwarz, Daniel R. *Conrad*: Almayer's Folly *to* Under Western Eyes. Ithaca: Cornell Univ. Press, 1980.

_____. Conrad: *The Later Fiction*. London: Macmillan, 1982.

Senn, Werner. *Conrad's Narrative Voice: Stylistic Aspects of his Fiction*. Bern: A Franke, 1980.

Sherry, Norman, ed. *Conrad: The Critical Heritage*. Critical Heritage Series. London: Routledge and Kegan Paul, 1973.

_____. *Conrad's Eastern World*. London: Cambridge Univ. Press, 1966.

_____. *Conrad and His World*. London: Thames and Hudson, 1972.

_____. *Conrad's Western World*. Cambridge: Cambridge Univ. Press, 1971.

Watt, Ian. *Conrad in the Nineteenth Century*. Berkeley: Univ. of California Press, 1979.

Watts, Cedric. *The Deceptive Text: An Introduction to Covert Plots*. Sussex: Harvester, 1984.

_____. ed. *Joseph Conrad's Letters to R. R. Cunninghame Graham*. Cambridge: Cambridge Univ. Press, 1969.

_____. *A Preface to Conrad*. Preface Books. London: Longman, 1982.

Zabel, Morton Dauwen. *Craft and Character in Modern Fiction*. New York: Viking Press, 1957. 147–227.

ARTICLES AND ESSAYS

Conrad in His Historical Perspective

Zdzisław Najder*

It is now over a hundred years since Conrad was born, seventy since he published his first novel, and over forty since he died. This lapse of time constitutes, I suppose, a distance sufficient to see him in a historical perspective. It allows us to ask, without excessive fear of having our picture blurred by the closeness of the object, what is Conrad's place in the history of literature. This problem, as I see it, involves three groups of questions — what were the traditions, intellectual and artistic, which nursed Conrad's creative talent? What was the position of his work within the contemporary literary and spiritual trends and movements? and thirdly, who were his followers and what sort of inheritance has he left to them? Of course, within the scope of a brief essay, one can hope only to open a few vistas on the problem so boldly announced by its title.

Luckily, for us historians of literature, most writers, including those of the first rank, fit more or less neatly into some general pattern of artistic and intellectual life of their time. Even when "exceptional," "outstanding," and "breaking new ground," they allow themselves to be arranged in groups and sequences. They loyally contribute to the "temper of the era" and make it possible to draw dividing lines between periods and to talk about typicality and representativeness. Occasionally, however, we encounter figures which are so peculiar, so aberrant, that it is virtually impossible to fit them into the general formula of their time. Conrad seems to be a fairly safe candidate for the first place among these freaks.

He published his most important books between the years 1897 and 1911. It was the time, when on the Continent Maeterlinck and Strindberg, D'Annunzio and France, Bourget and Chekhov, and also Andreiev, Björnson, Sudermann, Sienkiewicz and Hauptmann reached the peak of their fame. Gorki, Thomas Mann and Gide were just beginning their great careers. European intellectuals were idolizing Nietzsche and Bergson. In England Bennett, Galsworthy, Hardy, James, Kipling, Wells and Wilde were recognized as the leading writers.

*Reprinted with permission from *English Literature in Transition 1880–1920* 14 (1971):157–66.

With the sole exception of Henry James, another expatriate and spiritual solitary, there is not another name on this list which we could link with Conrad's to form a distinct "micro-group." Therefore it should not be surprising that the early critics of Conrad had great difficulties in classifying him and were almost compelled to resort to obviously superficial formulas, as for example "Kipling of the Malay Archipelago" or "writer of the sea and adventure." Evidently, he was not an epigone; but he was not one of the "normal" contemporaries either. Even Conrad himself, surely feeling not a little lost and lonely, towards the end of his life tended to succumb to the temptation of easy self-labelling and described himself, against the evidence of his best work, as a promoter of simple and unquestioned ideals.

Conrad's exceptionality as a writer was, of course, connected with the peculiarity of his biography. He was fluent in three languages but wrote all his books in the language he learned last, at the age of twenty. Born into a Polish gentry family in the Ukraine, at the age of four he had to accompany his parents to exile in Russia. Early orphaned, he never regularly attended any school. He left Poland at the age of seventeen, and for the next twenty years led the life of a sailor, beginning as a simple seaman and reaching the rank of a captain. He started to write his first book when he was already thirty-two, and published it six years later. When his sea-years were over, he settled in England; but even at the height of his creative power he would confess to a friend: "English is still a foreign language to me, requiring an immense effort to handle."[1]

As Jocelyn Baines, Albert J. Guerard and many other critics have pointed out, Conrad's immediate literary predecessors were French: he was a diligent disciple of Flaubert and Maupassant. From Flaubert he took the idea of the novel as a laboriously shaped work of art; from Maupassant the impressionistic elements of his literary manifesto in the famous Preface to *The Nigger of the "Narcissus."* Also, some characteristics of his narrative method are best explained by reference to Flaubert's programme of restrained objective realism. The writer, advised Flaubert, should be like God: present everywhere, nowhere visible.

However, we find in Conrad's work elements which cannot be explained by reference to either his French masters, or his English contemporaries. For clues, we have to look to Conrad's biography which reveals that there were in his attitude and background some factors conflicting with Flaubert's model of fiction.

Firstly, and this is perhaps the most important factor of all, the influence of the French realists clashed with the tradition of the Polish Romantics. Secondly, Conrad, a philosophical agnostic, was also sceptical as to the possibilities of a full understanding of the motives of human actions; the monadic separatedness of every individual and the inscrutability of forces governing our behaviour formed according to him an obstacle not to be overcome by any amount of intellectual analysis. And thirdly, writing was for him an obviously compensative action: to create meant to make up for the shortcomings, psychological as well as external, of real life.

The two other factors are usually, although in various ways, taken into account by English and American critics; the first one tends to elude or baffle them. In fact, traces of the Polish inheritance are not difficult to identify.[2] The evidence consists of numerous motifs, scenes, even particular sentences borrowed from Polish romantic poetry. It is also easy to recognize in many of Conrad's heroes a family likeness to the typical hero of Polish romantic literature: a lonely, uprooted individual, endowed with an outstanding awareness of his moral obligations, very self-conscious but not self-centered.

Of the same origin, and of infinitely greater consequence, is the notion, underlying Conrad's whole work, of the writer's role as analyst of basic moral issues — stated in terms not only psychological, but primarily socio-political. In spite of all ostentatious individualism of the "typically Polish" behaviour, Polish literature has been traditionally a literature of solidarity. Man as a member of his social group and of his nation, conscience as a reflexion of communal responsibility — are in this literature archetypal. "Movement from alienation towards commitment," which Ian Watt discerns in Conrad's work in his admirable essay,[3] is also something characteristic for Polish literature, from the sixteenth century onwards. Therefore, to take issue with Watt's essay, Conrad's national background not only enforced his alienation, but was at the same time giving him an original impulse to fight it.

All three factors, national, philosophical and psychological, worked in the direction of anything but dispassionate objectivism and traditional, direct realism. Consequently, Conrad's novels and short stories have, as a rule, some distinct moral focus, and it is impossible to overlook their ideological involvement. Furthermore, his heroes are not studies in character, not unrepeatable individuals — but types; he conceives them not as psychologically unique personalities, but as symptomatic cases.[4] Such [a] "typological" approach has behind it an old and glorious tradition, but evidently runs counter to the trends prevailing in the European prose of the last hundred and fifty years.

To what extent Conrad was conscious of these disparate components and influences is a question which interests mainly a psychological biographer. We do not need, however, any psychological hypotheses to see that these elements had to be somehow adapted to blend into an artistically congruous whole; and not biography, but structural analysis suggests that this is precisely the function of his two most characteristic devices: the narrator within the story and the time-shifts. The result of these devices is a sort of "sceptical realism." The convention of the omniscient narrator is abandoned (why it does not happen in all Conrad's books — is another matter); what is being told is not too far removed from

[the] possible experience of a living person. What is understood and explained is also carefully limited and distilled; in the place of the author's direct comments, or his porte-parole's pronouncements, we are faced with a subtle interplay of points of view, varying scopes of knowledge and insight, flashes of moral revelation. The time-shifts create an illusion of a gradual getting-at-the-truth about facts and about the character of the heroes. Both devices focus our attention on problems rather than personalities, and they also make it possible to achieve the impression of tragic necessity so important in Conrad's work and so difficult to attain in realistic novels, which at any moment present us with innumerable possibilities of a further development of action.

This is perhaps how we can describe, in most general terms, the peculiar artistic result of the merger of Conrad's manifold cultural tradition. His unusual, polycentric background and aesthetic taste made him an exceptional, even unique writer. Still, we can not say that he was not a man of his time.

By the time of Conrad's début the growth of industrial society, the progress of science and the crisis of religious beliefs resulted in a widespread break-down of established moral codes. Most of contemporary writers were conscious of this process — but nobody more deeply than the desperately probing Dostoevsky, who summed up the age's predicament in a cry, which was supposed to open anew the road to Christianity: "if God does not exist, everything is permissible." Conrad, who hated Dostoevsky and rejected his positive programme, was nevertheless very close to him in the intensity of being aware of the crisis in morality.

The reaction of unrest and alarm was by no means universal in literature. Naturalistic novelists were ready to supplant, without qualms, the newly discovered laws of biology for the old moral dogmas. Popularized Nietzsche and fashionable Wilde were understood as champions of the idea that the rules of the moral game can and should be changed at will: a strong, independent, self-sufficient man's will. And many a writer was inclined to the escapist gesture of turning his back on the whole hideous and nasty world.

Conrad belonged to neither of these groups. He was, like Turgenev and James, conscious that the traditions of enlightened generations were falling apart. Like Flaubert, Maupassant, France and Strindberg, he was shocked by the hypocrisy of the contemporary bourgeois morality. Like Hardy, he was dismayed by the moral plight of man, left defenceless at the mercy of heredity and natural forces. But, unlike Wells, he did not believe in the almost automatically beneficent influence of scientific progress.

Being, thus, by no means exceptional in his awareness of the general crisis of morals, he was probably unique in his response to it. It would be rash and presumptuous to attempt to describe this response in any simple terms, or to extract from Conrad's books some straightforward recipe or programme. But we can perhaps analyse his attitude by distinguishing its three aspects, corresponding to three possible levels of understanding and appreciating his work.

First, we have the most obvious level of the famous "simple principles": fidelity, honour, friendship, obeying the sailor's code, etc. To many unwary readers, and even to many a critic, unreserved trust in these plain rules is *the* Conrad message. But if it is debilitating to stay on this level of interpretation even with regard to a comparatively simple story like "Typhoon," it makes the more complex ones, like "Heart of Darkness" or *Nostromo*, virtually incomprehensible.

The second aspect or level consists in pitiless confrontation of the "simple principles" with their actual working in life. This confrontation is conducted on two planes: individual and general, and in both cases the outcome is highly disconcerting. Although the "simple principles" are supposed to provide ethically dependable guide lines for individual behaviour, the individual's ability to grasp them, to stick to them and to preserve their purity and human meaning turns out to be rather doubtful. This is why whenever Conrad uses the expression "true to himself" — he does so ironically; and to the notion of "being sure of himself," he retorts: "it is the last thing man should be sure about." Moreover, there exists an eternally gaping chasm between man's intentions and the results of his actions. As the examples of Kurtz and Charles Gould show, even the most idealistic intentions can become corrupt, if they are not constantly controlled by reference to the social results of the ensuing actions.

This highly dispiriting picture is also frequently taken to represent *the* Conrad view of man's situation in the world. With regard to some of his works, as "Heart of Darkness," such [a] critical conclusion seems to be justified. Conrad, an explorer of the "extreme situations,"[5] had no illusions about man's natural virtues or the world's moral order. However, there is also the third aspect, or level of understanding. The acceptance of the "simple principles" does not imply a belief in their "objective" truth or ontological necessity; man is not "naturally" good; history does not follow a rational and just course; contemporary society is materialistic and debased; and, whatever men do, the surrounding universe is equally indifferent to their heroic efforts and to their failures. But still, Conrad seems to maintain [that] the code of honour and fidelity, of the "few very simple ideas . . . as old as the hills," is the best we can hope for. It does not guarantee anything: neither success, nor sympathy, nor righteousness — but it is the only code worthy of the ancient dignity of mankind's traditions. In other words, these human values are not natural laws but only postulates difficult to meet and impossible to justify pragmatically, perhaps even illusory — but still worth our stubborn, if stumbling, adherence.

At this point it is perhaps fitting to say a few words about the problem of Conrad's "pessimism." That he was a pessimist, most of his critics readily pronounce. But pessimism is not a simple notion, and it is worth while to look at it a little more closely. An average pessimist seems to be a person who thinks, or says, something to the effect: "the world could have been good, it can be good — but it won't be." Now Conrad is plainly not this kind of pessimist, since he suggests rather that "the world has never been good, it cannot be good, but there is some possibility of our diminishing the amount of evil."

The idea of an autonomous morality, man-created, secular and related to social life, is not a new one; among Conrad's contemporaries we find it, for instance, in Jean-Marie Guyau. It is rather unlikely that Conrad knew his work. But, whatever theoretical predecessors he might have had, Conrad is undisputably one of the leading pioneers of moral thinking in fiction. To a large extent it is to him that we owe the vision of man as facing the indifferent or even hostile universe with his own code of behaviour, his own concept of moral order.

However, the content of the code, the body of values, were not of Conrad's own making — but represented a continuation of an ancient tradition philosophically based on the notions of loyalty, honour and mutual responsibility, and socially connected with the nobility and military. In literature it is the tradition of the *Iliad*, *Chanson de Roland*, Calderon, Corneille's *Le Cid*, Walter Scott and Alfred de Vigny's *Servitude et Grandeur militaires*. This also is a literature of extreme situations, of violent conflicts and decisive choices, of physical defeats from which man's dignity has to be rescued. There is no easy consolation to be found there, but only an enthusiasm of the in-spite-of-everything type. The foundations of the moral code, embodied in this tradition, are anti-pragmatic and secular (in spite of accidental religious affiliations).

But Conrad was not a simple inheritor of the "chivalric" tradition. He introduced a major novelty: most of his heroes are neither noblemen nor soldiers. The moral code remained basically the same, but its social ramifications disappeared. Preserving the principles while shedding their genetic and environmental basis has struck many critics as odd and anachronistic,[6] but it turned out to be very fruitful, as the example of Conrad's literary followers will show.

The impression of Conrad's strangeness has been grounded, however, mainly in the contrast he presents against the background of the nineteenth-century European novel. He was, in his mature work, opposed to the whole middle-class spirit of modern fiction and far removed from both the literary heritage of Rousseau (whom he disliked) and Richardson, and the heritage of Balzac. Peculiarities of individual psychology, extensive introspection, analysis of strange emotions and unusual human relationships, the liberation of man from the shackles of communal constraints concerned him as marginally as did the descriptions of social intercourse, revelations about the primacy of economic and political over moral motivations, or explorations of the possibly infinite number of marital geometrical figures.

To talk about "influences" with regard to contemporary literature is rather risky and perhaps even trivial; it is safer and potentially more illuminating to talk in terms of shared affinities, of trends and common legacies. The most conspicuous part of Conrad's legacy in twentieth century literature forms perhaps the revival of the ethics of honour, with its peculiar problems: conflict of honour and emotional attachment, contrast between principles and success in life, fidelity and personal interest, etc. It was to him and, on a lower level of sophistication, to Henryk Sienkiewicz, a superb story-teller, that this revival has been due.[7]

Not that Conrad's "formal" achievement has not been followed. F. Scott Fitzgerald was perhaps the most effusive in his confessions of how much he owed to Conrad in the shaping of his work, and the influence is most easily discernible in *The Great Gatsby*.[8] Also, Faulkner's type of narrative is evidently a development of Conrad's—a development in two directions. On the one hand, in *The Sound and the Fury* Faulkner contrasts personal points of view more sharply than Conrad ever did; on the other, the almost continuous and stylistically homogenous yarn of *Absalom, Absalom!* goes even farther than Conrad's *Chance* in its conventionalized use of various scopes of heroes' awareness. Also, "always Faulkner's style resembles Conrad's in its rhythms as well as in its dependence on sonorous Latinism, on abstractions paired in paradoxical phrases, on word-motifs, and on 'negative ultimates'—negative words of ultimate degree. Finally, the function of Faulkner's style is the same as that of Conrad's, to draw the reader into the compelling trance of the language."[9]

But even in the case of Faulkner the real affinity consists in something else: in the tensely dramatic concept of life, in the insistence on moral involvement, and in the basically analogous hierarchy of values stressing honour, loyalty, endurance and friendship. Hemingway's vision and values, although differently expressed and clothed, belong to the same sphere; and his fundamental moral problem of an autonomously defined code of behaviour is a continuation of Conrad's quest. His heroes, enveloped in their painful consciousness of *nada*, the metaphysical void within which we are condemned to act, embrace principles which are neither egocentric nor utilitarian.

In the writings of Antoine de Saint-Exupéry, who crossed as many skies as Conrad had seas, we find not only techniques deliberately paralleling Conrad's, but also a generally similar attitude, which finds its most remarkable expression in the words of Guillaumet, the crashed pilot who saved himself, in an incredible effort, because he remembered his comrades' trust in him: "Ce que j'ai fait, je te le jure, jamais aucune bete ne l'aurait fait!" And Camus' idea that man's only salvation in the face of besieging evil is a desperate solidarity and preservation of honour also recalls Conrad's message about man's tragic and heroic dignity.[10]

Conrad's political novels, *Nostromo*, *The Secret Agent*, *Under West-*

ern Eyes, rather neglected during his lifetime, in the last forty years have been attracting more and more attention and, if it would be difficult and risky to talk about their influence, they present an approach to political problems which has become quite common in contemporary literature.

A part of Conrad's legacy as a political novelist consists simply of the themes he raised, some of them for the first time: the themes of ineffectual liberalism and degenerating revolution, of "material interests" corrupting both their exploited victims and their supposed beneficiaries, of political provocation and terroristic idealism, of the state demanding a total loyalty and still distrusting those who are loyal not because of a feeling of absolute dependence but from personal conviction. In our time they would become only too frequently not literary motifs, but elements of everybody's life, and we have been compelled to experience them on a painfully grand scale.

Political problems were for Conrad moral problems, fundamentally. "The French Revolution"—he wrote—"was not a political movement at all, but a great outburst of morality."[11] This way of looking at a political conflict as at a massive outburst of moral indignation or depravity was characteristic for many liberal and conservative thinkers. It was, however, usually coupled with a certain degree of either benevolent naiveté, or social ignorance or selfishness. Conrad, unfair as he was to the anarchists, showed an awareness of the existing social conflicts and their sources, and did not have many illusions about the convergence of interests of the haves and the have-nots. For him moral evaluation was not a screen, hiding real social and political issues.

His mistrust of purely political terms of reference was undoubtedly determined by the fact that he looked at all abstract political programmes as at a many-headed body of false promises. Political theories of the bourgeois world deceptively suggested that all was well and shall be better. Political theories intending to change this world seemed to endanger the national spirit (which he cherished) and threaten to upset this precarious structure we call human civilization, a structure delicately balanced on the surface of a vulcanic swamp.

This is why he seems to be the only major European writer of his time whose outlook did not have to change as a result of World War I, and perhaps the only one who would not have been surprised by the emergence of the modern totalitarian state.

On the larger plane of the general development of fiction, Conrad has bolstered anti-psychologic and anti-naturalistic trends—at a time when naturalism and psychology in the novel ruled supreme. Paradoxically, this avowed individualist and agnostic left a heritage of social and metaphysical concerns. The concentration on types and problems rather than exceptions and psychological subtleties is also a part of his legacy. Whenever we encounter a contemporary novel which deals with moral issues—not by way of emphasizing the biological and psychological uniqueness of every person, but by way of looking for the core of [the] common human condition — we may suppose that it runs parallel, or even belongs to the Conrad tradition.

Concentrating on general problems and typical situations is in Conrad's work one of the means to overcome the oppressive consciousness of man's loneliness. He was intensely aware of the all-pervading problem of uprootedness and isolation; more so than any of his contemporaries or any writer since, with the possible exception of Kafka. "We live, as we dream — alone." Solitude was for Conrad an element of the human condition that is inescapable — but against which we should fight relentlessly (here he differed from the fatalistic Kafka). In view of our present preoccupation with alienation and with the individual's loneliness within mass society and in the face of a universe expanding in all directions — Conrad seems to be a prophet. But not a despairing prophet of helplessness in the face of unavoidable doom.

Notes

1. Conrad to Marguerite Poradowska, 5 January 1907 (*Letters of J. Conrad to M. Poradowska*, ed by J. A. Gee and P. J. Sturm, [New Haven: Yale U P, 1940], p. 109).

2. The risks involved in discussing Conrad's psychological makeup without a firsthand knowledge of his national background justify perhaps a moment of special attention. They may be illustrated by a fragment from Frederick Crews's' "The Power of Darkness," *Partisan Review*, XXXIV (Fall 1967), 507–25. Analyzing the autobiographical and subconscious content of "Heart of Darkness," Professor Crews maintains that the hero, Kurtz, "in many ways amounts to a vindictive reconstruction of Conrad's father," Apollo Korzeniowski. He supports his assertion by pointing out that the names Kurtz and Korzeniowski "are alike." They may appear so only to a person unaware of the rules of Polish pronunciation: the only analogous sound in both names is "k." As a matter of fact, in the MS of "Heart of Darkness" Kurtz bears originally the name of the person on whom he was, physically at least, based: Klein. In the course of writing, Conrad substituted the German "short" for "small." However, even if the names had been really similar, Conrad might have had in mind simply himself: legally, he was a Korzeniowski till his death.

Furthermore, Crews argues that Conrad's father, like Kurtz, "refused an offer of rescue" and in his youth "experimented with dissipation." There is no shred of evidence that it ever was so. And while it is indeed true that Apollo Korzeniowski had "messianic political ambitions" — if the word "messianic" means anything, this assertion cannot be applied to Kurtz.

The real point here is that, pursuing on uncertain ground his thesis of Kurtz being for Conrad an effigy of his father, Crews misses a very interesting indication that Kurtz was endowed by Conrad with at least one important autobiographical trait. In a letter sent in 1890 to the Congo, Tadeusz Bobrowski, Conrad's uncle and guardian, wrote to him: "You are probably looking around at people and things as well as at the 'civilizing' (confound it) affair in the machinery of which you are a cog." (*Conrad's Polish Background*, ed by Z. Najder [Oxford U P, 1964] p. 128[9]). Every reader of "Heart of Darkness" remembers well that the idea of a "civilizing mission" was what originally obsessed Kurtz and made him go to Africa. This biographical detail enables us to see more clearly that "Heart of Darkness" is primarily an ideological, not a psychological, parable.

3. Ian Watt, "Joseph Conrad: Alienation and Commitment", *The English Mind*,

Studies in the English Moralists Presented to Basil Willey, ed. H. S. Davies and G. Watson (Cambridge: Cambridge U P, 1964), pp. 257–78.

4. Norman Douglas, who knew Conrad well, noted a little angrily: "I have heard the late Joseph Conrad called a great psychologist. . . . Well, Conrad was first and foremost a Pole and, like many Poles, a politician and moralist *malgré lui*. These are his fundamentals. He was also a great writer with hardly an ounce of psychology in his composition" ("A Plea for Better Manners," *A Selection*, ed by D. M. Low [Lond: Chatto and Windus; Secker and Warburg, 1955], p. 308).

5. Cf. J. Burkhart, *Das Erlebnis der Wirklichkeit und seine künstlerische Gestaltung in Joseph Conrads Werken* (Marburg: 1935).

6. Perhaps the most perfect example of total misunderstanding, resulting from a thoroughly middle-class attitude of the critic, can be found in H. G. Wells' remarks on Conrad in his *Experiment in Autobiography* (Lond: Macmillan, 1934), p. 526. F. M. Ford (at that time still Hueffer), Conrad's literary partner and for many years his close friend, offered an intuitive explanation of his anachronism: "I have thought very often that Conrad is an Elizabethan. That is possibly because he is a Pole—and the Poles have the virtues and the powers that served to make nations great in the sixteenth and seventeenth centuries. Roughly speaking, that was when Poland was a great Empire. They were Romantic, they were heroic, they were aristocrats—they were all the impracticable things" (F. M. Hueffer, "Joseph Conrad," *English Review*, X [Dec 1911], p. 69). Conrad's admiration for Shakespeare, a writer thoroughly saturated with the ideas and problems of the chivalric code (as Mr C. B. Watson's excellent study *Shakespeare and the Renaissance Concept of Honor* shows), had certainly a lot to do with his "Elizabethan" outlook.

7. Cf. Faulkner and M. Cowley on Sienkiewicz, in *The Faulkner-Cowley File* (NY: Viking P, 1966), p. 115.

8. Cf. Fitzgerald to Mencken in 1925 (*The Letters of F. Scott Fitzgerald*, ed by Andrew Turnbull (NY: Scribners, 1963), pp. 362, 363, 482, 510. Conrad's influence on Fitzgerald is discussed in detail by R. E. Long, "*The Great Gatsby* and the Tradition of Joseph Conrad," *Texas Studies in Literature and Language*, VIII (Summer and Fall 1966), 257–76, 407–22.

9. J. E. Tanner, "The Twentieth Century Impressionistic Novel: Conrad and Faulkner," *Dissertation Abstracts*, XXV (1964), p. 1927.

10. ". . . honor, like pity, is the irrational virtue that carries on after justice and reason have become powerless." Camus talking to J. Bloch-Michel, *Reporter*, 28 Nov. 1957.

11. *A Personal Record* (Dent Collected Ed.), p. 95.

Conrad: The Presentation of Narrative
Edward W. Said*

> *There are no words for the sort of things I wanted to say.*
> —Lord Jim

In this essay I hope to be able to show that both in his fiction and in his autobiographical writing Conrad was trying to do something that his experience as a *writer* everywhere revealed to be impossible. This makes him interesting as the case of a writer whose working reality, his practical

*Reprinted with permission from *Novel: A Forum on Fiction* 7 (1974):116–32.

and even theoretical competence as a writer, was far in advance of *what* he was saying. Occurring at the time at which he lived and wrote, this irony of Conrad's writing therefore has a critical place in the history of the duplicity of language, which since Nietzsche, Marx and Freud has made the study of the orders of language so focal for the contemporary understanding. Conrad's fate was to have written fiction great for its presentation, and not only for what it was representing. He was misled by language even as he led language into a dramatization no other author really approached. For what Conrad discovered was that the chasm between words saying and words meaning was *widened*, not lessened, by his talent for words written. To have chosen to write then is to have chosen in a particular way neither to say directly nor to mean exactly in the way he had hoped to say or to mean. No wonder that Conrad returned to this problematic concern repeatedly, a problematic concern that his writing dramatized continuously and imaginatively.

I

Conrad's narratives pay unusual attention to the *motivation* of the stories being told; this is evidence of a self-consciousness that felt it necessary to justify in some way the telling of a story. Such attention to the motive for telling a story exactly conflicts with his account in *A Personal Record* of Conrad's beginning as a writer. Instead of a reasoned process by which a sailor became a writer, Conrad says that "the conception of a planned book was entirely outside my mental range when I sat down to write." One morning he called in his landlady's daughter: " 'Will you please clear away all this at once?' I addressed her in convulsive accents, being at the same time engaged in getting my pipe to draw. This, I admit, was an unusual request . . . I remember that I was perfectly calm. As a matter of fact I was not at all certain that I wanted to write, or that I meant to write, or that I had anything to write about. No, I was not impatient."[1] "This" is breakfast. Once cleared away, *Almayer's Folly* was begun: so much for an event of "general mysteriousness." Conrad's narratives deal simultaneously with actions without obvious rational motivation like this event in *A Personal Record*, and such actions as the telling of a story motivated by ascertainable causes. A clear example of what I am trying to describe is found in *Heart of Darkness*. Marlow's desire to visit the dark places is longstanding but really unexplained and yet his account of the journey to a group of listeners is related exactly to an occasion that motivates it. Marlow's "hankering after" blank spaces doesn't have a sequential history and it doesn't develop. It is fairly constant; even in *A Personal Record*, as he describes his "birth" as a writer, Conrad tells the same story as this one of Marlow's: "Now when I was a little chap I had a passion for maps. I would look for hours at South America, or Africa, or Australia, and lose myself in all the glories of exploration. At that time there were many blank spaces on the earth, and when I saw one that looked particularly inviting on a map (but they all look that) I would put my finger on it and say, When I grow up I will go there" (VI, 52). Years later one blank space "had become a place of darkness. But there was in it one river especially, a mighty big river, that you could see on the map, resembling an immense snake uncoiled, with its head in the sea, its body at rest curving afar over a vast country, and its tail lost in the depths of the land. As I looked at the map of it in a shopwindow, it fascinated me as a snake would a bird — a silly little bird" (VI, 42). If we compare this story of stupefied fascination with the occasion that gives rise to Marlow's telling of his African adventure we notice how, from even the tale's first paragraph, a rationale and a motive for the narration are described. The *Nellie* is forced to "wait for the turn of the tide" (XVI, 45), the five men have a common history of sea-faring, the lower reaches of the Thames suggest, not a snake fascinating a dumb bird, but a thread leading back to "the great spirit of the past . . . the dreams of men, the seed of common-wealths, the germs of empires" (XVI, 47) and then there is Marlow, with his well-known "propensity to spin yarns." Before the narration begins (and how unlike Conrad's inability to conceive of a planned book before he became an author) "we knew we were fated, before the ebb began to run, to hear about one of Marlow's inconclusive experiences" (XVI, 51).

As Conrad surveyed his novels for the Author's Notes he wrote at a late point in his career he was often impressed with the way his narratives resembled a species of gratuitous emanations. Frequently then he provided his reader with originating reasons for the story he had written. More often than not these reasons were an appealing anecdote, a bit of personal experience, a newspaper story and so on. Norman Sherry's prodigious labors have unearthed far more of that evidence than Conrad revealed, not only because Conrad was forgetful and evasive, but also because he was concerned mainly with *justifying* what he did as being reasonable. Conrad, I think, judged that to be more important than supplying clues to his methods of work. Hence, I think we ought to take seriously Conrad's protest in the Note to *Lord Jim* that Marlow's narration *could* have been spoken during an evening of swapping yarns. It is a very surprising line to take, but Conrad was addressing what was to him always an important point, the dramatized telling of the story, how and when it was told, for which the evidence was an integral part of the novel as a whole: "Men have been known, both in the tropics and the temperate zone, to sit up half the night 'swapping yarns.' This, however, is but one yarn, yet with interruption affording some measure of relief; and in regard to the listeners' endurance, the postulate must be accepted that the story was interesting. . . . That part of the book which is Marlow's narrative can be read through aloud, I should say, in less than three hours. Besides . . . we may presume that there must have been refreshments on that night, a glass of mineral water of some sort to help the narrator on" (XXI, vii).

Quite literally, therefore, Conrad was able to see his narratives as the place in which the motivated, the occasional, the methodical and the rational are brought together with the aleatory, the unpredictable, the inexplicable. On the one hand, there are conditions presented by which a story's telling becomes necessary; on the other hand, the essential story itself seems opposite to the conditions of its telling. The interplay of one with the other — and Conrad's attention to the persuasively realistic setting of the tale's presentation enforces our attention to it — makes the narrative the unique thing it is.

Such an interplay of antitheses moreover ought to be characterized as doing for Conrad what no other activity, whether verbal, plastic, or gestural, could have done for him. I attach a great importance to this observation. Too often Conrad's text is searched for supervening sub-texts or privileged meanings of the sort that seem more important than the book itself. Whereas not enough care is given the near-truism that the text such as it is, was for Conrad a produced thing, *the* produced thing — something he returned to as author, critic, defender, spectator or victim. The text was the never-ending product of a continuing process. For him, as many letters testify, the *necessity* of writing, once he had become an author, was pre-eminently the problem; for all the "general mysteriousness" of the "Rubicon" crossed into authorhood, he viewed his career as writer as a physical process and as a particularly onerous task that was his fate. "La solitude me gagne: elle m'absorbe. Je ne vois rien, je ne lis rien. C'est comme une éspèce de tombe, qui serait en même temps un enfer, où il faut écrire, écrire, écrire."[2] Loneliness, darkness, the necessity of writing, imprisonment: these are the pressures upon the writer as he writes, and there is scarcely any writer I have read who seems so profligate in his complaining. How different in tone this is from the aesthetic credo delivered by Conrad in his 1896 Preface to *The Nigger of the 'Narcissus'*. He speaks there of the artist's capacity for communal speech, and for the clarity of sight he affords the reader; those are achievements presumably won after much struggle with the writing itself: "To snatch in a moment of courage, from the remorseless rush of time, a passing phase of life, is only the beginning of the task. The task approached in tenderness and faith is to hold up unquestioningly, without choice and without fear, the rescued fragment before all eyes in the light of a sincere mood. It is to show its vibration, its colour, its form; and through its movement, its form, and its colour reveal the substance of its truth — disclose its inspiring secret: the stress and passion within the core of each convincing movement" (XXIII, xiv).

Yet this is no set of euphemisms. To rescue a fragment and give it shape and form, to make the reader *see*, to do this by overcoming rational choice at the outset and fear during the performance: as imperatives they are much more formidable when we insist, as Conrad does a little earlier, that the medium is words. To produce or to read words is something quite different, obviously, than the more *visual* (and more well-known) goals

Conrad formulates for his work. Indeed the perceptual transformation that occurs when writing or reading result in *sight* is very drastic, even antithetical. So antithetical in fact that one tends to forget the whole sentence in which Conrad formulates his primary ambition. "My task which I am trying to achieve is, by the power of the written word to make you hear, to make you feel—it is before all, to make you *see*" (xiv). Conrad's narratives thus embody (provide a locale for) the transformation in the act of taking place. Conrad's own efforts, he says, are to employ the power of *written* words, with their origin in the painstaking craft of writing, in order to make his reader experience the vitality and the dynamism of *seen* things. Most often, however, this happens through the mediation of spoken words.

For the dramatic protocol of much of Conrad's fiction is the swapped yarn, the historical report, the commonly exchanged legend, the musing recollection. This protocol implies (although often they are implicitly there) a speaker of course and a hearer and, as I said earlier, a sometimes very specific enabling occasion. If we go through Conrad's major work we will find, with the notable exception of *Under Western Eyes*, that the narrative is presented as transmitted orally. Thus hearing and telling are the ground of the story as it were, the tale's most stable sensory activity, the measure of its duration, whereas *seeing*, in marked contrast, is always a precarious achievement and a much less stable business. Consider, for a couple of examples, Kurtz and Jim. Both are heard about and spoken about more than they are seen directly in the narrative setting. When they are seen—and Jim is a particularly striking instance: "for me that white figure in the stillness of coast and sea seemed to stand at the heart of a vast enigma"—they are less clear than enigmatic, and in some curious way, grossly distorted. "Kurtz looked at least seven feet long . . . I saw him open his mouth wide—it gave him a weirdly voracious aspect, as though he had wanted to swallow all the air, all the earth, all the men before him" (XVI, 134). As Marlow speaks, furthermore, his voice remains steady as his listeners' sight of him fades. So frequent is that sort of disappearance that Conrad's stated goal in the 1896 Preface was for him an especially challenging one, since the course of narrative words seems frequently not only to run counter to vision, but to protract the silence of "an impenetrable darkness," despite the insistence of words either on the page or between speaker and hearer.

Perhaps it is useful to schematize some of what I have been saying. Narratives originate in the hearing and telling presence of people to each other. In Conrad's case this is usually true whether or not the narratives are told in the first person. Their subject is illusory, or shadowy, or dark: that is, whatever by nature is not easy to see. So much at least is ascertainable by the sheer telling of the tale, for what the tale usually reveals is the exact contours of this obscurity. Much of the time obscurity, regardless of even extravagant outward splendour (as is the case with

Nostromo or Jim or the Black Mate), is a function of secret shame. Paradoxically, however, the secret is all too easily prone to the wrong kind of exposure, which Conrad's notoriously circumspect methods of narrative attempt to forestall. The reflective narrator is always a narrator preventing the wrong sort of interpretation. His narrative invariably assumes the currency of a rival version. For example, the whole of *Nostromo* is built out of competing histories of Costaguana, each claiming to be a more perspicacious record of momentous events, each implicitly critical of other versions. The same is true of *Under Western Eyes, Lord Jim*, and so on.

One can conceive of Conrad's narratives abstractly as the alternation in language of presence and absence. The presence of spoken words in time mitigates, if it does not make entirely absent, their written version; a speaker takes over the narrative with his voice, and his voice overrides the fact that he is absent (or unseen) to his listeners as he speaks; Conrad's goal is to make us see, or otherwise to transcend the *absence* of everything but words, so that we may pass into a realm of vision beyond the words. What is that realm? It is a world of such uncomplicated coincidence between intention, word and deed that the ghost of a fact, as *Lord Jim* has it, can be put to rest. There, rifts in the community of man, or in the damaged ego, are healed, and the space separating ambition from activity is narrowed. Retrospective time and events are corrected for divergences. Or, still more radically, the writer's intention of wishing to say something very clearly is squared completely with the reader's seeing — words bound to the page are, by the labors of a solitary writer, become the common unmediated property of the reader, who penetrates past the words to their author's visual intention, which is the same as his written presentation.

For Conrad the meaning produced by writing was a kind of *visual* outline to which written language can approach only from the outside and asymptotically. We can perhaps ascribe this hobbling limitation upon words to Conrad's concurrent faith in the supremacy of the visible and his radical doubt of the mimetic power available to written language. His use of such devices as the inquiry (*Lord Jim*), historical reporting (*Nostromo*), methodical quest (*Heart of Darkness*), the translation (*Under Western Eyes*), the ironic investigation (*The Secret Agent*) incarnates the process of drawing near in retrospective language to a sight (pun intended with "site") for which language might no longer be necessary. In all his narratives Conrad assumes that there is a central *place*, a heart of darkness which may be somewhere in central Africa, in Central America, or central London, that is better located, more centrally, for understanding action whose tendency is to proliferate from that place. To think of Conrad's fiction in those terms is to be hit by how compulsively the whole complex of ideas associated with "the center" (approach to the center, radiations away from the center) keeps appearing, especially since *writing* a narrative is the translation of a told narrative, which itself is a means for reaching that center. Thus in *Heart of Darkness* Marlow's trek inwards makes Kurtz the goal. Why? Because Kurtz is at the Inner Station and he is much spoken about; Marlow hopes by reaching him to put a stop to all the rumors, and finally to *see* (silently) for himself what exactly it is that Kurtz is and has done. Most of the time, however, the reader like Marlow must finally be satisfied with *fewer* words rather than no words once the center has been reached. Hence the haunting power in Conrad of minimal phrases such as "the horror" or "material interests": these work as the still verbal center glossed by the narrative and around which our attention turns and returns. *See* the thing they announce, and you have done with words. *Find* their visual equivalent, and you have a total presence for which the duplicitous order of language has made absent in the narrative. Not for nothing is Conrad's first extended narrative, *Almayer's Folly*, about a structure called folly, designed to house the acquisition of gold brought out from the interior, gold never seen, never brought out, only spoken about.

So irrational must the coincidence between the effacement of words and the unmediated visual presence of meaning have become by the time of *The Secret Agent* (1907 — twelve years after *Almayer*) that Conrad's use of a deranged boy's habitual activity to represent the coincidence is, I think, strongly self-commenting: ". . . innocent Stevie, seated very good and quiet at a deal table, drawing circles, circles; innumerable circles, concentric, eccentric, a coruscating whirl of circles that by their tangled multitude of repeated curves, uniformity of form, and confusion of intersecting lines suggested a rendering of cosmic chaos, the symbolism of a mad art attempting the inconceivable. The artist never turned his head; and in all his soul's application to the task his back quivered, his thin neck, sunk into a deep hollow at the base of the skull, seemed ready to snap" (XIII, 45–6).

Mr. Verloc merely "discloses the innocent Stevie" when he opens the kitchen door, for Stevie's autistic art intends no hearer, and it is unspoken. It is just a ceaseless, intense application to a repeated action whose meaning is unchanging. Conrad's choice of the word *task* here was probably an unintended quotation from the 1896 Preface whose moral seriousness he drew upon frequently. The solitary, repetitive, uniform, and confusing nature of Stevie's art parallels Conrad's description of writing ("un enfer où il faut écrire, écrire, écrire"), just as the concentric, eccentric circles suggest the interplay of antithesis and the alternation in language of presence and absence to which I referred above. What is most remarkable is the *silence* of the whole scene and its "general mysteriousness." Can we say that Stevie is being overlooked, or overheard? For indeed it is hard to know whether Mr. Verloc's "grunt of disapproving surprise" means anything more than the merest awareness. Circles do not speak, they tell only of the inconceivable and that by a very attenuated symbolism, and they enclose blankness even as they seem partly to be excluding it. Moreover, Stevie's circles are pagebound; they tie him to a blank white space, and they exist no place else. I think it entirely likely that Conrad imagined Stevie as a kind of writer viewed *in extremis* who in being taken for a sort of pointless idiot is limited terribly to two poles: inscribing a page endlessly, or blown to bits and without human identity. (There are rough, but affecting antecedents for Stevie and the Verlocs in "The Idiots," a short story completed by Conrad in 1896. The story opens in very much the same way as "Amy Foster" [1901], which also deals with an alienated figure who appears to be insane, with the narrator *seeing* the vestiges of an old story as he visits a locale new to him. The story—"at last [it stood] before me, a tale formidable and simple"—is of a peasant couple who unaccountably produce four idiot children. The wife's hurt perplexity and rage drives her to kill her husband. She then kills herself by jumping off a cliff into the sea; a witness to the suicide hears "one shrill cry for help that seemed to dart upwards . . . and soar past, straight into the high and impassive heaven" [VIII, 84].

Still later, the language teacher in *Under Western Eyes* (1911) will comment further upon the attempt to transcend language by vision. Now, however, that folly has a political meaning as well, despite its formulation by him in verbal terms. "That propensity" he says "of lifting every problem from the plane of the understandable by means of some sort of mystic expression, is very Russian" (XXII, 104). Elsewhere he remarks on what it is like to listen to Russians speaking: "The most precise of her [Natalia Haldin's] sayings seemed always to me to have enigmatical prolongations vanishing somewhere beyond my reach" (XXII, 118). The verbs of physical action and perception to describe language put to extra-verbal use are thoroughly consistent with Conrad's usual practice. *Lifting* of course suggests the *holding up* of the 1896 Preface, but it is associated here with the derogatory *mystic expression*, an unreliable instrument at best. The net effect of this kind of communication, no matter how precisely formulated, is to extend meaning so far away from the words that it disappears completely. What the old teacher constantly reiterates is that the tendency in Russian to mystic expression is a kind of ontological flaw present to a much lesser degree in the Western languages. Razumov feels the flaw hysterically when Haldin throws himself upon the poor student's mercy. Order is associated with the careful study and use of language (and after all it is not fortuitous that both the teacher and Razumov are students of the word), whereas disorder, transcendence and a kind of political aestheticism are linked to Haldin's revolutionary wish directly to see, to change, to embrace.

By the time *Chance* (1913) gave him an unexpected popularity Conrad had determined that he was after all an English writer, not as some critics had alleged a French one *manqué*, nor a crypto-Slav. In the second, much later preface (1919) to *A Personal Record* he wrote this astonishingly "Russian" account of his use of English. I quote it at length for its passion and its determination not to press rationality too far:

> The truth of the matter is that my faculty to write in English is as natural as any other aptitude with which I might have been born. I have a strange and overpowering feeling that it had always been an inherent part of myself. English was for me neither a matter of choice nor adoption. The merest idea of choice had never entered my head. And as to adoption — well, yes, there was adoption; but it was I who was adopted by the genius of the language, which directly I came out of the stammering stage made me its own so completely that its very idioms I truly believe had a direct action on my temperament and fashioned my still plastic character.
>
> It was a very intimate action and for that very reason it is too mysterious to explain. The task would be as impossible as trying to explain love at first sight. There was something in this conjunction of exulting, almost physical recognition, the same sort of emotional surrender and the same pride of possession, all united in the wonder of a great discovery; but there was on it none of the shadow of dreadful doubt that falls on the very flame of our perishable passions. One knew very well that this was for ever.
>
> A matter of discovery and not of inheritance, that very inferiority of the title makes the faculty still more precious, lays the possessor under a lifelong obligation to remain worthy of his great fortune. . . . All I can claim after all those years of devoted practice, with the accumulated anguish of its doubts, imperfections and falterings in my heart, is the right to be believed when I say that if I had not written in English I would not have written at all. (VI, vii–viii)

Even if this is not the most lucid treatment of the problem at least one gets from this passage an inkling of how complex, and how close to "Impossible" (the capital is Conrad's), the problems were for Conrad as he considered the dissemination, reception, and perception of language.

His letters portray Conrad perpetually struggling with language. His narratives always dramatize how a story happens to someone else: he is either told it or, if he is the protagonist, he experiences it like Jim with its rationale herded under the heading Romance. "Romance had singled Jim for its own — and that was the true part of the story, which otherwise was all wrong." Written language was essentially a *passive*, retrospective transcription of action. As author therefore Conrad presented his writing as methodically overshadowed by the speaking voice, the past, vision, and restful clarity. How revealing is this moan in a letter of January 4, 1900 to Cunninghame Graham: "But difficulties are as it were closing round me; an irresistible march of blackbeetles I figure it to myself. What a fate to be so ingloriously devoured."[3]

Conrad *seemed* to have *overestimated* language, or at any rate its power over him. I do not intend this as a judgment against him since from this overestimation derives the extraordinary care Conrad took with the way his narratives are delivered. *Heart of Darkness*, for instance, is a complex structure with half a dozen "languages" in it, each with its own sphere of experience, its time, its center of consciousness. To say that Conrad wrote in English therefore is to say really that Conrad makes highly imaginative distinctions within English, distinctions no other writer before him would have thought necessary, distinctions that were "physical recognition" of verbal sources for a story that always lay just beyond and outside him. These distinctions were Conrad's defence against the assault of language: by redisposing and re-dispersing, then reassembling language into voices, he could stage his work as a writer. The plurality of narrative components is then imagined as encircling a subject in many different ways. The net effect, as Mallarmé says in *Crise de vers*, is finally to concede "l'initiative aux mots, par le heurt de leur inegalités mobilisés."[4] What gets left out of the words is that intransigent remnant of the writer's identity that is not amenable to language. By a curious irony, which doubtless appeals to a writer who wishes to make you see, the excluded remnant is the actual inscribing *persona* himself, the author, and yet Conrad pretended that the author was secondary. Once again we note how voices leading to vision efface what Conrad called "the worker in prose," whose disappearance, according to Mallarmé, ought to yield *l'oeuvre pure*. Unlike both Mallarmé and Flaubert, however, this does not happen in Conrad's case. Let us now try to see why not.

II

Walter Benjamin's reflections on Leskov's storytelling takes it that the success of narrative art has traditionally depended upon a sense of community between speaker and listener, and on the desire to communicate something useful. Those two conditions are interdependent. Information is useful only because it can be put to use by others with the same set of values, and a set of values is perpetuated only by the adherence to it of more than one individual. That this is no longer true in modern times, according to Benjamin, "is a concomitant symptom of the secular productive forces of history, a concomitant that has quite gradually removed narrative from the realm of living speech and at the same time is making it possible to see a new beauty in what is vanishing. . . . The storyteller takes what he tells from experience—his own or that reported by others. And he in turn makes it the experience of those who are listening to his tale. The novelist has isolated himself. The birthplace of the novel is the solitary individual, who is no longer able to express himself by giving examples of his most important concerns, is himself uncounseled, and cannot counsel others. To write a novel means to carry the incommensurable to extremes in the representation of human life."[5]

Conrad's personal history made him acutely sensitive to the different status of *information* in the sea life, on the one hand, and in the writing life on the other. In the former, community and usefulness are essential to the enterprise; in the latter the opposite is true. Thus Conrad had the dubious privilege of witnessing within his own double life the change from storytelling as useful, communal art to novel-writing as essentialized, solitary art.

What does the change specifically entail? First of all, since the status of information has become problematical, the medium of its delivery is given greater prominence. Second, the speaker has to vary his words and his tone enough to compensate for his doubts of the usefulness of what he is saying. James and Wilde, Conrad's contemporaries, repeatedly referred to this sort of variation as the creation of interest; interest in such an instance depends closely upon an uncertainty towards (or even an ignorance of) the usefully practical. Conrad's virtuosic skill in narrative management, which reached its apex in *Chance*, is always as important as — and usually more interesting and important than — any information the tale conveys. One can say this without any way belittling either the sea lore in Conrad's fiction or its devotees among his readers. Third, the narrative no longer merely assumes a listener. It dramatizes him as well, so that frequently the author himself appears to be participating in the tale as an audience, or more precisely in Conrad's case, as the dramatized *recipient* of impressions. Fourth, narrative is conceived, in what Frye calls its radical of presentation, as *utterance* rather than as useful information. In Conrad's case the refinement of information into narrative utterance, as well as the fact that his language is usually in the mode of reported speech, are signs that the content of what is said need not by definition be as clear as who says it, why, and how.

I think that this last change has to be considered as an aspect of the general loss of faith in the mimetic powers of language to which I referred earlier. I said then that it was possible for the writer to lose such a faith and still to retain a belief in the supremacy of the visible. Writing therefore cannot represent the visible, but it can desire and, in a manner of speaking, can move towards the visible, without actually achieving the unambiguous directness of the visible. Michel Foucault has studied this apparent contradiction in his *Les mots et les choses* by treating it as a specific historical phase embodied in the work of de Sade, Mallarmé and Nietzsche: Conrad's narratives, I believe, offer particularly rich illustrations of it. Only within a general perspective of the sort Foucault draws can we understand the deep necessity of Conrad's decision to ground narrative epistemologically in utterance — that is, speech reported or spoken during periods dramatized as *enforced calm* — and not in action, community, or information.

The springs of Conrad's narrative utterances are what I shall call a) wanting-to-speak and b) the need to link a given utterance with other utterances. What makes a Conradian character the special creature he is comes from something he possesses that is in need of telling about. Often he possesses a guilty secret; at other times he is a man or woman of whom other people talk obsessively. At still other times he is a taciturn man, like

James Wait, or Charles Gould, or MacWhirr, or Axel Heyst whose entire life *speaks* in an exemplary way to other men. Thus Conrad's tales are about such personages as all these but they are presented as *taken note of*. The internal continuity of each tale, however, derives from the utterance's sense of its own difference which, as I said above, is an awareness of conflicting or complementary utterances. In a sense therefore every narrative utterance in Conrad stands against another one: and Marlow's lie to Kurtz's Intended is only the most notable instance of a common enough habit. Nostromo's great ride out of Sulaco is the subject of Mitchell's admiring reports, but these must be judged to be but a few of the reports that generally treat the *capataz de cargadores* as Sulaco's savior. Then too Decoud's notes personify the cynic's attitude, in deliberate contrast to Gould's sentimentalism. Avellanos, Emilia, Giorgio Viola, Sotillo — each perceives and reports events in a manner turned either explicitly or implicitly towards other perceptions. In no place more than in *Chance* can the reader see Conrad make tension and conflict, and thereby a dynamic narrative texture, out of utterance at odds with and yet ineluctably linked to other utterance.

Lord Jim is one of the first of Conrad's extended narratives to make knowledge, intelligibility, and vision into functions of utterance. The novel "takes off" in "the act of intelligent volition" that directs Marlow's eyes to Jim's during the Inquiry. After a period of "endless converse with himself" and at a time when "speech was no use to him any longer" Jim at last meets a man whose presence loosens the tongues "of men with soft spots, with hard spots, with hidden plague spots." Marlow not only listened, but is "willing to remember Jim at length, in detail and audibly." True, Jim has "influential confidences" to confess, yet Marlow's propensity to tell and remember is at least as important to the book: ". . . With the very first word [of his narrative] Marlow's body, extended at rest in the seat, would become very still, as though his spirit had winged its way back into the lapse of time and were speaking through his lips from the past" (XXI, 33). Marlow's generosity towards Jim is rooted in precisely that same tendency to romantic projection because of which Jim so embarrassingly prefers courageous voyages in time to voyages in actuality. Neither man, whether hearer or storyteller, truly inhabits the world of facts. First Jim, then Marlow wanders off "to comprehend the Inconceivable," an activity so urgent and rarefied at the same time as to involve "A subtle and momentous quarrel as to the true essence of life." Ultimately Conrad points out that Jim does not speak to Marlow, but rather *before* him, just as Marlow cannot (by definition) speak to the reader but before him.

What first seems like a meeting of minds turns into a set of parallel lines. Moreover Marlow explicitly says later that Jim exists for him, as if to say that Jim's confession before Marlow mattered more than what Jim confessed (both Marlow and Jim seem just about equally confused anyway). Only because of that performance — not just because of Jim's exploits in and of themselves — does Jim exist for his listener. I have already commented on Conrad's practice, which is evident in what Marlow says of Jim's enigmatic appearance and his need to talk, of alternating the visual and the oral modes: the way the narrative shows how "Romance had singled out Jim for its own" follows directly from this practice. Jim's appetite for disastrous adventure, like Marlow's narrative, like our attention to the tale, corresponds not to any communicable pattern of linear progress from, say, ambition to accomplishment, but rather to a more abstract impulse. The impulse can find no expression in action, and no image, other than the vague rubric of Romance, conveys the aim of Jim's troubled quest. The impulse resolves itself into the duration of reported speech or utterance whose exigencies are such relatively ethereal things as pattern, rhythm, phrase, sequence. What is the pressure upon Jim that makes him favor death over life, and which urges Marlow and Conrad towards "inconclusive experiences" that reveal less to the reader than he is entitled normally to expect? In all cases there exists a fatalistic desire to behold the self passively as an object told about, mused on, puzzled over, marveled at fully, in utterance. That is, Jim, Marlow and Conrad having everywhere conceded that one can neither completely realize one's own nor fully grasp someone else's life experience, are left with a desire to fashion verbally and approximately their individual experience in the terms unique to each one. Since invariably this experience is either long gone or by definition almost impossible, no image can capture this, just as finally no sentence can either.

Nevertheless the utterance is spoken, if not only to, then before another. Words convey the presence to each other of speaker and hearer but not a mutual comprehension. Each sentence drives a sharper wedge between intention (wanting-to-speak) and communication. Finally wanting-to-speak, a specifically verbal intention, is forced to confront the insufficiency, and indeed the absence, of words for that intention. It is not too extreme, I think, to say that in a very complex way Conrad is dramatizing the disparity between verbal intention apprehendable and possible, grammatically and formally, and verbality itself, as a way of being in the world of language with other men. In no place more than in "Amy Foster," that most poignant of all his stories, is the disparity spelled out in particular human detail. Washed ashore in England, Yanko Goorall lives amongst people who cannot make him out and to whose language he is always a foreigner:

> These were the people to whom he owed allegiance, and an over-whelming loneliness seemed to fall from the leaden sky of that winter without sunshine. All the faces were sad. He could talk to no one, and had no hope of ever understanding anybody. It was as if these had been the faces of people from the other world — dead people he used to tell me years afterwards. Upon my word, I wonder he did not go mad. He

didn't know where he was. Somewhere very far from his mountains—
somewhere over the water. Was this America, he wondered?

. . . The very grass was different, and the trees. All the trees but
the three old Norway pines on the bit of lawn before Swaffer's house,
and these reminded him of his country. He had been detected once,
after dusk, with his forehead against the trunk of one of them, sobbing,
and talking to himself. They had been like brothers to him at that time,
he affirmed. Everything else was strange . . .

Many times have I heard his high-pitched voice from behind the
ridge of some sloping sheepwalk, a voice light and soaring, like a lark's,
but with a melancholy human note, over our fields that hear only the
song of birds. And I would be startled myself. Ah! He was different;
innocent of heart, and full of good will, which nobody wanted, this
castaway, that, like a man transplanted into another planet, was
separated by an immense space from his past and by an immense
ignorance of the future. His quick, fervent utterance positively shocked
everybody. (XX, 128, 129, 132)

Conrad's excruciatingly detailed understanding of this predicament
makes utterance something far more urgent than a comfortable aesthetic
choice. It is clear he believed that only a fully imagined scene between a
speaker and a *watching* hearer could present—continuously, directly, and,
since it occurs in story after story, repeatedly—the fundamental divorce he
stood for as a writer: the rift between a fully developed but, with regard to
other people, an intentional or virtual capacity, and an inescapable
human community. "There are no words for the sort of things I wanted to
say." Hence, for example, Conrad's penchant for repeating phrases like "he
was one of us" together with reminders of how unique each individual and
his experiences were. Moreover the text Conrad worked at ceased simply to
be a written document and became instead a distribution of utterances
around both sides of the rift. They are held together by the reader's
attention to both sides. In its duration for the length of the book such
overarching attention binds together Jim's verbal intention with Marlow's
forbearance as a witness. In the domain of intention and fantasy to which
Conrad's heroes have what appears to be a fatal attraction, and only there,
can there be completion for schemes of the kind Jim devises for himself;
but such a place is apprehendable only during the constantly progressing
narrative of his doom and failure. When Marlow sees Jim for the last time,
there is the following passage:

Jim, at the water's edge raised his voice. "Tell them . . ." he began. I
signed to the men to cease rowing, and waited in wonder. Tell who? The
half-submerged sun faced him. I could see its red gleam in his eyes that
looked dumbly at me . . . "No—nothing," he said, and with a slight
wave of his hand motioned the boat away. I did not look again at the
shore till I had clambered on board the schooner.

. . . He was white from head to foot, and remained persistently
visible with the stronghold of the night at his back, the sea at his feet,

the opportunity by his side — still veiled? I don't know. For me that white figure in the stillness of coast and sea seemed to stand at the heart of a vast enigma. The twilight was ebbing fast from the sky above his head, the strip of sand had sunk already under his feet, he himself appeared no bigger than a child — then only a speck, a tiny white speck, that seemed to catch all the light left in a darkened world . . . And suddenly, I lost him. . . ." (XXI, 336)

Much is brought together here. Jim's terminal silence indicates that once again "a silent opportunity" takes over his life. He seems for a moment to have become the point of visual, as well as intellectual, reference for which words are both inadequate and never relinquished. Then he disappears. His life is covered over with the minimal traces — a letter, an incomplete narrative, a patchy oral report — that Marlow can garner much later. But at least Jim holds the privacy of his intentionality intact, something Axel Heyst, for example, cannot hold to himself for very long. Heyst is the last of those substantial Conradian figures to attempt a life of almost pure virtuality and, almost by definition, the last of men whose passivity is an invitation to the assaults of Romance. Yet in *Victory* (1915) Heyst's insular seclusion is of itself no guarantee. No man, in short, can become invisible so long as he retains even the slenderest contact with the actual. The subject of Schomberg's malicious gossip, of Ricardo's venality, of the Archipelago's gossip, Heyst cannot use his father's philosophy of detachment to much purpose. Besides, Heyst's attraction to Lena is too strong for him, just as earlier his sympathy for Morrison's plight crushes his reserve.

Of course there is an important sexual theme in *Victory*, yet Conrad's deliberate juxtaposition of Morrison's boat with Lena as objects of Heyst's romantic intervention into the world belongs, I think, to another, more strictly verbal enterprise of his, one easily found in many other places in the fiction. I have said that Conrad's primary mode, although he is a writer, is presented as the oral, and his ambition is to move towards the visual. These are the situations that employ yarns, tales, and utterances for their depiction, and which in the end present us with the disparity between intention and actuality, or in sensuous terms between hearing on the one hand, and seeing and comprehending on the other. In my discussion of *Lord Jim* I had been indicating also the *play* of all this in the text, as well as the intense attraction to each other, despite the gulf between them, of intention (not silence) and actuality. But, it needs hardly to be said, Conrad is a novelist, not a philosopher, and not a psychologist. This brings me to my final point, which I'd like now to sketch briefly. I imagine that during the writing of his fiction Conrad had certain substantial quantities or qualities in mind, for both his memory and his senses, though transmuted into words as he wrote, were focussed on material objects. Despite what I have said about utterance and presentation one remembers *objects* in Conrad's fiction, not merely words. In his fiction an essential place is filled by substances around which a great deal of the action in the utterance is organized: Lingard's gold, Kurtz's ivory, the ships of sailors, Gould's silver, the women that draw men to change and romance, and so forth. A large proportion of the tension in Conrad's fiction gets generated as the author, or the narrator, or the hero tries to make us *see* the object that draws out the writing, the thought, the speech on and on. I said earlier that with telling or reporting as their basis, these activities approach substantiality. But why? And why, after all, did Conrad ground all these activities, given verbal form, in utterance, or reported speech, and not for example in the impersonal purity adopted by Mallarmé or Joyce?

The main interest of this question is, I think, that it purports to distinguish, however minimally and schematically, between Conrad's psychology (which is really the exclusive subject of psychoanalytic studies like *Joseph Conrad: A Psychoanalytic Biography*, by Bernard C. Meyer) and the psychology of Conrad's writing. As a source of evidence for the man's psychohistory, fiction is "finished" by literary process in a way that everyday behaviour, itself conditioned by culture and history, is not. Moreover, as I have tried to show elsewhere,[6] there is a particular psychological dynamic to a literary career and a literary text that is very doubtfully construed as either direct or indirect evidence of a *man's* psychology considered *tout court*. But does a literary career or text, and consequently an *author*, mean confirmation or denial of psychopathology? Is there any relatively useful and non-trivial way of separating "the man who suffers and the mind which creates?" To be more specific, is there an exact analogy between an author's personal writing and artistic writing on the one hand, and, on the other hand, the same man's discourse and his dreams?

Writing, whether personal or artistic, and dreams are subject to different sorts of control than the ones governing a man's spoken discourse. Yet it is difficult to conceive of writing-work done under conditions that resemble those of dream-work. Wakefulness, a pen or a typewriter, paper, one's past writing, a plan for what is being written, a set of physical gestures, what one has consciously learned about writing: these, I think, count importantly in differentiating writing and dreaming, at least if one is to insist that the two activities are valid as psychoanalytic evidence. The differences become more interesting, however, when writing is denied its importance in the writer's work itself, especially by the writer like Conrad for whom it was sheer agony.

If we say, as I think we must, that Conrad in his writing is generally unhappy, with the idea of writing, so much so that when he is not complaining about it he is always turning it into substitute speech, then we can go as far as saying that Conrad's writing tries in fact overtly to negate itself *as writing*. Of negation Freud has said that it is a way of affirming what is repressed. But what does it mean for a writer to affirm writing that is repressed? Again Freud is helpful. "By the help of the symbol of negation the thinking-process frees itself from the limitations of repression and enriches itself with the subject-matter without which it could not work efficiently."[7] Writing, and its negation in the ways I have discussed, was for Conrad a way of *permitting himself* a number of things otherwise impossible. Amongst these things are the use of English, the use of experiences from out of his past that are reconstructed and, most of the time, de-formed into "fictional" novels and stories, the use of events about which no explanation can (or need) be satisfactory.

Let us continue a step further with Freud's argument. Negation is the result of an intellectual judgment made on two grounds. First there is a judgment as to whether a thing has, or has not, a particular property. Second, a judgment is made as to whether or not an image exists in reality. In both cases criteria of internality (respectively: I want this inside me, or, that image is inside me) and criteria of externality (respectively: I reject this, or, that image also has an existence in reality outside me) are used, both of them making reference to the judging ego. Freud had been led to these discoveries because, he says, "in the course of analytic work we often bring about a further very important and somewhat bewildering modification of the same situation. We succeed in defeating the negation too and in establishing a complete intellectual acceptance of what is repressed — but the repression itself is still not removed" (182). Therefore when a *negative* reality-judgment about an image is made the ego may still be affirming the image's existence by repression; for an *image* is a rediscovery of what has already been lost. Thus only when "the symbol of negation has endowed thought with a first degree of independence from the results of repression and at the same time from the sway of the pleasure principle" (185) is there a proper judgment.

Writing for Conrad was an activity that constituted negation — of itself, of what it dealt with — and was also repetitive. That is, writing negated, re-constituted, negated again, and so forth indefinitely; hence the extraordinarily patterned quality of Conrad's writing. The utterance is the *form* of the negation. As such therefore its function is to postpone judgment indefinitely, on itself and its subject matter: it too is repetitive, for we see Conrad imagining narrative *being uttered* from one tale to the next while the reality of what Marlow calls "life-sensation" remains private, developed, uncommunicable except by negatives (e.g. "we live, as we dream — alone . . ."). But Conrad's characters, at some stage in their lives, are powerfully affected by material objects: women, treasure, ships, land, etc. Most of the time, however, these objects are at the outset passively endowed with force. Charles Gould inherits his father's mine. Only after that does he build the imperial power of the San Tomé Mine. At the point in Conrad's fiction that that process of mythical building becomes apparent, an important cleavage appears between the character reported about and the report. The fact of utterance from being a form of negation becomes then the instrument of Conrad's judgment. Writing transforms the writer from failed speaker, the character or the "narrating pen" who has direct, visual and even material goals passively accepted because of heritage or convention, into the reflective writer, the *author* who *takes on* the form of utterance habitually from novel to novel and forces it through a maximum of different and interesting developments. In each tale therefore Conrad's autobiographical presence plays numerous roles: first as man to whom events happened, as speaker, as listener, then finally as author who at one moment *presents* narrative, negates it by pretending it is speech, then negates that (in his letters) by denouncing its difficulties, then negates even that (late in his career) by sounding like Everyman's Favorite Old Novelist. My argument, put very bluntly, is that Conrad's writing was a way of repeatedly *confirming* his authorship amidst a variety of narrative and quasi-narrative contingencies, and not simply a way of representing his neuroses.

Conrad in short tried to use prose for the transcendence of writing and the *embodiment* both of direct utterance and vision. Every experience begins for him in the presence of speaker to hearer and vice versa; consequently each speaker tells of action whose goal is clarity, or realized intention. Yet in almost every case, what enables the latter fulfillment is an inert substance like silver given power over life. Such a substance is felt mistakenly to be capable of embodying the visible, the timeless, the unmediated sensory possession of all reality. But also in each case, this substance turns out to embody the ego's nearly limitless capacity for extension. Surely this insight is what makes *Nostromo* the impressively pessimistic edifice that it is, for the novel reposes upon the impregnation of silver with an imaginative conception of its power. The totality of this conception encompasses both life and death, and thus the Goulds, for all their pretention to humanity are no different from the Professor in *The Secret Agent* or Kurtz in *Heart of Darkness*. ". . . By her imaginative estimate of its power she [Amelia Gould] endowed that lump of metal with a justificative conception, as though it were not a mere fact, but something far-reaching and impalpable, like the true expression of an emotion or the emergency of a principle. . . . For the San Tomé mine was to become an institution, a rallying point for everything in the provinces that needed order and stability to live. Security seemed to flow upon this land from the mountain range" (IX, 107, 110).

Matter is transmuted into value as, in an ideal world, emotion can be converted into "true expression." Matter for Conrad's heroes becomes a system of exchange underlying language. The self, which is the source of utterance, attempts the reconciliation of intention with actuality; words are really being bypassed as a direct embodiment in material sought by the imagination, at the same time that the ego reports its adventures and its disappointments. If language fails ultimately to represent intention and analogously, if the mimetic function of language is sorely inadequate to make us see—then by using substance *instead of words* the Conradian hero, like Conrad himself, aims to vindicate and articulate his imagination. Every reader of Conrad knows how this aim too is bound to fail. In the end the hero, like the dying Kurtz, becomes a talking insubstantiality. For every brief success like Gould or Verloc there is a Nostromo or a Stevie whose destroyed body tells on. And for every Kurtz and Jim there is a Marlow by whose memory a body can be recaptured in all its splendour and youth. That this takes place only in "the lapse of time" and because the speaker's words are being written does not diminish its achievement except as words diminish, without actually delivering, a man entire. Conrad is the writer whose work exactly is this fertile irony.

Notes

1. All references to Conrad are to the *Complete Works*, 26 vols. (Garden City, New York: Doubleday, Page and Company, 1925) VI, 70. Volume and page numbers are noted parenthetically.

2. *Lettres françaises* (Paris: Gallimard, 1930), p. 50.

3. *Joseph Conrad: Letters to Cunninghame Graham*, ed. C. T. Watts (Cambridge: Cambridge University Press, 1969), p. 129.

4. *Oeuvres Complètes* (Paris: Gallimard, 1945), p. 366.

5. *Illuminations*, ed. Hannah Arendt, trans. H. Zohn (New York: Harcourt, Brace, 1968), p. 87.

6. "Notes on the Characterization of a Literary Text," MLN, 85, No. 6 (1970), 765–790.

7. *Collected Papers*, Vol. 5, trans. Joan Rivière (New York: Basic Books, 1959), p. 182.

Language and Silence in the
Novels of Joseph Conrad   Martin Ray*

"The art of our time," Susan Sontag cryptically remarks, "is noisy with appeals for silence."[1] Silence must indeed appear an attractive if paradoxical alternative for the writer haunted by the inadequacy of language, and the promise of cathartic release which silence holds has influenced many writers' attitudes to language in the past two centuries. While most of the references to the pursuit of silence which we shall study are favorable, it is important to acknowledge an opposite tradition which views silence as a kind of cosmic terror bringing only the annihilation of the writer's achievement. This alternative school of thought would appear to derive from Pascal, for whom "*le silence éternel de ces espaces infinis m'effraie.*"[2] In the work of Joseph Conrad, the status of silence is highly ambiguous and, as we shall see, partakes of both these opposing traditions.

*Reprinted with permission from *Conradiana* 16 (1984):19–41.

"Speech is great; but Silence is greater."[3] Thomas Carlyle's eulogy of silence, which is repeated throughout his work, is part of the most extensive study of its nature and effects in the nineteenth century. Carlyle's frequent comments on silence are unreservedly favorable: "Let us honour the great empire of *Silence*, once more! The boundless treasury which we do *not* jingle in our pockets, or count up and present before men! It is perhaps, of all things, the usefulest for each of us to do, in these loud times" (XII, 118). The fiscal imagery here is an ironic anticipation of Conrad's *Nostromo*, where the great empire of silence, together with the literal treasure, join forces not to liberate Martin Decoud from the "loud times" in which he lives, but to engulf him. Carlyle's later praise of taciturnity is also of interest for *Nostromo*: "The great *silent* men! Looking round on the noisy inanity of the world, words with little meaning, actions with little worth, one loves to reflect on the great Empire of *Silence*.[. . .] Silence, the great Empire of Silence: higher than the stars; deeper than the Kingdoms of Death! It alone is great; all else is small. I hope we English will long maintain our *grand talent pour le silence*" (XII, 264–65). Conrad's Charles Gould elevates taciturnity into a principle of moral conduct, and he establishes a "school of uncompromising silence" (165) which protects him from the "deadly futilities of pronunciamentos" (182). It is his "dumb reserve" (239) which alone can, he believes, preserve his integrity: "Charles Gould assumed that if the appearance of listening to deplorable balderdash must form part of the price he had to pay for being left unmolested, the obligation of uttering balderdash personally was by no means included in the bargain" (92). At the end of the novel, Nostromo similarly embraces silence, but this time it is as a way of concealing his deceitful theft of Gould's treasure. Both men, however, find it impossible to *use* silence in the manner that Carlyle recommends. Far from mastering silence and making it their servant, they become its prey. Following the death of Martin Decoud, Gould realizes, "there must be an end now of this silent reserve, of that air of impenetrability behind which he had been safe-guarding his dignity" (378). Carlyle's praise of "the great *silent* men" is parodied in the figure of the dead Hirsch, swaying on a rope from the ceiling—" 'Behold'," as one of his torturers declares, " 'a man who will never speak again' " (449). Conrad on occasions can approximate closely to the consensus of opinion as represented by Carlyle, while on others his novels work to refute the notion of the benignity of silence which Carlyle promotes.

It is tempting, although inconclusive, to suggest that Conrad was acquainted with Carlyle's work. Some evidence has been forthcoming of his knowledge of *Sartor Resartus* (mentioned in *Youth*) and *Past and Present*, but this is mainly of a circumstantial nature.[4] What is of relevance in this respect is that Carlyle was the foremost representative and disseminator of a certain school of thought, namely that silence was benign and consoling. Whether or not Conrad was responding directly to Carlyle, the latter may be taken as typical of a certain Victorian tradition which Conrad both extended and partially rejected. There are certainly some passages in Carlyle's work which would have struck Conrad as personally relevant had he known them — the suggestion, for example, in *Past and Present* that "*in*eloquence" and the " 'talent of silence' " are preferable to eloquence in three languages (XIII, 120). Similarly, Carlyle's criteria for the aspiring sailor would have sounded a receptive chord in Conrad: "There shall be a depth of Silence in thee, deeper than this Sea, which is but ten miles deep: a Silence unsoundable; known to God only" (XIII, 249).

Carlyle's preference for "good *work* with lips closed" (XIX, 212) in *Latter-Day Pamphlets* is characteristic of the Victorian disdain for mere eloquence, a contempt which Conrad shared. The view that language and labor were exclusive (to the detriment of the former) is seen also in Cardinal Newman's work: "That a thing is true, is no reason that it should be said, but that it should be done."[5] It is interesting to note that Marlow in *Heart of Darkness* seems to express this traditional division between language and labor, the dazzlingly immoral eloquence of Kurtz contrasting with the silent efficiency of Marlow's own work in repairing the boat. Indeed, his conscientious toil protects him from Kurtz's captivating fluency of speech. Not all writers, however, followed Carlyle in his traditional separation of noble silence, good work and futile words, and some commentators tried to reconcile the Protestant work ethic with language, which had for centuries suffered from the Platonic dismissal of it as empty rhetoric, as superfluous addition. Ralph Waldo Emerson's essay, "The Poet," in 1844 attempts to resurrect writing as a valid and noble labor in its own right, for "words and deeds," he says, are "quite indifferent modes of the divine energy. Words are also actions, and actions are a kind of words."[6] Conrad makes a similar point when he reminds E. V. Lucas that "a good book is a good action."[7] In this respect, Conrad is much closer to Hegel than to Carlyle, although his portrayal of Marlow in *Heart of Darkness* would *appear* to indicate the reverse. It was Hegel who first proposed that language and labor were comparable forms of the same activity, in that both give an objective standing to the individual identity: "language and labour," Hegel writes, "are outer expressions in which the individual no longer retains possession of himself *per se*, but lets the inner get right outside him, and surrenders it to something else."[8] Hence the ambiguity of Conrad's portrayal of Marlow; the Marlow who sails upriver concentrates on the rivets and bolts of his ship and tries to be a model of silent efficiency in order to retain his self-possession, but the older Marlow who narrates is in fact much *more* eloquent than the rather curt Kurtz whom he met. This ambiguity undercuts any simple opposition between language and labor, and consequently the status of eloquence or silence is, in Conrad's writing, much more problematic than Carlyle's neat division between them would suggest.

In the years immediately preceding the beginning of Conrad's literary career, the pursuit of silence gained prominence in the work of the French Symbolists. Mallarmé's ambition, for instance, to become the *"musicienne du silence"*[9] parallels Rimbaud's assertion that *"Je suis maître du silence."*[10] Indeed, it is in the French literary tradition that the preoccupation with silence as a release from the inadequacy of language has most flourished. Paradoxically, however, as Albert Camus has illustrated, it is precisely this inadequacy of language which prevents the attainment of silence: "We live for something that goes further than morality. If we could only name it, what silence."[11] The procedure of the artist therefore, says Maurice Blanchot, must be to *"ne rien dire, parler pour ne rien dire."*[12] The ambition to "arrange an endlessly recreated bubble of silence"[13] is of significant interest for a study of Conrad's work, and the French Symbolists, especially, appear to have influenced his writing in many respects, not least in this matter of the "black silence beyond the massacre of words,"[14] as Sartre describes it. The presence of Mallarmé and Rimbaud can be glimpsed behind the first draft (at least) of Conrad's Preface to *The Nigger of the "Narcissus,"* in which he described the role of the artist as a discloser not of life's "inspired secret," as it later became, but of its "convincing silence."[15]

Conrad's highly ambiguous attitude towards silence, which we shall examine shortly, reflects a comparable ambiguity which recurs throughout the nineteenth century. Even Thomas Carlyle, the chief advocate of silence as a moral principle is not without the occasional demur. In the context of his society's increasing reliance upon language and communication, he acknowledges that silence "means annihilation for the Englishman of the Nineteenth Century" (XIX, 232). It is this threat of extinction which Conrad repeatedly demonstrates. Far from the beneficial silence of Carlyle, this absence of words may prove instead the negation of that linguistic framework which at least supports (if it is not commensurate with) our sense of reality. The increasing fear of silence in the latter half of the nineteenth century parallels the increasing recognition of language's central role in human activity. The possible consequences of a retreat into silence are graphically described by J. L. Hevesi: "If words should fail us, we would be condemned to silence — a silence in which presumably would collapse not only the fabric of social relations in which we move, but also the structure of reality which, with the help of words, we build out of the raw material of experience. [Silence] seems to rebel proudly against the tyranny of words, but, in reality, constitutes a surrender to the forces of silence, treason to the intellect, and a condemnation to inescapable isolation."[16] The absence of language leads only to an annihilating detachment, an ethical independence comparable, as Brice Parain remarks, to that of Dostoevsky's Idiot, Prince Myshkin: "Réduisez-vous au silence, même intérieur, vous verrez à quel point certains désirs du corps grandissent, jusqu'à en être obsédants, et à quel point vous perdez la notion du social. A quel point vous ne savez plus vous conduire, à quel point vous cessez de comprendre pour sentir, à quel point vous devenez idiots, au sens où Dostoïewsky l'entend. Vous vous êtes séparés de l'expérience collective."[17]

All of the writers discussed so far have assumed that silence occupies a definite, autonomous realm which the author may at least strive to reach, if he does not actually succeed in attaining it. There is a school of thought, however, which argues that it is fallacious to conceive of silence as occupying an area independent of language. Wilhelm von Humboldt was one of the first to suggest that "language plays a decisive part even in silence."[18] One cannot then hope to escape the confines of language completely, since even in silence language continues to enjoy its determining role. This insight is particularly common among French writers who add an interesting dimension to the argument, an extension of the Victorian polarity between language and silence which Conrad, as we shall see, suspected. Sartre, for instance, echoes Humboldt in his suggestion that silence exists only by reference to language, which provides the defining framework: *"le silence n'avait de sens que par le langage, qui le nomme et le soutient."*[19] Silence may continue to be the paradoxical culmination of a writer's work, ratifying and completing what he has written, but, as Samuel Beckett asks in *The Unnameable*, how is one to achieve it? "This silence they are always talking about, from which supposedly he came, to which he will return when his act is over, he doesn't know what it is, nor what he is meant to do, in order to deserve it."[20] Although an author may be only too aware of the provisional status of the language which he is obliged to employ, the silence which he seeks may itself be equally provisional and arbitrary, determined as it is by that which he strives to escape, a temporary haven which, as Paul Valéry describes it, is but *"une comédie de silence."*[21]

The apocalyptic tradition of language, which holds that it will become extinct, irrespective of man's wishes, adds a new dimension to the quest for silence. To strive for silence in this context is simply to make a virtue out of an unavoidable fate, a willing complicity in the death of language. Paul Valéry has proposed the interesting idea that language contains within itself the seeds of its own destruction, in that effective communication depends on the ability of language to cease being *merely* language and become instead, in the mind of the hearer, those very objects or thoughts which it conveys. Words are simply disposable aids, not an end in themselves, and their adequacy is commensurate with their facility in becoming something else: *"la tendance est de provoquer ce qu'il faut pour annuler entièrement le langage même. Je vous parle, et si vous avez compris mes paroles, ces paroles mêmes sont abolies."*[22] Valéry's idea is of particular interest for Conrad's use of first-person narrative. It is possible to suggest, for instance, that the dilemma of *Heart of Darkness* is Marlow's conflict between a wish to communicate to his audience (in order to control or exorcize his experiences) and a knowledge that successful communication entails the annihilation of that language by which he seeks to support or re-establish a stable vision of reality. He must maintain language while acknowledging that communication demands its extinction. Words must not remain merely words but must give way to the things they denote. The very act of narration, therefore, may be a kind of self-immolation, committing oneself to a medium which one knows will expire. A further distinction to be made here is between Marlow's oral narrative and Conrad's written narrative which contains it. The structure of the story thus enacts the paradoxical desire both to uphold language (via the written, substantive narrative) and to extinguish it (via the oral, temporal narrative which is followed by a return to silence). Only the written narrative can survive as a defence against the engulfing silence, but only the oral narrative can disappear and thereby communicate successfully.

The writer, Paul Valéry suggests, must compensate for the necessity of using a fallacious and distorting medium by trying to make that medium destroy itself, by seeking to make language describe a world in which it has no part. In short, language must be made to express the silence of the universe, a realm uncorrupted by words: "*il faut que le langage s'emploie à produire ce qui rend muet, exprime un mutisme.*"[23] The language of a writer must strive to recreate that silence from which it emerged; as Stéphane Mallarmé remarks, it is the nullity of the blank page, the *tabula rasa* beneath the words of his text, which the writer should seek to communicate: "Appuyer, selon la page, au blanc, qui l'inaugure son ingénuité, à soi, oublieuse même du titre qui parlerait trop haut: et, quand s'aligna, dans une brisure, la moindre, disséminée, le hasard vaincu mot par mot, indéfectiblement, le blanc revient, tout à l'heure gratuit, certain maintenant, pour conclure que rien au delà et authentiquer le silence."[24]

To Conrad, the blank page is not so welcome as it is to Mallarmé. On the contrary, as we shall see, it is the object of his despairing laments during those frequent bouts of creative paralysis which afflicted him throughout his career. Although they obviously differ in this respect, what Conrad and Mallarmé do have in common is a shared terminology for the expression of their respective problems and ambitions. As F. R. Karl has remarked of Conrad's occasional inability to write, "He calls such 'blankness' visitations, whose presence fills him with dread. When he recovers from the blankness, he calls it a 'resurrection', which goes on until the next attack. The symbolistic-religious imagery is compelling, that use of nineteenth-century *symboliste* terminology: blankness, death, resurrection, as a way of defining art and the artist."[25]

In Conrad's novels, this perception of the blank and silent nullity which underlies existence is not the prerogative of the literary or even the sensitive man, but is instead a fate common to all. Indeed, Conrad writes in *A Personal Record*, this sense of blank annihilation is felt equally by that "band of the totally unimaginative," those "unfortunate beings in whose empty and unseeing gaze (as a great French writer has put it) 'the whole universe vanishes into blank nothingness' " (92). One of Conrad's characters who may confidently be included in the "band of the totally unimaginative" is Winnie Verloc in *The Secret Agent*, and it is true that for her the universe does indeed vanish into "blank nothingness." On learning of Stevie's death, Winnie finds that her kitchen is transformed for her, and she "gazed at the whitewashed wall. A blank wall perfectly blank" (244), an attribute which Conrad stresses several times. Verloc wonders what she is looking at, and he follows her gaze, but "there was nothing behind him: there was just the whitewashed wall. The excellent husband of Winnie Verloc saw no writing on the wall" (240). Conrad repeats this curious reference to a common idiomatic expression in his description of Winnie's "frozen, contemplative immobility addressed to a whitewashed wall with no writing on it" (241). Shortly after the murder of Verloc, we learn that "the vast world created for the glory of man was only a vast blank to Mrs. Verloc" (270). Winnie has unwittingly achieved precisely what the Professor, for all his efforts, failed to achieve, the latter being frustrated by his inability to "make a large enough blank to bring into existence his new conception of life."[26]

Many characters in Conrad's novels experience this feeling of blank annihilation. Lena, in *Victory*, feels "an awful mental tension which was like blank forgetfulness" (299), while "a sort of blankness" (326) afflicts Tom Lingard in *The Rescue*. Similar experiences are to be found in "The Return," "A Smile of Fortune," and *Almayer's Folly*.[27] More significant, however, is the recurring relation between blankness and writing. In *Lord Jim*, Marlow on one occasion finds that he has no control over the words he writes, and "all at once, on the blank page, under the very point of the pen, the two figures of Chester and his antique partner," whom Marlow has been trying to forget, "dodge into view with strides and gestures" (174). The enigmatic Flora in *Chance*, following the imprisonment of her father, is "not so much unreadable as blank" (207), and Almayer, at the end of *An Outcast of the Islands*, loses faith in the influence of his ledgers and his handwriting over the natives. Sitting amidst the ruins of his office, "He could not guide Patalolo, control the irrepressible old Sahamin, or restrain the youthful vagaries of the fierce Bahassoen with pen, ink, and paper. He found no successful magic in the blank pages of his ledgers; and gradually he lost his old point of view in the saner appreciation of his situation. The room known as the office became neglected then like a temple of an exploded superstition" (300).

The blank page with which Almayer ends is the starting point for Razumov in *Under Western Eyes*. Just as Stevie's circles in *The Secret Agent* suggest "a mad art attempting the inconceivable" (45), Razumov wishes to write the "inconceivable history" (33) of Russia: "Under the sumptuous immensity of the sky, the snow covered the endless forests, the frozen rivers, the plains of an immense country, obliterating the landmarks, the accidents of the ground, levelling everything under its uniform whiteness, like a monstrous blank page awaiting the record of an inconceivable history" (33). Razumov vows to answer his country's call. It is he who will write his homeland's history, which required "not the babble of many voices, but a man — strong and one" (33). Possessing all the necessary attributes of eloquence and resolution, Razumov meets with some success but, as Sophia Antonovna tells him, " 'So far you seem to have been writing it in water' " (263). Razumov performs the especially modernist task of creating an identity for himself through his writing, and Sophia Antonovna compares this self-affirmation to literary creation. His fame, she encourages him, " 'May become a fact written all over that great land of ours' " (263). The betrayal of Haldin leads Razumov, however, to abandon his ambition to win an identity, and, in the same way that his anonymity guarantees his safety in Geneva, after his flight from Russia, his self-preservation now depends on the blank page of his own history remaining blank. He asks the terrorists in Geneva if they had conducted any investigation into his background, to which Sophia replies, " 'No, no. . . . There you are again with your sensitiveness. It makes you stupid. Don't you see, there was no starting-point for an investigation even if anyone had thought of it. A perfect blank!' " (277). Slowly, Razumov is absorbed into the formless immensity of Russia, which he had hoped to conquer, until "his existence was a great cold blank, something like the enormous plain of the whole of Russia levelled with snow and fading gradually on all sides into shadows and mists" (303). Royal Roussel extends this development and sees the fate of Razumov as a complex metaphor for the structure of the novel as a whole: "Like Razumov's return to the emptiness of Russia [*UWE* is] completed at the point where the final sentence dissolves into the blankness of the margin; the narrative voice is completed in the silence which follows its last words."[28]

Conrad himself appears to have experienced these feelings of nullity and annihilation similar to those of his characters. After completing *An Outcast of the Islands*, for example, he wrote to Edward Garnett that "since yesterday life seems a blank — a dumb solitude from which everything, even the shadows, have completely vanished."[29] Of especial interest, in relation to the recurring image of the blank page throughout his work, are Conrad's paralyses of creative ability, which he expresses in analogous terms. Again with reference to *An Outcast of the Islands*, he describes to his aunt the nature of this torment: *voilà trois jours que je' m'assois devant une page blanche — et la page est toujours blanche,"* a mental state which endured for some time, for he wrote to her shortly after that *"je viens d'écrire XI en tête d'une page blanche et blanche elle restera peut etre dix jours ou je ne me connais pas."*[30] Such were the problems he faced in his protracted efforts to complete *The Rescue*, and he describes to Garnett in

1896 how "I went about thinking and forgetting—sitting down before the blank page to find that I could not put one sentence together" (*LL*, I, 192). Thirteen years later, as he was preparing to write *Under Western Eyes*, Conrad is still troubled by those "moments of cruel blankness when one's writing life seems to come to an end. I live in the constant dread of these visitations. They have been too frequent of late."[31] The blank page is a challenge to Conrad, as to Razumov, and he tells André Gide, during the writing of *Victory*, that *"Je n'ose pas quitter ma table avec la page blanche etalée dessus, la première page que je contemple avec des frissons. Car une fois le premier mot tracé, voyez-vous, il faudra marcher—et je ne m'en sens pas la force."*[32]

The compulsion to write imposed on Conrad by the writing of the first word is yet designed to return him eventually to that blankness from which he began, and this curious equation between completion and self-immolation has something in common with the fates of Razumov and Winnie Verloc. In this context, his literary advice to Edward Noble, as early as 1895, is especially significant. "You must do it sincerely, at any cost: you must do it so that at the end of your day's work you should feel exhausted, emptied of every sensation and every thought, with a blank mind and an aching heart, with the notion that there is nothing,—nothing left in you" (*LL*, I, 183). The work of art appears to exist tentatively, as it were, in parentheses, between the blank page from which it originates and the blank exhaustion which the author must seek.

II

"Woe to those that keep silent."[33] St. Augustine's warning finds support throughout the nineteenth century, and even Thomas Carlyle, the leading advocate of the cult of silence, acknowledges in *Latter-Day Pamphlets* that a commitment to life demands a commitment to language—"Vocables, still vocables" (XIX, 232). Carlyle's satirical analysis of the ideas which motivate Victorian man notes his veneration of language, his compulsion to speak, not eloquently or sensibly, but simply to speak, as a defence against the unworded darkness which would otherwise consume him: "To speak in various languages, on various things, but on all of them to speak, and appropriately deliver ourselves by tongue or pen,—this is the sublime goal" (XIX, 209). Carlyle's vision of the eloquent polyglot points towards Conrad's Kurtz, if not towards Conrad himself. Indeed, as Ezra Pound has suggested, literature may be the product of a fundamental compulsion to speak not qualitatively different from Kurtz's eloquent defiance of the silent darkness; literature, Pound remarks, is "made for no man's entertainment, but because a man believing in silence found himself unable to withhold himself from speaking."[34]

To speak or not to speak: in Conrad's attitude to language, one finds a curious and paradoxical accommodation of both these opposing demands.

Throughout his career, Conrad admires the taciturn and the efficient, men like MacWhirr or Singleton, and in *Under Western Eyes* he even chooses a man for whom words are "the great foes of reality" (3) to be his ironically eloquent narrator. The suspicion and deep distrust of language which this preference for silent men would seem to indicate is, however, opposed by that almost neurotic addiction to language and writing which is revealed in his letters and essays, and which several of his leading characters are made to share. In terms of the historical context which was sketched earlier in this article, Conrad can be seen to agree with Carlyle's view of silence as beneficial, while simultaneously he is acutely aware of the view represented by Pascal and St. Augustine, who regard silence as the negation and annihilation of consciousness, which only a commitment to language can prevent. In the remainder of this essay, each of these two contradictory attitudes will be examined in turn.

"No angel watches us at our toil" (*LE*, 43). The writer, Conrad laments, is an isolated creature, "forgotten by Providence" (*LE*, 43), obliged by his calling to spend his days producing "a varied lot of prose with a quite ridiculous scrupulosity and an absurd seriousness" (*LE*, 41). Conrad's caricature of himself as a writer is contained in his essay "Outside Literature," in which he contrasts the futile indulgence of his literary career with the practical consolations of his former life as a sailor. The two occupations, Conrad explains, require quite different approaches to language. The artist seeks words which will capture the fleeting and evanescent impressions of an imaginatively apprehended reality. For the sailor, however, language is a precise and practical tool, a medium which can be perfectly adequate for its task, since the demands upon it are finite and utilitarian. While the most precious possession of the artist is his "liberty of imagination" (*NLL*, 7), it would be a perilous gift for a sailor: "An imaginatively written Notice to Mariners would be a deadly thing. I mean it literally. It would be sure to kill a number of people before its imaginative quality had been appreciated and suppressed" (*LE*, 39). The language of the Notice to Mariners confines itself strictly to the practical surface of reality; indeed, the author of such Notices must exhibit a rigorous concern for the precision of his style comparable to the literary artist's regard for *le mot juste*. "Just suppose," Conrad muses, "the author of Notices to Mariners acquiring convivial habits and sitting down to write a Notice in that happy frame of mind when nothing matters much and one letter of the alphabet is as good as another" (*LE*, 40). Conrad himself, he recalls, steadily improved at writing these Notices "up to the moment when stepping ashore for the last time I lost all touch with the most trusted kind of printed prose" (*LE*, 43).

The language of the sea is contrasted by Conrad not only to literary language but also to the language of the shore, for Conrad, on leaving his ship for the last time, becomes a landlubber, albeit a literary one, and the language of the landlubber is an infectiously mendacious one. In *The*

Mirror of the Sea, Conrad berates those "poor, miserable, 'cast-anchor' devils" (15) who imagine that a sailor throws an anchor overboard. It is overboard already, Conrad explains, and a sailor simply releases it. "To take a liberty with technical language," he continues, "is a crime against the clearness, precision, and beauty of perfected speech" (13). Such vocabulary is "a flawless thing for its purpose" (13), the ideal adaptation of words to actions. A term like "the growth of the cable" cannot be improved upon as the expression of a precise activity, and it consequently possesses "all the force, precision, and imagery of technical language that, created by simple men with keen eyes for the real aspect of the things they see in their trade, achieves the just expression seizing upon the essential, which is the ambition of the artist in words" (21).

The "international language of the sea" (26), as Conrad calls it in *Youth*, functions so excellently because its area of reference is strictly limited. One does not dwell on the merits of such technical language, for its vocabulary is subservient to the actions which it describes. The words, as it were, must be ignored if they are to perform their function, and it is this ready translation of language into action which Conrad so admires. The medium is self-effacing, its willingness to remain so being the guarantee of its success. Technical language, within the very limited range of its application, works admirably, although, as we shall see, the self-effacing quality of such language is not a desirable attribute for all kinds of language. In the language of the sea, communication is secondary to the maritime duties which it assists. The technical words enjoy a direct correspondence with the objects which they describe; they are like counters, and in the process of communication the hearer simply exchanges the word for the thing. Such efficient and economical adjustment of the word to its meaning is, Conrad laments, precisely what is lacking in literary language. In contrast to the writers of fiction, sailors "deal in things and face the realities — not the words — of this life" (*NLL*, 217). Any language beyond the purely factual appears to a sailor mendacious and decadent; indeed, a "capacity for vivid language," as Conrad explains in *The Mirror of the Sea*, may be an admirable attribute of a writer, but to a sailor such a fluency of speech is accompanied by a "shadiness of moral character and recklessness of disposition" (102).

This opposition between silent efficiency and depraved eloquence is prominent in such stories as *Typhoon* and *The Nigger of the "Narcissus."* In the latter, the contrast is between Singleton, whose "generation lived inarticulate" (25), and James Wait, who, together with his ally Donkin, possesses a depressing and insidious eloquence. Singleton the mate is one of those "voiceless men — but men enough to scorn in their hearts the sentimental voices that bewailed the hardness of their fate" (25). His only friend is another veteran sailor, to whom he is bound by a silent fraternity of the sea: "those two understood one another, though they hardly exchanged three words in a day" (97). Apart from this single ally, Conrad notes, "the men who could understand his silence were gone" (25). As for the present generation of seamen, "if they had learned how to speak they have also learned how to whine" (25). It is possible that Conrad's guilt about his literary activity originates in a suspicion that a writer has more in common with these eloquent "poll-parrot[s]" (110) than with a seaman like Singleton, of whom Conrad says, "the thoughts of his lifetime could have been expressed in six words" (25). Wait's voice, "hollow and loud" (35), has a seductive magnetism which anticipates Kurtz's captivating eloquence in *Heart of Darkness:* "We were always incurably anxious to hear what he had to say" (73). It is Wait's accomplice, "the fascinating Donkin" (100), however, who most closely resembles Kurtz. "We could not but listen with interest to that consummate artist" (100), as the narrator remarks, acknowledging reluctantly that Donkin's "impassioned orations" have come to replace the "impenetrable silence" (100) of Singleton's generation: "his picturesque and filthy loquacity flowed like a troubled stream from a poisoned source" (101). Donkin is an illustration of Conrad's belief, as he states it in his essay "Books," that "to have the gift of words" without an accompanying moral purpose "is no such great matter" (*NLL*, 9).

Donkin's demonic fluency is a threat both to the stable surface of reality, enshrined in the maritime code which he seeks to subvert, and to the technical language which describes that surface. His speech has its source far below the surface, and he utters his mutinous denunciations of the crew in a "bored, far-away voice, as though he had been talking from the bottom of a hole" (110). There is no single character in *Typhoon* who approximates to Donkin, but there is a group of people, the Chinamen whom the *Nan-Shan* is transporting, whose primitive and underworld speech threatens to subvert the ship's discipline. During a particularly violent phase of the storm the crew go below deck to comfort the coolies, who show their gratitude in "fierce denunciations [. . .], grunts and growls" (80). One of the Chinamen begins to speak: "his mouth yawned black, and the incomprehensible guttural hooting sounds, that did not seem to belong to a human language, penetrated Jukes with a strange emotion as if a brute had tried to be eloquent" (80).

In opposition to this absurd language, the negation of precise distinction and factual descriptions, stands the language of the sea. All shore-talk, in comparison, is superfluous and repetitive; Captain MacWhirr, the stoical skipper of the *Nan-Shan*, despises landlubbers, who " 'Must be saying the same things over and over again' " (18). Indeed, the sea appears antagonistic towards mere human language, which can never hope to rival its own succinct and mute mastery of expression. Jukes, the ship's officer, attempts to write up the log, but the "continuous, monotonous rolling of the ship" defeats his efforts. It is as if the sea seeks to frustrate any attempt to describe its motions in human language, and the manner in which the inkstand slides away from Jukes suggests to him that it possesses a "perverse intelligence in dodging the pen" (26).

The sea finds its closest ally in MacWhirr, the dogged skipper for whom "to be silent was natural" (40). He is the antithesis of a writer, and his account of the typhoon, which he relates in a letter to his wife, is "completely uninteresting" (93). These regular letters to his wife, indeed, are his sole concession to language, which he otherwise despises. Only a meticulous attention to detail can overcome his aversion to expression of any kind, and his letters to home, consequently, are composed in the technical language of a maritime report. His wife learns only minute details of MacWhirr's trips: "her master, faithful to facts, which alone his consciousness reflected, would set them down with painstaking care upon many pages" (14). Language, restricted to such a purpose, is perfectly adequate, but any more ambitious demand upon it (the expression of emotion, for instance) instantly reveals its shortcomings. MacWhirr ends his letters with "Your loving husband," but these words strike him as "worn-out things, and of a faded meaning" (15). Jukes's figurative speech strikes MacWhirr as similarly redundant and fallacious. The first officer remarks to his skipper that the foul weather "would make a saint swear," a phrase which MacWhirr interprets literally. In reply to Jukes's explanation that " 'It's a manner of speaking, sir,' " MacWhirr "expostulated against the use of images in speech": " 'Some of you fellows do go on,' " MacWhirr continues. " 'I wish you wouldn't talk so wild' " (25).

MacWhirr's contempt for words is justified by the conclusion of the tale, and his belief that " 'You don't find everything in books,' " which seems "the maddest thing, when you come to look at it sensibly" (34), enables him to save the *Nan-Shan*. He refuses to follow the advice of the definitive book (Captain Wilson's study of storm-strategy) and instead sails directly through the eye of the typhoon, a tactic which he feels intuitively will protect his ship. The conventional wisdom of Captain Wilson strikes him as mortally bankrupt, a skulking ploy which would have the *Nan-Shan* "running most of [its] time all over the sea" (33). Wilson's book is remarkably similar to Towson's *An Inquiry into Some Points of Seamanship*, which Marlow is delighted to discover in *Heart of Darkness*. To Captain MacWhirr, however, such a book of maritime conduct serves only to make him "contemptuously angry with such a lot of words and with so much advice, all head-work and supposition, without a glimmer of certitude" (32). In contrast to the superfluous verbiage of Wilson's book, it is MacWhirr's simple grasp of language which inspires the ship's crew with the courage to survive the typhoon. It is the steadfast simplicity of his speech which defies the storm in an exulting cry of indomitable optimism. MacWhirr's is the language which triumphs:

> And again [Jukes] heard that voice, forced and ringing feebly, but with a
> penetrating effect of quietness in the enormous discord of noises, as if

sent out from some remote spot of peace beyond the black wastes of the
gale; again he heard a man's voice—the frail and indomitable sound
that can be made to carry an infinity of thought, resolution and
purpose, that shall be pronouncing confident words on the last day,
when heavens fall, and justice is done—again he heard it, and it was
crying to him, as if from very, very far—
    "All right." (44).

There are two groups of characters in Conrad's work for whom
silence is natural and desirable: one group, as we have seen, consists of
sailors and the second group is Conrad's lovers. To speak is always a
harrowing experience for the Conradian lover. Words are painful to him,
and he hesitates to commit his feelings to a medium which he senses is an
inadequate and belittling reflection of his ardour. Speech is equally
distasteful, however, to those for whom love had died, for it serves as a
ghastly reminder of the hypocrisy which loveless communication entails.
Alvan Hervey, the cuckold of "The Return," longs for silence: "how much
better it would be," he believes, "if neither of them ever spoke again," since
language has become simply a matter of "words that can be smiled at,
argued away, shouted down, disdained" (*TU*, 141). To those for whom
love is happier, silence is similarly attractive, for language brings with it
an intimation of mortality, signalling the invasion of the outside world into
their romantic haven. It is this fear of speech and the worldly corruption
attending upon it which encourage Rita and George in *The Arrow of Gold*
to "fall into a long silence, so close that the sound of the first word would
come with all the pain of a separation" (107).
    Silence is attractive to Conrad's lovers for the further reason that
speech may let loose the full force of their passion, or their concealed hate.
"The Return" again illustrates the awesome responsibility of breaking the
comforting silence; Alvan and his wife "were afraid to hear again the
sound of their voices; they did not know what they might say—perhaps
something that could not be recalled; and words are more terrible than
facts" (*TU*, 143). Alvan, fearing that he will unleash a demonic savagery,
desperately subdues the "howls and imprecations" (146) which he feels
rising within him. "Outspokenness," Conrad adds, can for the lover be
"nothing less than criminal" (165). Tom Lingard in *The Rescue* displays a
similar reluctance to talk which, he suspects, will lead only to a loss of
identity, an annihilating banishment of his self-possession: "He would have
to go in and talk to Mrs. Travers. The idea dismayed him. Of necessity he
was not one of those men who have the mastery of expression. To liberate
his soul was for him a gigantic undertaking, a matter of desperate effort,
of doubtful success" (211).
    Lovers in Conrad's work, however, struggle to overcome such reti-
cence, since the claims of fellowship, either with one's fellow men or with
a particular woman, continue to demand obedience. This is Falk's
dilemma: unwilling to declare his love, he "had existed and could have

existed without being married. Yet he told me that he had found it more and more difficult to live alone" (*TOS*, 200). With "so much being at stake," however, Falk is "afraid of putting it to the hazard of the declaration" (204), and he solves his dilemma only by a bizarre kind of silent immolation, offering himself for sacrifice before the object of his passions: "without a word, without a sign, without the slightest inclination of his bony head, by the silent intensity of his look alone, he seemed to lay his Herculean frame at her feet" (216). Falk's natural and mute proposal avoids the complicity and commitment which speech brings (as Lena rebukes Axel in *Victory*, " 'What did you want to speak to me for?' " [80]), but only at the cost of his identity.

Many of Conrad's characters who strive to remain silent are, perversely, the victims of a mad loquacity over which they have no control. They cannot be silent, but neither can they choose the words which they feel they must compulsively speak. Razumov, for instance, in *Under Western Eyes* must scrutinize every word he utters lest he betray his duplicity, and yet "on certain days he was afraid that any one addressing him suddenly in a certain way would make him scream out insanely a lot of filthy abuse" (298). Similarly, in "The Duel," it occurs to D'Hubert that "if he had to open his lips he would break out into horrible and aimless imprecations" (*SS*, 247), while the narrator of "A Smile of Fortune" remarks that "there were moments when I felt I must break out and start swearing" at Alice "till all was blue" (*TLS*, 51). There are also comparable scenes in *Lord Jim* and "The Planter of Malata."[35]

Several of Conrad's characters who believe their very lives depend on their ability to maintain this silence are nevertheless driven by a suicidal need to speak (Razumov's double confession is the best example of this). Some characters do succeed in remaining quiet, but their silence is invariably a sure sign of their guilt or their failure, and certainly does not ensure their safety as they believed. The secret guilt which haunts Nostromo after the theft of the silver results in an enforced silence: "he could only hold his tongue, since there was no one to trust" (471). This reference to holding one's tongue recurs throughout Conrad's work, and is frequently linked to guilt and villainy. Carlier in "An Outpost of Progress" is confident of his safety because, as he tells his accomplice Kayerts, " 'who will talk if we hold our tongues?' " (*TU*, 109). Razumov in *Under Western Eyes* reminds the terrorists during his confession that " 'I had only to hold my tongue' " (368) to preserve his former disguise. Winnie Verloc has "a devilish way of holding her tongue" (*SA*, 258) which serves only to provoke her husband and leads to her own eventual tragedy, while Tom Lingard in *The Rescue* discards his previous honest and open existence following the arrival of Edith Travers, and instead "learned to hold his tongue" (95), the better to conduct his future romantic intrigue with her.

Conrad himself, however, refuses to hold his tongue, and this rejection of silence is clearly seen in a letter of 1896 to Edward Garnett: "I can be deaf and blind and an idiot if that is the road to my happiness—but I'm hanged if I can be mute. I will not hold my tongue! What is life worth if one can't jabber to one's heart's content? If one can't expose one's maimed thoughts at the gate of some cemetery or some palace."[36] Conrad shares this determination to speak with some of his characters, notably Lord Jim, of whom Marlow says he could "no more stop telling now than he could have stopped living by the mere exertion of his will" (100). To continue to live requires that one continue to speak, since silence, as Conrad says in his essay on Henry James, "is like death" (*NLL*, 14). Equally, one must continue to speak in the knowledge that one cannot and *must* not achieve any conclusive or definitive statement, which would remove the need for any more words. The writer is obliged to create only incomplete, provisional utterances, although this inconclusive language would at least have the merit of being a faithful representation of the inconclusive nature of life as defined by Conrad in a letter to Edward Garnett: "the incomplete joy, the incomplete sorrow, the incomplete rascality or heroism—the incomplete suffering" (*LL*, I, 197). This inability to conclude gives an air of futility to all of one's actions and to all of one's words: as the anonymous narrator at the end of *Lord Jim* remarks, "the last image of that incomplete story, its incompleteness itself, and the very tone of the speaker, had made discussion vain and comment impossible" (337). In desperation, Marlow in fact had tried to make a virtue out of this failure to utter any definitive statement: "The last word is not said—probably shall never be said. Are not our lives too short for that full utterance which through all our stammerings is of course our only and abiding intention? I have given up expecting those last words, whose ring, if they could only be pronounced, would shake both heaven and earth! There is never time to say our last word—the last word of our love, of our desire, faith, remorse, submission, revolt. The heaven and the earth must not be shaken" (225). The kind of ultimate utterance which Marlow refuses to articulate is repeatedly associated in Conrad's writings with death and defeat. He praises Henry James' work, for example, on the grounds that it contains "no suggestion of finality, nowhere a hint of surrender" (*NLL*, 11), and indeed Conrad elevates this refusal to accept the validity of any single assertion into an aesthetic principle: "A work of art is very seldom limited to one exclusive meaning and not necessarily tending to a definite conclusion" (*LL*, II, 205).

This fear of concluding is particularly prominent during the composition of *Lord Jim*; at this period Conrad seems to have experienced a compulsion to continue writing similar to his hero's compulsion to continue speaking, and he tells his publisher that "it would be to my interest to cut it short as possible, but I would just as soon think of cutting off my head" (*WB*, 71). The same association of silence and suicide is present in Marlow's remark on Lord Jim that he would "no more stop telling now than he could have stopped living by the mere exertion of his will" (100). It is as if, despite the torment of writing and the consequent appeal of silence, Conrad was unable to welcome the finality of his novels, which may account for his feeling that "the end of a story is a very important and difficult part, the *most* difficult for me, to execute" (*WB*, 86–87). Conrad frequently expresses his insatiable desire to create, and he tells Mrs. Galsworthy, for instance, that "write I must, to stave off remorse, despair" (*LL*, II, 94). This characteristic need to practice a continual self-expression to avert the onset of silence may be the origin of those nervous breakdowns which he experienced on completing *Nostromo* and *Under Western Eyes*; as Conrad described the latter in the Author's Note to *'Twixt Land and Sea*, "the memories of 'Under Western Eyes' are associated with the memory of a severe illness which seemed to wait like a tiger in the jungle on the turn of a path to jump on me the moment the last words of that novel were written" (*TLS*, vii–viii).[37] In his essay on Henry James, Conrad describes "the subtle presence of the dead" which is felt "in that silence that comes upon the artist-creation when the last word has been read" (*NLL*, 19). This equation of silence and death for the writer is present also in a letter to Arthur Symons, in which Conrad declares that "once the last page is written the man does not count. He is nowhere" (*LL*, II, 73). Conrad must continue to write, but never conclude, in the hope that, as he tells Edmund Gosse, "there may be salvation, somewhere, before the last line is written" (*LL*, I, 300).

The appeal of silence is strengthened, it would seem, if the continuing exhaustion of language has reached a point where the author no longer possesses any words. "*Je ne sais plus parler*," laments Arthur Rimbaud, for there are "*plus de mots*,"[38] no more words. The search for *le mot juste* and the urgency of discovering the correct expression run parallel at this with the suspicion that not only *le mot juste* but the most familiar of words has become alien and beyond reach. "*J'ai presque perdu la raison*," says Stéphane Mallarmé, "*et le sens des paroles les plus familières*."[39] The artist seeks the uniquely correct expression while remaining sceptical of its existence: if only, Dostoevsky regrets, "I could bring myself to believe a single word of all that I have written."[40]

Joseph Conrad is frequently to be found lamenting in similar fashion both the elusiveness of language and its debilitation. "The hand is paralysed," he tells Garnett in 1898, "when it comes to giving expression" (*LC*, 132) to the action of *The Rescue*, and his agony of creativity, those phases when "I simply could not express myself artistically" (*LC*, 17), continues throughout his writing career. His suspicion that "I have forgotten how to think — worse! how to write," that "I simply can't find the words" (*LC*, 43, 226), makes him feel like "a man stricken dumb" (*LL*, II, 132). To stay silent may appear a curious way of relieving the agony of creative paralysis, but to strive against such blank vacuity merely increases its torment. Although Conrad never succumbed to the temptation of retirement for very long, vestiges of its appeal surface occasionally in his work. A cancelled opening to *The Arrow of Gold* bears witness to the attraction of a resigned silence for one who was obliged to be silent for long periods already. To cease to strive against it, thinks Monsieur George, may make the burden more tolerable: "In common parlance: once bit — twice shy. But there was something more there. He had been bitten all over as it were, enough to make him shy of expressing himself for ever."[41] A number of Conrad's characters, such as Jasper and Heemskirk in "Freya of the Seven Isles" and Cosmo Latham in *Suspense*,[42] experience Conrad's sense of being unable to express himself. Cosmo Latham attempts to write a letter to his family in England about his life in Naples: "he could write something about that but, after all, was it worth while?" (72). This weary resignation in the face of an insuperable disillusionment with writing may hold the key to the lassitude and muted achievement of Conrad's later work. "I am still like a man in a nightmare," he tells Richard Curle as late as 1917. "And who can be articulate in a nightmare?" (*RC*, 57).

The difficulties of expression which Conrad encountered in the majority of his finest novels are well documented,[43] and it is not surprising that he should frequently endorse Virginia Woolf's belief that "the wordless are the happy."[44] His preference for the "formless eloquence of a cry" over the superficial comfort of "words that can be smiled at, argued away, shouted down, disdained" (*TU*, 141), reveals a fundamental dissatisfaction with the function and purpose of language. So often, he suggests in *The Arrow of Gold*, words provide only an assurance of our well-being, a temporary and fragile refuge to distract us from our appointed end in an "eternal phantom-like silence" (305). "Every sort of shouting," Conrad explains in his essay "Confidence" (1919), is a "transitory thing. It is the grim silence of facts that remains" (*NLL*, 206). All human language appears an impertinent and incongruous affront to the "eloquent silence of mute greatness" (*TU*, 94). This suspicion of the absurdity of both speech and writing silences several of Conrad's characters whose words "remained on their lips as if checked by the fear of profanation" (*R*, 148). As Edith Travers suggests in *The Rescue*, " 'It's difficult to imagine that in this wilderness writing can have any significance" (325). In such a setting the "articulate language of mortals" is defeated, to be replaced by "animated and vocal" spectres who reproach the human trespassers not in mere words but in "faint sobs, deep sighs, and fateful gestures" (462).

"Silence claims the world," Edward Said believes, at the end of Conrad's novels, because his "English words could no longer cope either with truth or with its many deceiving ideas and images." It is, however, precisely the bewildering chaos of such ideas, Said continues, that compelled Conrad not to stay silent but to write — he "needed to talk in order to ward off a growing feeling of illusion and unreality."[45] The refuge of silence, attractive as it may be, was consistently shunned by Conrad, for the threat of "absolute silence," as J. Hillis Miller remarks, can become in Conrad's novels "a murmurous sound louder than any noise."[46] Conrad's attempt to erect a barrier of language against the impending silence is but one half of his ambiguous attitude to the forces of negation; much of his creative power may be said to originate in his direct confrontation with those forces, a confrontation which required him to transcend temporarily the barriers of language before retreating again into the shelter which they provide. Conrad's style, one critic has suggested, is the very embodiment of this tenuous and uneasy flirtation with the forces of annihilation; it is a style which alternates between the two spheres of language and silence, weaving a fusion of words and their negation which reconciles and holds them in harmony. Refusing to take language at face value, F. R. Karl believes, Conrad deliberately builds into his style the weapons of its own destruction, emphasizing the void between each word, gaining "cumulative effects through special awareness of both the sounds and silences inherent in language."[47] The medium is itself the record and the reward of Conrad's confrontation with the forces of silence.

"Write I must, to stave off remorse, despair" (*LL*, II, 94). Conrad's compulsion to write and "let out a howl upon things in general" (*LC*, 39) resembles Carlyle's reluctant recognition of the need for "vocables, still vocables."[48] Conrad is well aware that the artist "is so much of a voice that for him, silence is like death" (*NLL*, 14). His fear of silence is graphically recorded in his essay, "Well Done" (1918), in which he recalls the trepidation with which he set out on his early sailing voyages. At sea, he remarks, all language becomes transitory and superfluous, for one "can't conceive a vocal Eternity," and there remains only "an enormous silence, in which there was nothing to connect one with the Universe" (*NLL*, 182). Hazlitt's description of words as the "links in the chain of the universe, and the grappling-irons that bind us to it,"[49] perhaps illuminates the reason for Conrad's commitment to language as a means of overcoming this sense of a dislocated existence. It is through language that Conrad can avoid the fate of Kurtz, who had "kicked himself loose of the earth" (*HD*, 144). Conrad's fear of ending his novels and of the subsequent silence which envelopes his created world would appear also to have its origin in this wish to avoid becoming detached from his identity. While he approvingly cites Flaubert's dictum that *"le misérable écriviat toujours"* (*LL*, II, 64), it is perhaps fitting that, in his final novel *Suspense*, he appears to accept that he cannot ward off forever the eventual silence. Cosmo Latham attempts to write from Naples to his sister in England, but "It required all his courage to keep on, piling up words which dealt exclusively with towns, roads, rivers, mountains, the colours of the sky. It was like labouring the description of the scenery of a stage after a great play had come to an end. A vain thing" (188).

Notes

1. "The Aesthetics of Silence," in *The Discontinuous Universe: Selected Writings in Contemporary Consciousness*, ed. Sallie Sears and G. W. Lord (New York: Basic Books, 1972), p. 57.

2. *L'Oeuvre de Pascal*, ed. Jacques Chevalier (Paris: Editions de la Nouvelle Revue Française, 1936), p. 848.

3. *Thomas Carlyle's Collected Words*, 34 vols. (London: Chapman & Hall, 1870–87), XII, 127. Later references included in text.

4. See *Youth*, p. 7 for Conrad's reference to *Sartor Resartus*. See also Paul Kirschner, *Conrad: The Psychologist as Artist* (Edinburgh: Oliver & Boyd, 1968), p. 182; Norman Sherry, ed., *Joseph Conrad: A Commemoration* (London: Macmillian, 1976), p. 213, and C. T. Watts, ed., *Joseph Conrad's Letters to R. B. Cunninghame Graham* (Cambridge: Cambridge University Press, 1969), p. 26. Conrad and Carlyle are compared by Avrom Fleishman, in *Conrad's Politics: Community and Anarchy in the Fiction of Joseph Conrad* (Baltimore: Johns Hopkins University Press, 1967), pp. 36, 73–74 (but see p. 64), and by Eloise K. Hay, in Sherry, ed., *A Commemoration*, p. 213. The validity of the comparison is refuted by Zdzislaw Najder, in *Conrad's Polish Background: Letters to and from Polish Friends*, trans. Halina Carroll (London: Oxford University Press, 1964), pp. 78, 87.

Page references to Conrad's novels will hereafter be included in the text and are to the Collected Edition, 21 vols. (London: J. M. Dent, 1946–55). Abbreviated titles used in the text are as follows: *AF — Almayer's Folly; HD — Heart of Darkness* (in *Youth: A Narrative; and Two Other Stories*); *LE — Last Essays; LJ — Lord Jim; NLL — Notes on Life and Letters; R — The Rescue; SA — The Secret Agent; SS — A Set of Six; Su — Suspense; TLS — 'Twixt Land and Sea; TOS — Typhoon, and Other Stories; TU — Tales of Unrest; UWE — Under Western Eyes; WT — Within the Tides.*

5. John Henry Newman, *Parochial and Plain Sermons*, 8 vols. (Westminster, Md: Christian Classics, 1966–68), V, 45.

6. *Complete Works*, The Centenary Edition, 12 vols. (Boston: Houghton, Mifflin, 1903–04), III, 8.

7. Georges Jean-Aubry, *Joseph Conrad: Life and Letters*, 2 vols. (London: Heinemann, 1927), II, 89. Later abbreviated *LL*.

8. G. W. F. Hegel, *The Phenomenology of Mind*, trans. J. B. Baillie (1910; rpt. London: Allen & Unwin, 1971), p. 340.

9. *Oeuvres Complètes de Stèphane Mallarmè*, ed. Henri Mondor and Georges Jean-Aubry (Paris: Gallimard, 1945), p. 54.

10. *Oeuvres Complètes de Arthur Rimbaud*, ed. Roland de Renéville and Jules Mouquet (Paris: Gallimard, 1946).

11. *Camus: Essays*, trans. Justin O'Brien (New York: Random House, 1959), p. 145.

12. *La Part du Feu* (Paris: Gallimard, 1949), p. 327.

13. Jean Genet, *The Thief's Journal*, trans. Bernard Frechtman (London: Penguin, 1965), p. 98.

14. *What is Literature?*, trans. Bernard Frechtman (1950; rpt. London: Methuen, 1967), p. 109.

15. See David R. Smith, *Conrad's Manifesto: Preface to a Career: The History of the Preface to The Nigger of the "Narcissus"* (Philadelphia: Philip H. & A. S. W. Rosenbach Foundation, 1966), p. 67.

16. J. L. Hevesi, ed., *Essays on Language and Literature* (London: A. Wingate, 1947), pp. 18–19.

17. *Essai sur la misère humaine* (Paris: B. Grasset, 1934), p. 217.

18. *Humanist without Portfolio: An Anthology of the Writings of Wilhelm von Humboldt*, trans. Mariane Cowan (Detroit: Wayne State University Press, 1963), p. 289.

19. *Situations I*, 6th ed. (Paris: Gallimard, 1947), p. 229.

20. *Molloy. Malone Dies. The Unnameable* (London: Boyars, 1966), pp. 379–80.

21. *Oeuvres*, ed. Jean Hytier, 2 vols. (Paris: Gallimard, 1957–60), p. 863.

22. *Variété V*, 36th ed. (Paris: Gallimard, 1945), p. 143.

23. *Oeuvres*, p. 374.

24. "*Le Mystère dans les lettres*," in *Divagations* (Geneva: 1943), p. 293, trans. in Elizabeth Sewell, *The Structure of Poetry* (London: Routledge & Kegan Paul, 1951), pp. 155–56.

25. Frederick R. Karl, *Joseph Conrad: The Three Lives: A Biography* (London: Faber & Faber, 1979), p. 670.

26. J. Hillis Miller, *Poets of Reality: Six Twentieth-Century Writers* (Cambridge, Mass: Belknap Press of Harvard University Press, 1965), p. 54.

27. See *TU*, 126, 165–66; *TLS*, 68, and *AF*, 190.

28. *The Metaphysics of Darkness: A Study in the Unity and Development of Conrad's Fiction* (Baltimore: Johns Hopkins University Press, 1971), p. 188.

29. Aubry, *LL*, I, 108. See also Richard Curle, ed. *Conrad to a Friend: 150 Selected letters from Joseph Conrad to Richard Curle* (London: Sampson Low, Marston, 1928), p. 84. Later abbreviated *RC*.

30. René Rapin, ed., *Lettres des Joseph Conrad à Marguerite Poradowska* (Geneva: Droz, 1966), pp. 147, 157. The errors in Conrad's French are reproduced.

31. *LL*, II, 100. See also II, 74, and William Blackburn, ed., *Joseph Conrad: Letters to William Blackwood and David S. Meldrum* (Durham: Duke University Press, 1958), p. 27. Later abbreviated *WB*.

32. Georges Jean-Aubry, *Lettres Françaises de Joseph Conrad* (Paris: Gallimard, 1929), p. 122. Later abbreviated *LF*.

33. Quoted in Kenneth Burke, *The Rhetoric of Religion: Studies in Logology* (Boston: Beacon Press, 1961; rpt. Berkeley: University of California Press, 1970), p. 55.

34. *Literary Essays of Ezra Pound*, ed. T. S. Eliot (London: Faber & Faber, 1954), p. 64.

35. See *LJ*, 67 and *WT*, 35.

36. Edward Garnett, ed., *Letters from Conrad, 1985–1924* (London: Nonesuch Press, 1928), p. 21. Later abbreviated *LC*.

37. See also *LL*, I, 316 and *WB*, 192.

38. *Oeuvres*, pp. 242, 223.

39. *Propos sur la poésie, recueillis et présentés par Henri Mondor* (Monaco: Editions du Rocher, 1946), p. 82.

40. F. M. Dostoevsky, *Letters from the Underworld*, trans. C. J. Hogarth (London: J. M. Dent, 1929), p. 41.

41. Quoted in Kirschner, p. 10. See also *LL*, I, 26.

42. See *TLS*, 153, 214, and *Su*, 72.

43. See, e.g., *LL*, I, 192 and II, 14; *LF*, 50; *LC*, 126; Watts, *Letters*, p. 131 and Rapin, *Lettres*, p. 136.

44. *A Writer's Diary, being extracts from the diary of Virginia Woolf*, ed. Leonard Woolf (1953: rpt. London: Hogarty, 1974), p. 345.

45. *Joseph Conrad and the Fiction of Autobiography* (Cambridge: Harvard University Press, 1966), pp. 163, 97.

46. Miller, pp. 59–60.

47. "The Significance of the Revisions in the Early Versions of *Nostromo*," *Modern Fiction Studies*, 5 (Summer 1959), 133.

48. *Collected Works*, XIX, 232.

49. *The Complete Works of William Hazlitt*, Centenary Edition, ed. P. P. Howe, 21 vols. (London: J. M. Dent, 1930–34), XII, 337.

Conrad's Covert Plots and Transtextual Narratives
Cedric Watts*

Conrad was a master of the covert plot. Various of his novels and tales are characterised by the presence within the main narrative of smaller or larger plot-sequences which are so subtly and obliquely presented, with elisions or hiatuses, that they may be overlooked at the first or even second reading; indeed, some readers may never see them at all, but may only have the feeling that some narrative enigma has been posed and left unresolved. When once the covert plot is perceived, various consequences ensue. The narrative as a whole is seen to be more intelligently artful in its exposition; the work becomes more ironic; and certain themes gain richer presentation. Generally the mode of concealment of elements of the plot is that we see through the eyes, or "over the shoulder," of a protagonist or narrator who is being deceived or circumvented, and who is slow to perceive, if he perceives at all, the web that others are weaving around him. The covert plots of Conrad are therefore covert in two senses: concealed from a central observer, and largely concealed (at least at the first reading) from the reader.

The elision or withholding of logical connections preoccupies Conrad the story-teller as it preoccupies Conrad the descriptive artist. He developed to sophisticated extremes the art of "delayed decoding" (Ian Watt's phrase) in descriptive passages: he presents the effect while withholding or delaying the knowledge of the cause; and the result is that the event gains in vividness of impact while initially seeming strange, random or absurd, a quality diminished but seldom erased by our subsequent perception of the rational explanation. There are hundreds of possible examples, including the presentation of the death of Marlow's helmsman in *Heart of Darkness*, the explosion of the coal-gas in "Youth," and the onset of rain in *The Shadow-Line*. I cite the last example because of its convenient brevity: "By an effort which absorbed all my faculties I managed to keep my jaw still. It required much attention, and while thus engaged I became bothered by curious, irregular sounds of faint tapping on the deck. They

*Reprinted with permission of the author from *Critical Quarterly* 24 (1982):53–64.

could be heard single, in pairs, in groups. While I wondered at this mysterious devilry, I received a slight blow under the left eye and felt an enormous tear run down my cheek. Raindrops."[1] This instance shows that there may be three stages in the registration of material. First stage: the sense-data, undeciphered ("curious, irregular sounds of faint tapping on the deck"); second stage, first or inaccurate decoding (here, a Poltergeist or alien spirit at work—"mysterious devilry"); third stage: eventual accurate decoding—"Raindrops." I have suggested previously[2] that the concept of delayed decoding applies not only to many of Conrad's most vivid descriptive passages but also to longer narrative sequences—and perhaps even to the main narrative strategies of whole works, as in *Heart of Darkness*, where Marlow is attempting to decipher, to comprehend, the meaning of his journey into the Congo, and as in *Nostromo*, in which the reader must overcome moral myopia by ordering and reconciling the jumbled chronology and viewpoints of the text. It is clear that a novelist who is interested in modes of delayed decoding will also be interested in covert narrative sequences: often the two will go together and will entail kindred scrutinies.

A good example of the delayed decoding of a narrative sequence is provided by the long first section of *The Shadow-Line*, in which, at first reading, the reader's mystification is probably maintained almost as long as the narrator's. What is overt is that the steward at the Officer's Home is being reduced to desperation by Hamilton, who stays there as a brooding, sulky and arrogant presence, refusing to pay his bills. What is covert is that upon receiving a message from Captain Ellis which offers a command to the young hero, the steward passes the message not to the hero but to Hamilton, hoping that Hamilton will take the command and that the Home will thus be rid of its parasitic incubus. However, wise Captain Giles has seen the arrival of the message and guesses the deception; he takes the hero aside and hints to him—rather too subtly—the nature of the deception. The hero initially makes a false decoding of the hints: he assumes that Giles is half mad, gaining "the impression of mild, dreary lunacy"—"It flashed upon me that high professional reputation was not necessarily a guarantee of sound mind." Next, the hero makes a truer but not adequate decoding: after accosting the steward, he learns that the latter has intercepted a notification of a command; but it is not until Giles urges him to hurry to the Harbour Office that the hero tardily realises that the letter was intended specifically to invite him to the command. So eventually he just succeeds, though late, in gaining the position.

As the covert is perceived and surfaces as the overt, so multiple ironies emerge. Giles, who had seemed so tedious and vague, had in fact been astutely observant; and he has done more than save a command for the hero: he has virtually saved the hero's maritime soul, for the tale has indicated that the latter is beset by the temptation of becoming an aimless drifter, like others at the seamen's home. A further irony is that the command thus saved for the hero will prove to be for him a purgatorial ordeal on a vessel beset by calms and disease: whether on land or at sea, the seeming sanctuary may be a trap.

On the subsequent voyage in *The Shadow-Line*, a naturalistic reading of events provides the overt plot, while a supernatural dimension provides the covert plot. Though a characteristically evasive "Author's Note" by Conrad repudiates the supernatural, the text intermittently invites us to consider that the ship has been cursed by the spirit of the corrupt previous captain—a curse eventually exorcised by Burns's defiant laugh which (on this reading) ends the calm and permits the vessel to cross the latitude of 8° 20′ in the Gulf of Siam—the latitude at which, like a barrier, lies the body of that captain, who was buried at sea. In using the theme of curse and exorcism, Conrad is writing in a long tradition of sea-narratives which includes Coleridge's "Rhyme of the Ancient Mariner" and numerous versions (by Heine, Wagner, Marryat and Clark Russell) of the legend of the Flying Dutchman. Of course, all the events of Conrad's narrative have their natural explanation; but the supernatural elements, though not given dominance, are evoked and not refuted: this had been his strategy in *The Nigger of the "Narcissus"* and "The Secret Sharer," which also used the theme of curse and exorcism.

A subtler example of the covert narrative is provided by the tale "A Smile of Fortune" in *'Twixt Land and Sea*. So deeply is the narrator-captain entranced by Alice Jacobus that he never seems to come to conscious recognition of the extent of the plot that her father has woven about him, and it is certainly not until a second reading of the tale that we perceive how cunningly Jacobus has sought to ensnare the captain both with his daughter and with his trading schemes. The text plays on the verb "to procure," which links the mercantile with the sexual: "Procure— indeed! He's the sort of chap to procure you anything you like for a price."[3] Another theme is that familiar Conradian one of the seeming sanctuary which is really a baited trap. Alice is like the kid tethered in a trap to entice a free predator to its fate. It is overt enough that Jacobus is a shrewd businessman who hopes that the captain will become a suitor to his illegitimate daughter; but it is only in retrospect, as covert narrative connections surface, that we see how cunningly Jacobus has prepared the ground. He uses the family name, and the resulting confusion of identity with his accredited brother, to gain access to the captain on his ship; he quietly introduces samples of his wares, and particularly praises the potatoes (for his eventual coup will be to sell many tons of them to the hero); he asks whether the captain is unmarried, and is pleased to learn that he is not; he introduces flowers to the cabin in the hope of thus tempting the captain to the flower-garden where Alice waits; and eventually he insists that the captain should wait at his house (with Alice) while he, Jacobus, goes to search for bags to enable the captain to dispose of his cargo. Eventually, the hero agrees to buy a load of potatoes in his anxiety to spend time alone with the clumsily seductive Alice. Though Jacobus does not secure a husband for his daughter, he does succeed in the business deal. It can be argued, of course, that since the cargo of potatoes eventually brings a big profit to the hero, the tables are turned; but this is not how the hero sees the matter; for he feels corrupted and says "it was driving me out of the ship I had learned to love . . . I sat heavy-hearted at that parting, seeing all my plans destroyed, my modest future endangered. . . ."[4]

In *Heart of Darkness*, as I have shown in more detail previously,[5] the covert plot is the manager's plot to ensure the demise of Kurtz, his rival for promotion, by wrecking the steamer and delaying its repair, so that Kurtz's relief arrives too late. As Marlow tells his tale, he is in process of perceiving the full extent of the manager's plot: "I did not see the real significance of that wreck at once. I fancy I see it now, but I am not sure—not at all. Certainly the affair was too stupid—when I think of it—to be altogether natural. Still. . . ."[6] The manager estimates that the repair (which will be delayed by the lack of rivets) will take as long as three months. Marlow says: "I flung out of his hut. . . . He was a chattering idiot. Afterwards I took it back when it was borne in upon me startlingly with what extreme nicety he had estimated the time requisite for the 'affair.' "[7] Consequently, by the time the steamer reaches the inner station, Kurtz is deranged and dying.

The covert plot, when perceived, increases greatly the tale's ironies: among other things, it makes a sardonic comment on the belief of political Darwinians that the white man has a God-given right to invade and colonise tropical lands; for it shows that morally the Europeans, who treacherously scheme against their fellows, are no better and indeed probably worse (because of their hypocrisy) than those they purport to civilise. (We may recall Conrad's scorn for Lord Salisbury's view that the "living nations," such as Great Britain, must inevitably encroach upon and cut up the "dying.") If harmony between creature and his environment is a goal of the evolutionary process, that harmony has been attained not by the restless white men, who, with the exception of the abnormally healthy manager, tend to succumb to illness within months of arrival in Africa, but by the natives who so energetically paddle their canoe through the surf: "They shouted, sang; their bodies streamed with perspiration, they had faces like grotesque masks—these chaps; but they had bone, muscle, a wild vitality, an intense energy of movement, that was as natural and true as the surf along their coast. They wanted no excuse for being there. They were a great comfort to look at."[8]

But, if the covert plot thus contributes importantly to the tale's themes, the reader may well ask why it is covert instead of overt. The answer is that by the elliptical presentation of the manager's plot against Kurtz, Conrad can have his cake and eat it: he has the best of both possibilities. Through the elliptical presentation, which initially conceals the plot's logic from the reader, Conrad is able to preserve that important initial impression that Marlow has entered a region of irrationality, nightmare, and absurdity, a region of crass purposelessness: the theme of the futility of imperialism is thus emphasised, while the more general theme of the perils of crossing the threshold from the familiar to the unknown is maintained. When we eventually, in retrospect, see the covert plot, the theme of futile activity is modified by our recognition that some activity in the Congo may indeed be purposeful and effective — but since it is maliciously competitive activity by a European, it still supports the criticism of imperialism and the warnings about the dangers of the unknown. As Africa ambushes Europeans, so the narrative ambushes readers.

What commentators on Conrad have so far overlooked is that the covert plots and narrative obliquities of the later works have been boldly anticipated in Conrad's first novel, *Almayer's Folly*. As in *Heart of Darkness*, the overlooked material in *Almayer's Folly* concerns a treacherous scheme by one trader to defeat another in an exotic, remote region to which both have come from afar. Let us first recall the familiar overt plot of *Almayer's Folly* and then see how the covert plot interweaves it.

The overt plot. When the novel opens, Almayer is waiting for the return of Dain, his Balinese friend. He hopes that when Dain returns, the two will at long last make the journey into the interior, the journey on which (Almayer believes) they will find the gold whose whereabouts appeared to be indicated in the journals of Lingard. (Lingard has vanished while on a visit to Europe.) Almayer dreams that with the gold he will be able to live in Europe with his beloved daughter Nina. Dain does indeed re-appear and speaks briefly to him, but then travels on to see Lakamba. In a long retrospective sequence we learn of prior events, such as Nina's unhappy upbringing and the abortive proposal made by Reshid for her hand in marriage. Dain had befriended Almayer, originally for trading purposes (and evidently because of his need to trade in gunpowder, to which Almayer as a European has access, though officially forbidden to trade with natives), and subsequently the friendship has been a cover for Dain's courtship of Nina. He had also effected a reconciliation between Rajah Lakamba and Almayer, the latter having "spent his last dollar" in fitting out the boats of Lakamba and Dain for the gold-seeking journey into the interior. After the retrospective sequence, we learn that Dain has lost his brig during an ambush by the Dutch: he suspects that he was betrayed to the authorities by someone in Sambir — "The Orang Blanda [Dutchmen] have good friends in Sambir, or else how did they know I was coming thence?"

We learn that the Dutchmen are pursuing Dain; Lakamba is annoyed because of his involvement with Dain in the powder-smuggling project. Almayer, in response to Dain's blandishments, had bought gunpowder with Dain's money, the powder being brought out by Ford in the steamer and then transferred to the brig. Before Almayer would consent to this scheme, "Lakamba had to send Babalatchi over with the solemn promise that his eyes would be shut in friendship for the white man, Dain paying for the promise and the friendship in good silver guilders of the hated Orang Blanda." What Almayer gets in return is not money so much as Dain's assistance in the gold-seeking venture. (As for the gunpowder, Dain trades it to Malays for possible use against the Dutch — this is "at the time when the hostilities between Dutch and Malays threatened to spread from Sumatra over the whole archipelago.")

The morning after Dain's return, a mutilated corpse is found by the river, and, in a sequence of macabre delayed decoding, Almayer is led to believe that it is Dain's corpse. In reality it is the body of one of Dain's boatmen, drowned while they were crossing the river in darkness, which had been disguised by Dain and Nina and deliberately mutilated by Mrs Almayer so as to be mistaken for the body of his master. The pursuing Dutch seamen reach Almayer's house; we learn that in escaping from their ambush, Dain by blowing up his brig had killed two Dutchmen, who drowned as a result of the explosion. Nina elopes with Dain, but Taminah, jealous, reveals the elopement to Almayer. He sets out; later Taminah tells the Dutch officers, who also go in pursuit.

For highly ambiguous reasons (both to rid himself of the racial disgrace and to help a daughter whom he loves), Almayer takes Nina and Dain to the river-mouth, eluding the Dutch pursuers; he is tempted to overcome prejudice and pride and to follow his daughter, but stays; Nina and her lover embark for Bali. Lonely and disillusioned, Almayer returns, burns his house, moves into the Folly, and eventually dies the solitary death of an opium-addict, seeking oblivion. Abdulla, the Arab trader, supported by his nephew Reshid, comes to observe the body of his old rival — "this Infidel he had fought so long and had bested so many times": "And as they passed through the crowds that fell back before them, the beads in Abdulla's hand clicked, while in a solemn whisper he breathed out piously the name of Allah! The Merciful! The Compassionate!"

It will have been seen that among the whites and the other races there is a complicated and fluctuating mixture of loyalties and hostilities. Almayer is of Dutch origin, but he had hoped that the British, not the Dutch, would develop Borneo; indeed, the Folly had been begun in the hope that it would eventually accommodate men of the British Borneo Company. Dain, the Balinese, makes temporary working alliances with Almayer and the Malay, Lakamba, but Almayer he deceives (in the sense that he covertly courts Nina), while Lakamba would be quite willing to see both Almayer and Dain die if he could only learn the secret of the gold's location. Almayer's wife is of Sulu origin; naturally she schemes with the Sulu, Babalatchi, against her own hated husband. The Arab traders, Syed Abdulla and Reshid, hope to see all trade rivals defeated. The ruler of the Malays is Lakamba, who had been helped into power by the poisoning ("scientific manipulation") of his predecessor and by "having been well served by his Arab friends with the Dutch authorities." Inland, the Malays are "eternally quarrelling" with tribes of Dyaks or head-hunters.

The overt plot clearly merges with the Hobbesian theme. It is part of the originality of this novel of 1895 that it so thoroughly develops this pattern of the scheming by nations, races or individuals against each other: the law of the jungle prevails among men. Indeed, one of the main thematic statements is made by Nina's reflections—the reflections of one who has bitter experience of the prejudice and hypocrisy of the whites, and who, as a half-caste, is well placed to comment on the lives of white and black alike.

> It seemed to Nina that there was no change and no difference. Whether they traded in brick godowns or on the muddy river bank; whether they reached after much or little; whether they made love under the shadows of the great trees or in the shadow of the cathedral on the Singapore promenade; whether they plotted for their own ends under the protection of laws and according to the rules of Christian conduct, or whether they sought the gratification of their desires with the savage cunning and the unrestrained fierceness of natures as innocent of culture as their own immense and gloomy forests, Nina saw only the same manifestations of love and hate and of sordid greed chasing the uncertain dollar in all its multifarious and vanishing shapes.[9]

The outline of the overt plot has shown that a crucial point in the action is the ambush of Dain's brig by the Dutch authorities. All else stems from this—his flight, followed by the Dutch; his feigned death; and his precipitate elopement with Nina, leading to Almayer's realisation that he has been deceived both by Dain and by his beloved daughter and that the quest for gold must be abandoned and the daughter surrendered. Almayer's death stems from this demoralising recognition.

The covert plot is, virtually, Abdulla's; for it was through Abdulla that the ambush of the brig had taken place. Abdulla had wished to dominate trade on the Pantai and to overcome Almayer in one way or another. One way that he considered was a scheme of marriage: he had thought that his nephew Reshid might marry Nina, so that a rival, Almayer, would thus become a relative and partner. The apparently friendly meeting of the Dutch commission with Almayer strengthened this resolve. Abdulla and Reshid visited Almayer; Abdulla "made a polite allusion to the great consideration shown him (Almayer) by the Dutch 'Commissie,' and drew thence the flattering inference of Almayer's great importance amongst his own people"; and he offered 3,000 dollars as dowry if Nina would marry Reshid. Almayer was appalled at the idea and coldly declined the offer. After this, Reshid made a long trading voyage in quest of powder, at a time when the trade had been banned by the Dutch;

he brought some powder almost all the way back to Lakamba, but was stopped by the authorities and his cargo was confiscated. "Reshid's wrath was principally directed against Almayer, whom he suspected of having notified the Dutch authorities of the desultory warfare carried on by the Arabs and the Rajah with the up-river Dyak tribes." To Reshid's surprise, "the Rajah received his complaints very coldly" — because the Rajah knows that Almayer is innocent and has been reconciled to him by Dain, Dain being a new source of supply. Abdulla and Reshid then plan to turn the tables on Dain, we infer; and it is from the Dutchmen who visit Almayer in their pursuit of Dain that we learn how the tables were turned.

The Dutch lieutenant accuses Almayer of having sold to Dain the gunpowder that was stored in the brig.

> "How did you hear about the brig?" asked Almayer . . .
> "An Arab trader of this place has sent the information about your goings on here to Batavia, a couple of months ago," said the officer. "We were waiting for the brig outside, but he slipped past us at the mouth of the river, and we had to chase the fellow to the southward. When he sighted us he ran inside the reef and put the brig ashore. The crew escaped in boats before we could take possession. As our boats neared the craft it blew up with a tremendous explosion; one of the boats being too near got swamped. Two men drowned — that is the result of your speculation, Mr Almayer."[10]

The crucial statement here is "An Arab trader of this place has sent the information." At this point is the nexus of the overt and the covert plots. Abdulla and Reshid have turned the tables on Dain and Almayer; presumably Abdulla, the senior and wilier of the two Arabs, sent via Reshid the message to the authorities which resulted in the ambush, the deaths, the pursuit and the dénouement.

Readers who have read the text with the normal degree of attention will almost certainly not have noted that the fulcrum of the plot is provided by the Arab traders' betrayal of Dain, nor will they have noted, therefore, the element of ironic racial revenge: Arab betrays Balinese and European, as once European had prevented marriage of half-caste to Arab, and as once European had been thought to have betrayed Arab (Reshid) into ambush. Those who *do* see the covert plot will perceive that *Almayer's Folly* has a more intricate, intelligent and ironic plot-structure than at first seemed to be the case, and they will also perceive that the ending of the novel, far from being a quiet coda (as it may appear to the more casual reader) is a crowning irony, for the pious prayer at Almayer's death ("Allah! The Merciful! The Compassionate!") is uttered by the arch-rival, Abdulla, whose cunning had brought about the recognition, reversal and disillusionment which led to that death. Almayer is indeed the man whom "he had fought so long and had bested so many times." Furthermore, the initiate who is aware of the covert plot will also see that

Almayer's Folly, though in some respects a cumbered and laboured first novel, is in this respect more subtle than critics have recognized, and a worthy fore-runner of the later Conradian narratives whose obliquities and ellipses have long been a topic of discussion. Thus his or her sense of the continuity in Conrad's narrative preoccupations will be enhanced.

Just as there are logical relationships between delayed decoding and the covert plots (for in each case the reader supplies suppressed causal connections), so there are logical relationships between delayed decoding and what I term the *transtextual narratives* of Conrad. A transtextual narrative is one which exists in, across and between two or more texts. Sometimes it may offer *hysteron proteron* on a large scale. In delayed decoding, we encounter the later first and the earlier subsequently. The latter event in a sequence is thrust at us; subsequently we learn of the preceding events. So it is with some of Conrad's transtextual narratives, in which a later fictional stage may have been published years before the earlier.

We have previously noted, in the discussion of *The Shadow-Line*, the affair of Hamilton, the unpopular sponger at the Seamen's Home. This little story of Hamilton, inaugurated in that later work (for *The Shadow-Line* was first published in *Harper's Magazine* in 1916), had actually been completed in an earlier work, the tale "The End of the Tether," first published in *Blackwood's* in 1902. In "The End of the Tether" we learn how Hamilton was finally sent packing. Captain Eliott (a counterpart of Captain Ellis in *The Shadow-Line*) tells Whalley that the British Consul in Cochin-China had asked him to send a qualified master to take charge of a Glasgow ship at Saigon. Eliott had sent word to the Home, and at first there was no response.

> "You would think they would be falling over each other. Not a bit of it. Frightened to go home. Nice and warm out here to lie about a verandah waiting for a job. I sit and wait in my office. Nobody. What did they suppose? That I was going to sit there like a dummy with the Consul-General's cable before me? Not likely. So I looked up a list of them I keep by me and sent word for Hamilton — the worst loafer of them all — and just made him go. Threatened to instruct the steward of the Sailor's Home to have him turned out neck and crop. He did not think the berth was good enough — if you — please. 'I've your little record by me,' said I. 'You came ashore here eighteen months ago, and you haven't done six months' work since. You are in debt for your board now at the Home, and I suppose you reckon the Marine Office will pay in the end. Eh? So it shall; but if you don't take this chance, away you go to England, assisted passage, by the first homeward steamer that comes along. You are no better than a pauper. We don't want any white paupers here.' I scared him."[11]

And thus Conrad ends the yarn about Hamilton — approximately fourteen years before starting it!

Almayer's Folly inaugurates various transtextual narratives. If we ask how the Arab traders came to be located at Sambir in the first place — if, that is, we ask for an earlier stage in the narrative of Abdulla — we turn for answer to the subsequent novel, *An Outcast of the Islands*, which tells us how Abdulla was guided to Sambir through the vengeful treachery of Willems to Lingard. If, on the other hand, *Almayer's Folly* makes us curious about the earlier life of Lingard, the later works lead us into his earlier history: again we encounter a parallel to the *hysteron proteron* of delayed decoding. *An Outcast* tells us of the trading prowess of the younger Lingard; while *The Rescue*, which was not published until 1919 (in *Land and Water* magazine), twenty-four years after publication of *Almayer's Folly*, tells us of a Lingard younger still, and we see a tragically ironic life-pattern analeptically emerging, for in all three of the books we see a man who well-meaningly intervenes in the lives of others yet only, in the long run, with the effect of increasing the sum of misery and bitterness, whether it be the misery of Almayer, the bitterness of Willems, or the disillusionment of Hassim and Immada.

However, transtextualities are not always examples of *hysteron proteron*. The most important transtextual biography in all Conrad's works is one which proceeds in normal chronological order: the biography of Marlow, as we proceed from "Youth" (1898) to *Heart of Darkness* (1899), *Lord Jim* (1899–1900) and *Chance* (1912). It is a sad story, for as Marlow ages we hear him gradually become less intelligent and more garrulous; in the later part of *Jim* and for much of *Chance* he is too facile and waffling as philosopher-raconteur, and we regret his ageing. It is a sad story in another respect, too, for this man who had once felt love for Kurtz's Intended[12] never marries but settles into a long lonely bachelorhood. (There is a slight parallel with Tom Lingard, who after his infatuation with Mrs Travers, described in *The Rescue*, never marries but, like Marlow, gratifies a paternal instinct by adopting various protégés.) The critical biographies of Marlow and Lingard have yet to be written; and it may be felt that the importance of transtextual narratives in Conrad has not yet been appreciated. Not only Lingard and Marlow, but numerous other characters recur in his pages, figuring in two or even three of his works (Schomberg, Davidson, Burns and Ellis come to mind; and the narrator of *Heart of Darkness* reminds us that the very same group of hearers listened to Marlow in "Youth"), and this network of recurrences gives a special quality to Conrad's fiction.

First, and obviously enough, the network enhances the realism, for such recurrences are likely to occur when an author is recalling actual journeys and actual encounters. Sometimes the reason for the recurrence is indeed that Conrad is recalling a real person (Burns is based on the real mate, Born; Tom Lingard on the actual William Lingard); sometimes that he is re-using a convenient fictional construct based probably on several acquaintances (as seems to be the case with Marlow). But while one effect is to give an apparent warrant of authenticity to the fiction, another is to give a peculiar spaciousness to the fictional world. For, as tale is linked to tale, novel to novel, tale to novel and novel to tale by means of these recurrent characters (and locations), we sense behind the individual works a meta-narrative, one large imaginative territory closely related to actuality and from which all the individual existent fictions can be seen as selections. With most other major writers, we move from separate work to separate work, and though we gain cumulative knowledge of each writer's habits of mind and moral and technical preoccupations, we do not encounter that Conradian sense of the symbiosis of fictional worlds and lives.[13]

More obviously, transtextuality provides a gain not only in realism but also in economy; for Conrad can invoke in one tale recollection of matters given perhaps more fully in a previous tale (as when the opening of *Heart of Darkness* refers us to the character-descriptions at the opening of "Youth"); which suggests in turn that any reading of a single Conradian work which is not "contextual" in its range is likely to impoverish that work unjustly. If it be argued that to evaluate a work we have to regard it as a single entity, isolated from its fellows, the answer is that in deciding on the content and meaning of that work we naturally and properly take account of those parts of its context which seem to enrich it appropriately, rather as we relate to a Shakespeare sonnet or a Blake poem others in their respective sequences; and there are grounds for considering as one entity a narrative which extends across two or more tales or novels, just as we may consider the tetralogy of Shakespeare's histories from *Richard II* to *Henry V* as one entity for some of our critical purposes.

It may be felt, too, that Conrad's transtextual narratives generate a strong sense of Conrad as a living responsive author, responsive to the reader's curiosity: his narratives, apprehended as groups or clusters, invite and reward our interrogation. For example, near the beginning of "A Smile of Fortune," the narrator discusses the character of the mate, Burns: "Meantime the wind dropped, and Mr Burns began to make disagreeable remarks about my usual bad luck. I believe it was his devotion for me which made him critically outspoken on every occasion. All the same, I would not have put up with his humour if it had not been my lot at one time to nurse him through a desperate illness at sea. After snatching him out of the jaws of death, so to speak, it would have been absurd to throw away such an efficient officer. But sometimes I wished he would dismiss himself."[14] We interrogate the statement in various ways: one, by asking the narrator to tell us more about this interesting love – hate relationship (as he subsequently will in this tale), and particularly by asking for more information about the dramatic incident referred to ("snatching him out of the jaws of death"): and that second question will be answered not in this tale but five years later in *The Shadow-Line*, which gives an account of Burns's feverish illness and of his being tended by the captain. A further general consequence ensues: not only a sense of entry into an extensive and consistent fictional universe in which we have freedom to roam — and to re-encounter landmarks and acquaintances — but a sense that the narrator, where he is the anonymous presenter of a sea-tale, like the narrator of "A Smile of Fortune" (or of "Falk" or *The Shadow-Line*) is remarkably like an author who is intelligently responsive to our enquiries, and who is an astute friend in evoking and obliquely gratifying our curiosity; an olympian yet intimate raconteur. Recent critics who claim that literature is merely about itself shun many friendships and much wisdom.

Notes

1. Dent, London, 1950, p. 113. All subsequent Conradian quotations are also from the J. M. Dent Collected Edition.

2. In "Conrad's Absurdist Techniques: a Terminology," *Conradiana* IX (1977), pp. 141–8.

3. *'Twixt Land and Sea*, p. 19.

4. *Ibid.*, p. 88.

5. Cedric Watts, *Conrad's "Heart of Darkness": A Critical and Contextual Discussion* (Mursia International, Milan, 1977), pp. 82–5; also *Conradiana*, vol. VII (1975), pp. 137–43.

6. *Youth*, p. 72.

7. *Youth*, p. 75.

8. *Youth*, p. 61.

9. *Almayer's Folly*, p. 43.

10. *Ibid.*, p. 123.

11. *Youth*, pp. 199–200.

12. Conrad pointed out to Blackwood's adviser, Meldrum, that there was "a mere shadow of love interest just in the last pages [of *Heart of Darkness*]." W. Blackburn, ed., *Joseph Conrad: Letters to William Blackwood and David S. Meldrum* (Cambridge, London, 1958), p. 38.

13. Fiction-writers of various kinds use recurrent characters, but in the main these characters tend not to age; their settings may change and be up-dated, but they themselves remain the same. It is perhaps a sign of Conrad's realism that his recurrent characters do age; more important, it is a sign of the searching, questioning quality of his fiction that we feel the need to follow Marlow, for example, to learn more of him, sensing that perhaps some of the enigmas of personality that Conrad is so fond of posing will find resolution.

14. *'Twixt Land and Sea*, p. 4.

Conrad and the Power
of Rhetoric
John E. Van Domelen*

Throughout his literary career Conrad was impressed by the power of both the spoken and written word. Acknowledging their legitimate use, it was far more often their abuse that drew his attention. Eloquence is almost always a suspect quality in Conrad's characters; when a character is eloquent he is likely to prove a villain. Furthermore, rhetoric is associated with revolution: Conrad's revolutionaries are invariably either masters of visionary rhetoric or peculiarly susceptible to its power. Masters of words in Conrad are almost always either liars or visionaries whose rhetoric has few points of contact with moral or physical reality. Though one could trace this concern with the power of rhetoric throughout Conrad's writings, I shall confine myself in this analysis to five of the works where the collision between rhetoric and action is most conspicuous: *Almayer's Folly*, "Typhoon," *The Secret Agent*, *Under Western Eyes*, and *Chance*.[1]

Almayer, who is "gifted with a strong and active imagination" (I, 10),[2] is cursed with a "feebleness of purpose" (I, 25) that makes him merely a "grey-headed and foolish dreamer" (I, 35). His tragedy is his inability to realize that before he can enjoy the indolent life "the world had to be conquered first, and its conquest was not so easy as he thought" (I, 24). Almayer, like other romantic characters in Conrad, suffers from mental depression brought on by the discrepancy between his aspiration and reality, and from one such fit of dejection he rouses himself with talk: "Almayer came out of his despondency with another burst of talk" (I, 122). He is, like Kurtz, a dreamer intoxicated by the sound of his own voice.

As a romantic idealist he is convinced of the value of his word, and confuses its promissory nature with true gold; the worthlessness of his word is revealed when the lieutenant, demanding that Almayer deliver up Dain Maroola, sternly addresses the drunken dreamer as follows: " 'Hi! Almayer! Wake up, man. Redeem your word. You gave your word. You gave your word of honour, you know" (I, 139).

Nina prefers the words of her Malay kinsmen and of Dain Maroola, who speaks to her "with all the rude eloquence of a savage nature" (I, 69), to the hypocrisy of the whites; we are told that "the savage and uncompromising sincerity of purpose shown by her Malay kinsmen seemed at last preferable to the sleek hypocrisy, to the polite disguises, to the virtuous pretences of such white people as she had had the misfortune to come in contact with" (I, 43). Moreover, as Nina tells the Dutch lieutenant: " 'I hate the sound of your gentle voices. That is the way you speak to women,

*Reprinted with permission from *Conradiana* 8 (1976):172–78.

dropping sweet words before any pretty face. I have heard your voices before' " (I, 140–41). Ironically, it is Almayer who tells Nina that by eloping with Dain Maroola she will " 'live a life of lies and deception till some other vagabond comes along to sing' " (I, 180). Thus there is a contrast between the worthless words of the effete and hypocritical whites and the sincere though rude eloquence of the noble and savage Malays.

The Arabs or Moslems in *Almayer's Folly* are another matter. Neither traders nor diplomats are known for plain speaking, and consequently one does not expect veracity from Abdulla or Babalatchi. It is the wily Babalatchi who possesses serpentine eloquence; indeed, it is his prime characteristic. There are references to his "oratory" (I, 77) and his "polite eloquence" (I, 78); he is "eloquent and persuasive, calling Heaven and Earth to witness the truth of his statements" (I, 144). It is he who tells Almayer's violent native wife that "a man knows when to fight and when to tell peaceful lies" (I, 155). Conrad's valuation of eloquence can in part be determined by the kinds of characters to whom he assigns this quality; some examples, in addition to Babalatchi, are Schomberg, Donkin, and Kurtz.

Captain MacWhirr, on the other hand, is held up by Conrad as an ideal: "With a temperament neither loquacious nor taciturn he found very little occasion to talk. There were matters of duty, of course — directions, orders, and so on; but the past being to his mind done with, and the future not there yet, the more general actualities of the day required no comment — because facts can speak for themselves with overwhelming precision" (III, 9). It is not just his sparing use of words that saves MacWhirr: it is his almost total lack of imagination. The ship is saved because her master is "faithful to facts, which alone his consciousness reflected" (III, 14). The brute facts of actuality speak to him loud and clearly, and he listens to them attentively and obediently: "The China seas north and south are narrow seas. They are seas full of every-day, eloquent facts, such as islands, sand-banks, reefs, swift and changeable currents — tangled facts that nevertheless speak to a seaman in clear and definite language" (III, 15).

Language divorced from practical use and figurative, imaginative language are beyond MacWhirr's comprehension. Jukes writes of MacWhirr to his friend and quotes his skipper: " 'I can't understand what you can find to talk about,' says he. 'Two solid hours. I am not blaming you. I see people ashore at it all day long, and then in the evening they sit down and keep at it over the drinks. Must be saying the same things over and over again. I can't understand' " (III, 17–18). In a conversation with Jukes, Captain MacWhirr insists upon his using plain, unadorned, speech: "Captain MacWhirr expostulated against the use of images in speech" (III, 25).

The helmsman Hackett exclaims to the Captain that he can steer forever if nobody talks to him (III, 66), and thus the far-from-loquacious

Captain is reminded that words take one's mind off the duty at hand. The written word fares no better: MacWhirr tells Jukes that "These books are only good to muddle your head and make you jumpy" (III, 87), and these are not imaginative works but very practical books on navigation! Not only are books pernicious because they confuse and cause needless anxiety but also because they are inadequate; Jukes concludes his letter to his friend by mentioning that "the skipper remarked to me the other day, 'There are things you find nothing about in books' " (III, 102).

The Secret Agent contrasts the forensic skill of Mr. Verloc with the silence of Winnie. Of Mr. Verloc it is stated: "His voice, famous for years at open-air meetings and at workmen's assemblies in large halls, had contributed, he said, to his reputation of a good and trustworthy comrade" (X, 23). Satirically, "there was no uproar above which he could not make himself heard." Mrs. Verloc, on the other hand, "was a woman of very few words" (X, 245) who, in her moment of crisis, reacts as follows: "Mrs. Verloc had not sufficient command over her voice. She did not see any alternative between screaming and silence, and instinctively she chose the silence. Winnie Verloc was temperamentally a silent person" (X, 246). Just as his power with words fails him when Mr. Vladimir demands action, so his persuasive power fails him when it is pitted against the inarticulate feeling of his wife: "The self-confident tone grew upon Mrs. Verloc's ear which let most of the words go by; for what were words to her now? What could words do to her for good or evil in the face of her fixed idea?" (X, 250).

In addition to the opposition between speech and silence there is that between the word and the deed. Vladimir has nothing but contempt for Verloc's abilities as a speaker: "I daresay you have the social revolutionary jargon by heart well enough" (X, 24). Furthermore, the revolutionist must deliver action not words; Vladimir tells him: "Well, I am going to speak plain English to you. Voice won't do. We have no use for your voice. We don't want a voice. We want facts—startling facts—damn you" (X, 25). Vladimir wants no fiction in place of facts: "You are being called upon to furnish facts instead of cock-and-bull stories" (X, 31). The Professor tells Ossipon that "the condemned social order has not been built up on paper and ink, and I don't fancy that a combination of paper and ink will ever put an end to it" (X, 71). Ossipon is rebuked: "Here you talk print, plot, and do nothing" (X, 73).

Verloc's tragedy is that of one who is faced on both fronts, the revolutionary and the domestic, with crises that reveal the inadequacy of words, and the power of words is really all he has. If *Nostromo* indicates that ideology, law, culture, are the creatures of economic realities, then *The Secret Agent* shows that "the way of even the most justifiable revolutions is prepared by personal impulses disguised into creeds" (X, 81). Though the impulses of father and son are perhaps similar, the creeds they result in differ.

A new opposition is introduced in *Under Western Eyes*. The speaker is an old teacher of languages who ruefully acknowledges that not only are words "the great foes of reality" but that too long and intimate an acquaintance with them destroys "imagination, observation, and insight": "If I have ever had these gifts [imagination and expression] in any sort of living form they have been smothered out of existence a long time ago under a wilderness of words. Words, as is well known, are the great foes of reality. I have been for many years a teacher of languages. It is an occupation which at length becomes fatal to whatever share of imagination, observation, and insight an ordinary person may be heir to. To a teacher of languages there comes a time when the world is but a place of many words and man appears a mere talking animal not much more wonderful than a parrot" (XII, 3).

Conrad's fear and distrust of the Russian mentality is well-known, and in *Under Western Eyes* he provides a psycho-linguistic basis for this: "What must remain striking to a teacher of languages is the Russians' extraordinary love of words. They gather them up; they cherish them, but they don't hoard them in their breasts; on the contrary, they are always ready to pour them out by the hour or by the night with an enthusiasm, a sweeping abundance, with such an aptness of application sometimes that, as in the case of very accomplished parrots, one can't defend oneself from the suspicion that they really understand what they say. There is a generosity in their ardour of speech which removes it as far as possible from common loquacity; and it is even too disconnected to be classed as eloquence" (XII, 4). One can see that it was no accident that Kurtz's admirer was a young Russian. It should be noted, though, that it is not the perversion of truth or the unscrupulous application of persuasion that he notes in the Russians but rather an unbalanced romantic enthusiasm, an intoxication with words, that suggests the visionary who mistakes the signs of things for the things themselves.

Razumov is the atypical Russian; it is he who benefits from the observation that "amongst a lot of exuberant talkers, in the habit of exhausting themselves daily by ardent discussion, a comparatively taciturn personality is naturally credited with reserve power" (XII, 6). But, most ironically, it is the voluble Haldin who refuses to confess while the taciturn Razumov not only talks too much to Councillor Mikulin but also confesses to the revolutionaries! It is tragically ironic that the taciturn Razumov is forced to play the role of informer, the very idea of which he evidently loathes, as his statement to Peter Ivanovitch indicates: " 'Oh, we are great in talking about each other,' interjected Razumov, who had listened with great attention. 'Gossip, tales, suspicions, and all that sort of thing, we know how to deal in to perfection. Calumny, even" (XII, 206). Yet, ironically, it gives Razumov "a feeling of triumphant pleasure to deceive her [Sophia Antonovna] out of her own mouth. The epigrammatic saying that speech has been given to us for the purpose of concealing our thoughts came into his mind" (XII, 261).

Forced by circumstances to live a lie, Razumov acknowledges to himself that "all sincerity was an imprudence. Yet one could not renounce truth altogether, he thought, with despair" (XII, 209). Instead of renouncing the truth, he eventually sacrifices himself to it by, ironically, confessing. He seems to be thinking in terms of sacrifice earlier, and he does so in terms of progress and change.

Like Pedrito Montero in *Nostromo*, the revolutionary Julius Laspara has the gift of tongues: "he spoke and wrote four or five other European languages [in addition to Russian] without distinction and without force (other than that of invective)" (XII, 287). Conrad generously supplies his revolutionary Calibans with the ability to curse.

Under Western Eyes is notably rich in irony, and the ironic fate of Razumov is related to the power of words; the appropriateness of Razumov's punishment is obvious: the *listener* is *deafened*. Furthermore, Sophia Antonovna states that after Razumov's compulsive confession and terrible punishment " 'some of *us* always go to see him when passing through. He is intelligent. He has ideas. . . . He talks well, too' " (XII, 379). Unable to hear his own voice, he still talks. Moreover, he still has the fatal Russian habit: "however strongly engaged in the drama of action, they are still turning their ear to the murmur of abstract ideas" (XII, 294). One could add that they do this even after their eardrums have been burst.

The hero of *Chance*, Captain Anthony, "was a silent man" (XIV, 154), though his father was a poet, and he is himself "a great reader" (XIV, 413). Mr. and Mrs. Fyne are both authors, and "it was mostly 'conversation' which was demanded" of Flora de Barral by the German family with whom she for a time worked (XIV, 180). Reminiscent of *Romeo and Juliet*, Captain Anthony tells Flora: " '[Smith is] Not your name? That's all one to me. Your name's the least thing about you I care for' " (XIV, 223).

The power of the word, however, is stressed in *Chance*. Flora's father had achieved his financial eminence by riding the dominant word of the day, Thrift: "Just about that time the word Thrift was to the fore. You know the power of words. We pass through periods dominated by this or that word — it may be development, or it may be competition, or education, or purity, or efficiency, or even sanctity. It is the word of the time" (XIV, 74). The word of the hour is vigorously exploited by the press: "the greatest portion of the press was screeching in all possible tones, like a confounded company of parrots instructed by some devil with a taste for practical jokes, that the financier de Barral was helping the great moral evolution of our character towards the newly discovered virtue of Thrift" (XIV, 74). The mischievous power of words is to be feared: "See the might of suggestion? We live at the mercy of a malevolent word. A sound, a mere disturbance of the air, sinks into our very soul sometimes" (XIV, 264).

But it is the written word too that influences us: "We are the creatures of our light literature much more than is generally suspected in a world which prides itself on being scientific and practical" (XIV, 288). Light literature can intoxicate and seduce us away from reality, as it did in the case of Pedrito Montero. Marlow, whose literary proclivities were already suggested in "Youth," confesses to "a great liking for books. To this day I can't come near a book but I must know what it is about" (XIV, 413).

The relationship between one's true feelings and their expression and the danger of exposing one's true sentiments are both touched upon: "Young Powell recognized the expression of a true sentiment, a thing so rare in this world where there are so many mutes and so many excellent reasons even at sea for an articulate man not to give himself away, that he felt something like respect for this outburst" (XIV, 303). It was the expression by Kurtz of his true sentiment that won the admiration and respect of Marlow in *Heart of Darkness*. Yet in *Chance* it is Marlow who exclaims: "Never confess! Never, never! An untimely joke is a source of bitter regret always . . . and a confession of whatever sort is always untimely" (XIV, 212).

Marlow has evidently changed his mind about the nature of women since making his remarks in *Heart of Darkness*. Far from seeing women as being out of contact with reality, living in an ideal world of their own, he remarks: "I call a woman sincere when she volunteers a statement resembling remotely in form what she really would like to say, what she really thinks ought to be said if it were not for the necessity to spare the stupid sensitiveness of men. The women's rougher, simpler, more upright judgment, embraces the whole truth, which their tact, their mistrust of masculine idealism, ever prevents them from speaking in its entirety. . . . We could not stand women speaking the truth" (XIV, 144). The difficulties of Captain Anthony and Flora, are, like those of Charles Gould and his wife, and of Heyst and Lena, partly attributable to defective communications between the sexes.

In the preface to *A Personal Record* Conrad states that "He who wants to persuade should put his trust not in the right argument, but in the right word. The power of sound has always been greater than the power of sense. I don't say this by way of disparagement. It is better for mankind to be impressionable than reflective. Nothing humanely great — great, I mean, as affecting a whole mass of lives — has come from reflection. On the other hand, you cannot fail to see the power of mere words; such words as Glory, for instance, or Pity" (IX, xiii). He goes on to say: "Give me the right word and the right accent and I will move the world" (IX, xiv). Yet throughout his career Conrad emphasized the pernicious abuse of the word rather than its legitimate use. His writing continually displays his awareness of the ease with which the word can be used to pervert or distort the truth, and his rueful knowledge of the readiness with which people accept words as a substitute for reality itself.

Against the pernicious power of the word Conrad opposed action, though his attitude toward the efficacy of action was highly ambivalent: in referring to the French Revolution in his essay "Autocracy and War" Conrad declares that "it is the bitter fate of any idea to lose its royal form and power, to lose its 'virtue' the moment it descends from its solitary throne to work its will among the people" (XIX, 86). Yet, Conrad maintains, the primacy rests with the deed, not the word or the unrealized ideal: "A man is a worker. If he is not that he is nothing" (XIX, 190).

Notes

1. Three related essays by this writer have already appeared: "Conrad and Journalism," *Journalism Quarterly*, 47 (Spring 1970), 153–56; "In the Beginning Was the Word: or Awful Eloquence and Right Expression in Conrad," *SCMLA Studies*, 30 (Winter 1970), 228–31; and "A Note on the Reading of Conrad's Characters," *Conradiana*, 3:1 (1970–71), 87–89.

2. All references to Conrad's work are to the Medallion Edition (London: Gresham, 1925–28). Pagination is identical to the Dent and Sun-Dial.

The Ending of *Lord Jim*   Ian P. Watt*

Critical discussion of the last part of *Lord Jim* has largely concentrated on Jim's feelings and motives at three points in the narrative: during Marlow's visit to Patusan; during the Gentleman Brown episode; and during the final catastrophe. In all three cases Conrad's intentions seem to have been obscured by modern preconceptions.

Marlow's account of his month or so in Patusan is dominated by an atmosphere of gloomy foreboding. The enveloping jungle, the Stygian river, and the general prevalence of dusk, obscurity, and shadow compose a dark backdrop against which Jim, "white from head to foot," stands out in "total and utter isolation."[1] This persistent contrast is no doubt a way of emphasizing how, in Marlow's words, Jim's three years of fame took their "tone from the stillness and gloom of the land without a past, where his word was the one truth of every passing day" (272).

Jim's consciousness also has its sombre undercurrents; although he tells Marlow that he is "satisfied . . . nearly" (306), Jim still yearns to "frame a message to the impeccable world" (339). To some extent, therefore, one must agree with the judgment of many of the novel's best critics that Jim has not achieved "redemption"[2] or "atonement"[3] in Patusan, nor "transcended the world of the *Patna*."[4] But it may be playing with loaded dice to apply such terms to *Lord Jim*; they would certainly not have been accepted as appropriate by Conrad, whose scepticism firmly

*Reprinted with permission from *Conradiana* 11 (1979):3–21.

rejected the optimistic religious or transcendental assumptions about reality which they imply. Like Marlow, Conrad had very limited expectations about human possibilities, and neither of them would have hoped for much more than what has actually happened: that Jim "came on wonderfully" (224), and that his courage, work and self-discipline finally enabled him to feel "I am all right" (247).

It is in any case far from clear what "atonement" or "redemption" might mean for Jim. There is no one he could possibly make reparation to for his desertion of the *Patna*, since he was, and remains, its chief victim; while the fact itself can hardly be "redeemed." Very humanly, Jim had earlier hoped that he might begin again "with a clean slate" (185), but this was obviously impossible; Conrad emphasized the point in the manuscript by making Marlow say, "Once some potent event evokes before your eyes the invisible thing there is no way to make yourself blind again" (395).[5] On Patusan Jim faces the truth that none of his triumphs can ever wipe the slate clean; there is always, he says, "the bally thing at the back of my head" (306). "The world outside," Jim confesses, "is enough to give me a fright . . . because I have not forgotten why I came here. Not yet!" (305).

This inability to forget the *Patna*, however, will not seem to Jim's discredit to anyone who believes that the moral life depends, among other things, on treating our actions as in some sense permanent for ourselves and others. In any case, to wish otherwise would be to require Jim to accept the kind of celestial illusion on which the Intended relies in *Heart of Darkness*, and which, indeed, would have been needed to exorcise Jewel's continual terror that one day the outside world would rob her of Jim. Marlow knows very well that to kill such fears "you require . . . an enchanted and poisoned shaft dipped in a lie too subtle to be found on earth" (316); and to find that kind of deliverance, Marlow comments scornfully to his listeners, would be "An enterprise for a dream, my masters!"

The same ancient hunger for a magical transformation of reality has been at work in much of the psychological criticism of *Lord Jim*; it animates such objections, for instance, as that Jim fails to achieve full self-knowledge, that he is still "an outcast from himself . . . unable to recognise his own identity,"[6] or that he continues to exist in the "mist of self-deception" (G, 141). Here again there is much evidence to support these views: Marlow certainly says, for instance, that Jim "was not clear to himself" (177); but he also makes the important concession, "I did not know so much more about myself" (221); more generally, Marlow asserts that "no man ever understands quite his own artful dodges to escape from the grim shadow of self-knowledge" (80). Conrad was no more sanguine; and the question therefore arises whether Jim, or indeed anyone else, should be judged and found wanting by standards derived from the unsupported modern dogmas that full self-knowledge is possible, and that it can deliver us from the ignominious fate of being what we are.

Conrad's novels in general make clear that he regarded character as being almost as resistant to real change as to full comprehension. *Lord Jim* is not a *Bildungsroman*,[7] and insofar as it is essentially concerned with character, it is with character viewed from two resolutely sceptical points of view. Conrad's presentation of Jim's character is sceptical in the impressionist way because it is portrayed almost entirely through Marlow, who has no privileged knowledge of the "real" Jim such as an omniscient author might have claimed. Secondly, Conrad's portrayal is sceptical psychologically, because it does not show any very important change in Jim's character. His naive romanticism, his ingenuous and boy scoutish devotion to the importance of his role, his moody self-preoccupation — all these components of the old Jim are still there on Patusan; all that has changed is that they are no longer disabling: as Marlow nicely puts it, there is now "a high seriousness in his stammerings" (248).

In many respects, indeed, Jim is more than just satisfied; "Now and then," Marlow reports, "a word, a sentence, would escape him that showed how deeply, how solemnly, he felt about that work which had given him the certitude of rehabilitation" (248). Earlier, as a seaman, the only real reward, that of "the perfect love of the work," had "eluded him" (10); now Jim has found a form of this love: Marlow comments that "he seemed to love the land and the people," although he adds the qualification that he loved it "with a sort of fierce egoism, with a contemptuous tenderness" (248).

How seriously must one assess this reservation? Much has been made,[8] for instance, of the damaging implications of Marlow's observation that "all his conquests, the trust, the fame, the friendships, the love — all these things that made him master had made him a captive, too" (247). But this is not a sign of Jim's failure; in the real world, such a captivity is surely an unanticipated but almost inevitable result of assuming any responsibility — even that of literary criticism — seriously: the subjects are what they are, and make their own demands.

Many of the critics who take a severe view of Jim's failure to transform himself have centered their argument on his dealings with Gentleman Brown, the piratical ruffian who turns up in desperate straits and attempts to plunder Patusan. It has frequently been maintained that Jim is still psychologically crippled by an enduring sense of guilt, which leads him to identify unconsciously with Brown, and that this is the reason why he lets Brown escape and thus brings disaster upon himself and Patusan.[9] The various versions of this view, first put forward by Gustav Morf, and widely accepted — by Dorothy Van Ghent and Albert Guerard, for instance — argue that Jim's error is due to the "paralysing" and "immobilizing bond" brought about by his unconscious identification with Brown (G, 150), that he "simply cannot resist the evil *because the evil is within himself*,"[10] and that Jim's letting Brown leave is really a "compact with his own unacknowledged guilt" (*VG*, 235).

Marlow certainly stresses the moral intensity of the confrontation between the two men. On Brown's side the motives are conscious and very obvious. Brown, Marlow tells us, "hated Jim at first sight," because he "seemed to belong to things he had in the very shaping of his life contemned and flouted" (380). On Patusan Jim represents the established moral and social code and therefore provokes the ideological hatred of Brown, the lawless adventurer; on his deathbed Brown still exults in the thought that he had "paid out the stuck-up beggar" (344). As to Jim's reactions, he is certainly shaken when Brown tries to establish that they are equals, not only as English seamen, but as criminals; Jim is deeply wounded by the assumption that he, like Brown, had had to escape from civilization for discreditable reasons, and is in Patusan only in quest of "pretty pickings" (383); and Brown completely undermines Jim's self-possession when he asserts that if "it came to saving one's life in the dark, one didn't care who else went" (386).

Jim's consciousness of his own past, then, may well have strengthened his wish to spare Brown's life; as he comments to Jewel, "Men act badly sometimes without being much worse than others" (394). Jim may even have identified with Brown to the extent that he thought that, like himself, Brown ought to be given another chance. Nevertheless, the weight of the evidence is far from supporting the view either that Jim acted as he did out of guilt, whether conscious or unconscious, or that any other decision was possible in practical or moral terms.

When Gentleman Brown arrives with fourteen of his armed followers in a longboat, he is able to gain a foothold in Patusan because Jim is absent and the Rajah, Doramin, Dain Waris, and Jewel cannot agree on what to do. When Jim returns only two choices remain: to give Brown "a clear road or else a clear fight" (388). In a fight, Brown and his men would sell their lives dearly; they have already inflicted six casualties, and Jim feels "responsible for every life in the land" (394); the obvious way to avoid further slaughter is to let Brown go. Both *realpolitik* and local custom would no doubt dictate a more ruthless policy; but the deliberate extermination in cold blood of any human being is deeply offensive to anyone raised in the Western tradition; it would be especially so to Jim, the son of a parson; the decision, as Marlow sees it, essentially involves Jim's "truth" as against the "creed" of Patusan (393). The general moral argument is seconded by a more idiosyncratic psychological one: Jim has already shown that he prefers to take great risks rather than shed blood — as when he spared the three assassins who had been sent to kill him; and he still allows their accomplice, Cornelius, to live on nearby out of "absurd carelessness or else his infinite disdain" (285).

In practical and moral terms, then, Jim had no real alternative but to let Brown go, whatever he may have thought or felt. Of course, he must take the blame, as anyone in charge must be blamed when things turn out badly; but he cannot fairly be considered even imprudent. It is true that the catastrophe would not have occurred if Brown and his men had been disarmed; but Jim had originally stipulated this, and only yielded when Brown made it clear he would fight rather than surrender his arms. In any case the massacre of Dain Waris and his men could not have been predicted; as Marlow says, no one could have foreseen the combination of Brown's "almost inconceivable egotism" (394), which impels him to an otherwise pointless act of murderous revenge, with the "intense hate" (344) of Cornelius, who guides Brown to the backwater so that he can revenge himself indirectly against Jim, the man who has ousted him as Stein's representative.

A sense of guilt-ridden complicity in evil is not, then, a necessary hypothesis to explain why Jim lets Brown go; but the question of guilt has a larger importance, since it has been made central in some influential interpretations of Jim's character and fate.

From the very beginning, Jim puzzles and annoys Marlow because he seems to feel no guilt at having deserted the *Patna*. For Jim, we discover, this transgression of the code is an external matter which can be dealt with by taking his punishment in court; what really matters to Jim's inner self is something quite different: his failure to live up to his own ego-ideal in his own eyes. From this follows Jim's need to contest the opinions of others who assume that his real character is defined by his desertion of the *Patna*. Against such people Jim has only two reactions: to fight or to blush. We see both reactions succeeding each other on his first meeting with Marlow outside the courtroom: when Jim realizes his mistake about the yellow cur, he is foiled of his unconscious need to relieve his feelings by giving Marlow "that hammering he was going to give me for rehabilitation" (74–75); instead, Jim blushes and so deeply that "his ears became intensely crimson." Jim also blushes at Brown's first question; when asked "What made you come here?" we are told Jim went "very red in the face" (381).

In both cases Jim's blushing is surely a sign not of guilt, but of shame. The nature of the distinction remains moderately obscure, partly because the word "guilt" can mean so many things; but it is usually agreed that shame is much more directly connected than guilt with the individual's failure to live up to his own ideal conception of himself. As Gerhart Piers puts it in his psychoanalytic treatment of the distinction, "Whereas guilt is generated whenever a boundary (set by the Super-Ego) is touched or transgressed, shame occurs when a goal (presented by the Ego-Ideal) is not being reached. It thus indicates a real 'shortcoming.' Guilt anxiety accompanies transgression; shame, failure."[11]

Marlow uses this distinction in his condemnation of Jim: "The idea obtrudes itself," he says, that Jim "made so much of his disgrace while it is the guilt alone that matters" (177). Marlow is characteristically concerned with guilt, Jim with shame; and the case of Brierly establishes the contrast. It is because, like Jim, Brierly cannot bear the thought of falling short of his own ideal that he finds the enquiry a "disgrace" which is "enough to burn a man to ashes with shame" (67), and which eventually drives him to suicide.

The wider psychological implications of shame have been suggested by Max Scheler in terms which recall Stein's diagnosis of Jim. Scheler sees the origin of shame in the discrepancy between the individual's inward conception of himself and how his external appearance and acts seem to others. The most famous example of this discrepancy is the physical shame of Adam and Eve when they receive the burden of self-knowledge after the Fall;[12] for Jim the equivalent moment of self-knowledge and shame presumably came after his instinctive jump from the *Patna*; his intense suffering arose when he realized the total disjunction between his dreams and his act.

To return to Gentleman Brown, it is significant that, despite his own preconceptions, Marlow does not explain Jim's dealings as the result of guilt. Marlow is clearly referring to guilt in its common public sense of culpability for crime when he emphasises Brown's "sickening suggestion of common guilt" (387);[13] Jim is actually sickened by shame at having his failure on the *Patna* connected with Brown's deliberate crimes. Marlow also emphasises that Brown did not, as he thought, "turn Jim's soul inside out"; it was, Marlow affirms, "so utterly out of his reach" (385).

Marlow, then, does not question Jim's decision about Brown, and his testimony thus runs counter to the assumption that Jim's decision, and therefore his death, were the outcome of his guilt-ridden identification with Brown. If we seek to explain the basis of this widespread assumption, we must surely seek it not in the text, but in that strange Freudian mutation of the doctrine of original sin which has established as an *a priori* postulate that all errors are the result of unconscious guilt. This convenient moral melodrama makes it possible for us, unlike Conrad, to retain two comforting beliefs: that the world is just; and that despite all contrary appearances people who suffer really have themselves to blame. These doctrines make it our pleasurable duty as readers and critics to discover discreditable unconscious motives which prove that Jim deserved to be punished. Dorothy Van Ghent compares the fates of Jim and Oedipus, and asks the question, "Is one guilty for circumstances?" (*VG*, 239); through the privileged immunity to the complexities of other people's circumstances which is granted by modern psychology, we can return the unhesitating verdict of "Guilty."

On hearing that Brown had massacred Dain Waris and his followers, Jim's first thought is to avenge their death: but when Tamb'Itam says that the people of Patusan have turned against him, Jim realizes that this is out of the question. Three possible courses of action remain. If Jim is to keep Jewel and his followers with him, he must, like Brown, either fight or run. Both courses are hazardous; neither would benefit Patusan; fighting would cause much bloodshed; as for escape, it would only repeat the aftermath of the *Patna*, and Marlow surmises that Jim soon resolved that "the dark powers should not rob him twice of his peace" (409). The third possible course of action is to go to Doramin; and Marlow assumes that Jim decided on this almost at once; he would "defy the disaster in the only way it occurred to him such a disaster could be defied," and "conquer the fatal destiny itself."

Jim must have known that Doramin would want a life for a life— Jim's blood for that of his son, Dain Waris; and so Jim is in effect choosing a form of suicide. The mood in which Jim silently makes up his mind certainly suggests a defeated apathy somewhat similar to that which immobilized him on the *Patna*; and Marlow's comment on Jim's frame of mind then seems equally appropriate now: "The desire of peace waxes stronger as hope declines, till at last it conquers the very desire of life" (88). In the lifeboat Jim had wished for death partly out of revulsion from the defiling contact of the three other officers; and Cornelius and Brown are very like them in that they take the lowest possible view of life as egotistical survival. They represent what Tony Tanner has called the beetle view of the world (*TT*, 47–56); on this analogy, Jim's final choice is that of a butterfly who wants to fly away from the earth-bound corruption which has once again fouled his life.

Many actions, however, can be psychologically complex, and yet inevitable. This was the case with Marlow's lie to the Intended; and Jim's tendency to moody and suicidal self-withdrawal during his last hours need not in itself invalidate the view that he really had very little choice except to go to Doramin. To do so fulfilled Jim's primary and most explicit obligation, his formal promise to the people of Patusan that "he was ready to answer with his life for any harm that should come to them if the white men with beards were allowed to retire" (392). Great harm has come, and what Marlow calls "the sheer truthfulness of his last three years of life," that same truthfulness which had made the people agree to let Brown go, now demands that Jim be ready to keep his word whatever the consequence, and thus affirm his solidarity with those who had trusted him.

So Jim, telling what few of his personal followers who remain to go back to their homes, walks alone through the night to Doramin's kampong. When he arrives, the meaning of his intention is recognized: a voice in the crowd says, "He hath taken it upon his own head" (415); and thus the people of Patusan recognize that, just as Brown had taunted, Jim has indeed become "one with them" (381).

So, "stiffened and with bared head," Jim looks straight at Doramin; and he, without a word, "deliberately . . . shot his son's friend through the chest" (415). The crowd rushes forward, and, Marlow reports, "The white man sent right and left at all those faces a proud and unflinching glance. Then with his hand over his lips he fell forward, dead." Jim's "fixed from-under stare" has been transformed, and he dies facing the world in the posture of silent but resolute defiance.

In the brief commentary with which his letter ends, Marlow recapitulates some of his earlier doubts about Jim; but his main emphasis is on the positive realization of Jim's early dreams: "And that's the end. He passes away under a cloud, inscrutable at heart, forgotten, unforgiven, and excessively romantic. Not in the wildest days of his boyish visions could he have seen the alluring shape of such an extraordinary success!" Jim's boyhood dream of being "as unflinching as a hero in a book" (6) has finally come true.

Conrad began his career as a writer under something like the standard modern prescription — when fearful of self-exposure, take cover in irony: and so *Lord Jim* opens with a critical and sardonic view of its hero and his daydreams. This negative attitude is qualified by an increasing sympathy during Marlow's narrative; but it persists until the Stein episode; there Jim is elevated to an unexpected metaphysical dignity, and his very failure as an adventure-story hero becomes a symbol of the romantic world-view. This serves as a transition to an even more complete reversal of our picture of Jim, when he is given "a totally new set of conditions for his imaginative faculty to work upon" (218); in the apt terms of Jean-Jacques Mayoux: "A romantic finds his bearings again in a romantic situation; a devotee of unreality is at last at ease in an unreal and fabulous world where his imaginings precede and create the events instead of being surprised by them."[14]

Conrad's reversal of his original fictional assumptions no doubt reflects a prolonged irresolution in his own personal attitudes. If *Lord Jim* is the most romantic of Conrad's works it may be because he began it as a sad farewell to an earlier self, but then discovered that the parting would be too painful unless he first granted that romantic self some of the satisfactions it had dreamed of long ago. This change of direction impelled the last part of *Lord Jim* towards other literary models, and in particular towards the very different, though equally archaic, traditions of romance and tragedy. In Patusan, romance becomes the dominant spirit until that of tragedy supersedes it at the end.

Much of the action, the setting, the characters and the symbolism of Patusan suggest fable, fairy tale, and medieval romance. In Patusan, where "Romance had singled Jim for its own" (282), the land and its people "exist as if under an enchanter's wand" (330). Like a wandering knight, Jim arrives in an enchanted kingdom and there triumphs over incredible odds to deliver the people from their oppressors, notably Sherif Ali and his "infernal crew" (264). In addition, just as his mentor Stein had been rewarded for his "innumerable exploits" with the hand of a princess, so Jim wins the hand of a persecuted maiden, Jewel; they come together, we are told, "under the shadow of a life's disaster, like knight and maid meeting to exchange vows amongst haunted ruins" (312).

It can hardly be denied that these conventional elements of romance necessarily involve a marked falling off from the moral and dramatic intensity of the first part of *Lord Jim*. This led F. R. Leavis to place *Lord Jim* among Conrad's minor works on the ground that "the romance that follows" the *Patna* episodes, "though plausibly offered as a continued exhibition of Jim's case, has no inevitability as that."[15] The continuity between Jim of the *Patna* and Tuan Jim of Patusan is certainly not one of complete inevitability. On the other hand, Conrad is remarkably successful in adjusting the formulae of romance to quite different fictional premises. This can be seen, for instance, in the ingenuity with which the emblematic detail of the silver ring is used to bring about an ironic variation on the folk-tale motif of the poisoned gift, and thus to enact the transition from Jim's moment of chivalric glory to his fatal destiny.

The ring was given to Stein by Doramin, his old "war-comrade," as a token of "eternal friendship" (233). Stein gives it to Jim as his introduction to Doramin; and soon after his arrival in Patusan, when Jim is being pursued by his enemies, the ring becomes the magic emblem which causes Doramin to save his life and set him on the road of triumph. After that, however, the ring plays a less conspicuous role. Jim sends it by messenger to Dain to vouch for his order that Brown be allowed safe-passage to the sea; the ring is then returned to Doramin with Dain's corpse; and the cycle of friendship and trust comes to an end when, as Doramin rises to shoot Jim, the ring falls from Doramin's lap and rolls against Jim's foot. The talisman which had first "opened . . . the door of fame, love, and success" (415) to Jim, now closes it forever.

This symbolic reversal is complemented by another. Doramin owns a pair of huge ebony and silver flintlock pistols which Stein long ago gave him in return for the ring. Stein in turn had received the pistols from his early benefactor in the Celebes, a Scot called Alexander M'Neil; and it is out of gratitude to him that Stein plans the reciprocal gesture of adopting a Briton, if not a Scot, and decides to make Jim his heir. The continuity of this cycle of trust and friendship is also broken when Doramin avenges the death of his only son; he does it by shooting Stein's adopted son with the gift his old friend had given him to seal their friendship.

Both these romance motifs reflect the ancient warning that, in Marlow's words, "the imprudence of our thoughts recoils upon our heads" (342). The catastrophe itself, he comments, has "a terrifying logic to it"; it is "as if it were our imagination alone that could set loose upon us the might of an overwhelming destiny." Jim's romantic imagination has made him what he is; it has brought him to Patusan; and there his destiny is consummated with something of the spare and sudden brevity of Greek tragedy.

This fatal outcome has been immanent throughout the novel. Jim's conflict with himself and with the world can never be appeased or resolved; and the intensity with which Jim confronts this intractable conflict gives him something of the representativeness of the tragic hero.

Jim, as Marlow puts it, becomes an "individual in the forefront of his kind," because his problem is one where "the obscure truth involved" seems "momentous enough to affect mankind's conception of itself" (93).

In this respect also, Patusan constitutes a continuation rather than a new departure. Jim thinks that he can at last be wholly isolated from the corruptions and denials of the world; but, as we have seen, the *Patna* not only robs Jim of any inner peace, but also keeps him separate from Patusan and its people. No one can understand Jim: neither his adoptive family — Doramin and his wife — nor his friend, Dain Waris, knows his secret; and when Jim tells Jewel the story of the *Patna*, "she did not believe him" (320). Jewel can only see Jim's memories as an anguishing "hint of some mysterious collusion, of an inexplicable and incomprehensible conspiracy to keep her for ever in the dark." Marlow is finally forced to confront the source of this intractable division when Jewel asks him: "Has it got a face and a voice — this calamity?" (315); and Marlow's realization that the burden of their unhappy pasts irremediably isolates them from each other makes him see "their two benighted lives" as "tragic."

Jim's situation in Patusan, then, is one of insoluble conflict even before the advent of Brown; and the death of Dain Waris is only the last and decisive demonstration that Jim cannot possibly reconcile all the just claims upon him. It is this intractability of moral circumstance which goes far to justify Robert B. Heilman's claim that "Jim is that rare figure in English fiction — the tragic hero."[16] Several other critics, including Dorothy Van Ghent, have also considered him in this light, although usually to arrive at a qualified dissent.

The problem of whether we should see *Lord Jim* as tragedy is largely a matter of what we understand by the term. If we take as our main tragic criterion the hero's achievement of self-knowledge, Jim does not qualify. Heilman, it is true, speaks of Jim's having to go through "the tragic course of knowing himself and thus learning the way to salvation." Convincing evidence of Jim's final moral maturity, however, is surely far to seek. Marlow comments during his Patusan visit that "It's extraordinary how very few signs of wear he showed" (269); and what continues to make Jim attractive is largely his youthful surface of imperviousness to fortune's frown. In any case, Marlow's most explicit judgment on the issue of Jim's self-knowledge certainly runs counter to Heilman's view: Jim, Marlow says, "was overwhelmed by his own personality — the gift of that destiny which he had done his best to master" (341).

The postulate of tragic self-knowledge, however, may be yet another of the modern secularized versions of the consolations which religion offers in the face of suffering, waste, and evil. Heilman's use of the term "salvation" might be taken as confirmation of this, and so might Dorothy Van Ghent's argument that what distinguishes Jim's death from the "atonement" of the exile of Orestes or Oedipus is that the expiation of Jim's blood-guilt brings about not the "restoration" but the "destruction" of "community health" (*VG*, 232–33). Much could be said in general against the Hegelian theory that tragedy is socially reconstructive; but even if it were true of Greek tragedy, it is surely evident that both the form and the substance of *Lord Jim*, as of the modern novel in general, make a very different view of society their point of departure; to adopt Van Ghent's terminology, modern novels start from "the disintegration" of those very "moral bonds between men," which in classical tragedy are assumed to be the world's normative order.

In any case all the evidence suggests that the various Christian, Hegelian, or Marxist theoretical systems which present suffering, conflict, or death as necessary parts of some promised transcendental recompense or dialectical reconciliation were, or would have been, completely alien to Conrad's way of looking at the world. That at one moment Marlow sees a "terrifying logic" in the operation of Jim's destiny does not mean he sees it as part of an ultimately just or moral process; on the contrary, beginning with the *Patna* episode, Marlow suggests that Jim's fate may be as meaningless, accidental, and "devoid of importance as the flooding of an ant-heap" (93). Such a bleak perspective would not necessarily discount the view that *Lord Jim* is much closer to tragedy than most novels; but it would have to be tragic in other meanings of the term.

There is another much more archaic and less moralistic view of tragedy which sees it primarily as the expression of humanity's awed astonishment at the works of fate, and more especially at its remorseless dealings with individuals who are far above the common run, not only in their position and achievements, but in the resolution with which they confront suffering and death. Such a reaction is expressed by one of the men of Patusan at the fate of Dain Waris: he is "struck with a great awe and wonder at the 'suddenness of men's fate, which hangs over their heads like a cloud charged with thunder' " (411); this feeling is surely the essence of Marlow's own reaction to Jim's destiny almost from the beginning; and at the end Conrad probably intended the reader, like Marlow, to be left with a sense of half-comprehending but dazzled admiration very similar to the awe which the death of the tragic hero inspires.

Many theories of tragedy see it not as the resolution but as the culmination of conflict. Schopenhauer, for instance, whose general perspective on life was in many way very close to Conrad's, saw the "purpose" of tragedy as "the description of the terrible side of life . . . the wretchedness and misery of mankind, the triumph of wickedness, the scornful mastery of chance, and the irretrievable fall of the just and the innocent." Jim's state of mind before going to Doramin is consistent with Schopenhauer's view of the tragic protagonist who eventually refuses to be deceived by "the phenomenon, the veil of Maya," and whose "complete knowledge of the real nature of the world, acting as a *quieter* of the will, produces resignation, the giving up not merely of life, but of the whole will-to-live itself." Schopenhauer also dismissed the "demand for so-called poetic justice" as "a dull, insipid, optimistic, Protestant-rationalistic, or really Jewish view of the world." Jim's death would be tragic, in Schopenhauer's view, not as a just retribution, but as an example of "the guilt of existence itself." On this, Schopenhauer quotes the famous lines from Calderon's *La Vida es Sueño* which Conrad also used: "For man's greatest offence / Is that he has been born."[17]

A somewhat similar, but much more general, view of tragic conflict is that of Conrad's contemporary, Miguel de Unamuno, and it applies to the central theme of *Lord Jim* as a whole. The perspective of the three chief characters, Jim, Marlow, and Stein, is dominated by a sense of irremediable conflict: for Jim it is his preoccupation with the intolerable discrepancy between what he has done and what he would like to have done; for Marlow it is the distance between his faith in solidarity and the apparently random and amoral meaninglessness of the physical and social world; for Stein it is the radical and inexorable disjunction between the individual's ego-ideals and the world he struggles to realize them in. All three of these intractable disjunctions exemplify what Miguel de Unamuno called the tragic sense of life;[18] and Jim's struggles embody Unamuno's affirmation that, despite the awareness of foredoomed defeat, the individual should nevertheless, like Don Quixote, live as though his inward faith were more real than any of the negations by which reason and experience alike demonstrate its futility.

Marlow's closeness to Jim can be seen as grounded in the same disjunction. The pathos of Jim's presence sends Marlow's memory back to the defeated aspirations of his own youth; and this continual reminder is complemented by Marlow's increasingly bitter awareness that what has since taken their place, the code of solidarity, is usually supported on grounds that are complacent or prudential if they are not actually hypocritical; solidarity is really the code of those whom experience has brought into an unprotesting conformity with the attitudes of their group. "The wisdom of life," Marlow remarks ironically, "consists in putting out of sight all the reminders of our folly, of our weakness, of our mortality; all that makes against our efficiency" (174). But everything in Patusan exposes the triviality of such wisdom; there, Marlow discovers, "the haggard utilitarian lies of our civilisation wither and die" (282), and in their place is revealed "a view of a world that seemed to wear a vast and dismal aspect of disorder." Of course, a more limited vision, Marlow ironically reassures his comfortably established hearers, presents "in truth, thanks to our unwearied efforts . . . as sunny an arrangement of small conveniences as the mind of man can conceive" (313).

Marlow's desolate irony at modern Western civilization as a system of "small conveniences," aligns his private sympathies with Jim rather than with his listeners; and this is an indication not only of Marlow's tragic sense of life, but of a much larger transformation in the way in which he comes to see the essential moral and social meaning of Jim's existence.

This changed perspective is suggested in Marlow's letter to his privileged friend. The friend had argued that "we must fight in the ranks or our lives don't count" (339), and that Jim's "kind of thing" in Patusan could only be "endurable and enduring when based on a firm conviction in the truth of ideas racially our own, in whose name are established the order, the morality of an ethical progress." Marlow replies that on this general position he can "affirm nothing," but that Jim's death forces him to wonder whether Jim, who "of all mankind . . . had no dealings but with himself . . . at the last . . . had not confessed to a faith mightier than the laws of order and progress."

Marlow does not name Jim's faith, but the immediate context makes it clear that it belongs to a different and much older phase of civilization than that of modern "order and progress." The only faith which has been mentioned in connection with Jim is Stein's diagnosis of him as romantic; but Marlow has earlier tended to equate "romantic" with an unrealistic, irresponsible, and self-indulgent placing of the individual self above social norms. This equation, however, hardly does justice to Jim on Patusan, as Marlow realizes. When Jim repeats his promise, "I shall be faithful," at their last parting, Marlow recalls Stein's romantic injunction "to follow the dream, and again to follow the dream — and so — always — *usque ad finem*"; and this leads Marlow to conclude of Jim that "He was romantic, but none the less true" (334).

If we seek to find an ancient ideal of individual behavior which can be called romantic, but which emphasizes the obligation of being "true" and "faithful," it is surely to be found in the ideal values of medieval romance, which gave Europe not only the word *romantic*, but also, and long before, its most distinctive and enduring ideal of personal conduct. That ideal has already been named, and given a kind of transcendental status, by the French Lieutenant: "The honour . . . that is real — that is!" (148).

Honor is primarily associated both in the chivalric romances and in common parlance with the fame earned by exceptional exploits. Here Jim, who has filled Patusan "with the fame of his virtues" (243), obviously qualifies. It may be objected, of course, that the *Patna* episode raises serious doubts as to Jim's possession of the supreme value in the code of honor, the warrior quality of courage. In the elaboration of this code during the Renaissance, however, momentary cowardice was apparently not considered an insuperable bar, especially when it arose out of inexperience.[19] In any case Jim's going to face Doramin constitutes the most public, dramatic, and voluntary refutation of the charge that on the *Patna* he had put his life above his honor; and this is surely the consideration which persuades Marlow that Jim's death may have been "that supreme opportunity, that last and satisfying test for which I had always suspected him to be waiting" (339).

Jim's final test also involves two of the other supreme values of knightly honor: friendship and keeping faith. Jim's death is, in its way, an act of friendship for Dain Waris — Roland must not survive his comrade-in-arms Oliver; and Jim is keeping faith not only with Doramin, but with both Stein, Doramin's sworn comrade, and, less directly, with Marlow.

Keeping faith with these four men necessarily means betraying Jewel. Hers is the "jealous love" that Marlow must have in mind when he gives his final verdict on Jim: "We can see him, an obscure conqueror of fame, tearing himself out of the arms of a jealous love at the sign, at the call of his exalted egoism" (416). The "sign" and the "call" refer back to Jewel's question about the nature of the mysterious power that would rob her of Jim: "Will it be a sign — a call?" (315), she asks Marlow. But when Jewel afterward asserts that Jim's death proved that "he was false," Stein protests: "Not false! True! true! true!" (350). The contradiction reflects how the code of honor makes an ideal of public conduct into an absolute, and thereby exalts it above domestic or other private ties; it is this which produces the classic literary conflict between the woman, representing love, and the man, representing honor. The depth of Jim's feeling for Jewel is not at issue: he "love[s] her dearly," and finds being "absolutely necessary" to her "wonderful" (304); the determining force, as Stein well understands, is the absolute nature of Jim's pledge. Jim obviously has this in mind when he says to Jewel that, if he were to respond to her appeal and flee Patusan, "I should not be worth having" (412). The argument is a commonplace in the literature of honor; as Richard Lovelace put it in "To Lucasta, Going to the Wars": "I could not love thee (Dear) so much / Loved I not honour more."

When Marlow refers to Jim's faith as "exalted egoism," he is in effect repeating the common Stoic and Christian objection to the code of honor, an objection repeated in such later political and ethical philosophies as those of Montesquieu, Rousseau, and Kant.[20] The basis of their objections is essentially that suggested by Marlow's statement that Jim "had no dealings but with himself": honor encourages a personal pride and self-sufficiency which leads the individual to put his primary trust in himself, instead of relying on divine grace, moral virtue, civic duty, or personal feeling.

That such charges can fairly be made against Jim, and against the code of honor in general, is incontestable; on the other hand the gravity of the charges is not indisputable. It can be argued that Jim's egoism and pride are not the main determinants of his behavior on Patusan, and that contradictions arise when any theoretical system of behavior is brought to the test of practice. In any case there can be little doubt either that Conrad himself endorsed the code of honor, or that its characteristic strengths are inseparable from the greatness of his novels, and especially of *Lord Jim*.

Honor inevitably has two main aspects, the external, which is primarily concerned with the esteem of others, and the internal, which is primarily concerned with the esteem of the self. For Jim it is the latter which matters by far the most; throughout the novel he is "trying to save from the fire his idea of what his moral identity should be" (81); but Jim's internal sense of identity, his sense of what he should esteem himself for, has clearly incorporated a loyalty to many of the values both of solidarity and of the Western ethical tradition. This is made particularly clear in Jim's dealings with Brown: for instance, when Brown says "even a trapped rat can give a bite," and Jim immediately returns an answer "Not if you don't go near the trap till the rat is dead" (381). Jim realizes well enough what the safest practical course would be; but chivalric honor inherited from Christianity the idea that an enemy should be treated with charity and as a human equal. So Jim merely asks "Will you promise to leave the coast?" (387); when Brown agrees, and then breaks his word, it is not Jim who is dishonored, as he would have been had he gone against his inward sense of proper action. Jim's romantic conception of personal honor, then, has incorporated a strong social and ethical component derived from the ideals of Western civilization: and it is this component, rather than the "pride and egoism" of which Guerard speaks (G, 144), that brings about both his triumphs in Patusan and his disasters. Jim's personal allegiance to the heroic ideal is directly involved only to the extent that, when all is lost, he prefers to die rather than live on with the sense that he has broken his troth, and thus — this time consciously and intentionally — betrayed his conception of himself.

When Marlow speaks of Jim's "pitiless wedding with a shadowy ideal of conduct" (416), the words "pitiless" and "shadowy" reveal that Marlow remains sceptical about some aspects of the code of honor. His doubts reflect how the whole modern intellectual and psychological outlook tends to view the code of honor as rigid, coercive, and retrograde; it suggests the stuffy and hypocritical moralism of the Victorian public school, as we are incidentally reminded in Jim's only use of the word, when he swears by the old schoolboy oath of fidelity, "Honour bright" (269); and many features of Jim's character no doubt exemplify Hannah Arendt's view that the psychological effect of the British colonial system tended to "a certain conservation, or perhaps petrification, of boyhood noblesse which preserved *and* infantilized Western moral standards."[21]

Conrad, however, would probably have regarded a degree of intellectual callowness as a small price to pay for honorable conduct, and all the evidence suggests that he saw Jim's character in this perspective. In his preface to *The Red Badge of Courage*, for instance, Conrad discusses its hero in terms which apply quite closely to Jim's sense of shame at his failure on the *Patna*. Crane's Young Soldier, Conrad writes, is "the symbol of all untried men"; his fear does not make "him a morbid case" because "the lot of the mass of mankind is to know fear"; and Conrad then specifies that he means "the decent fear of disgrace."[22] The fear of disgrace, in a somewhat different form, is also defended in Conrad's "Author's Note" to *Lord Jim*. There he mentions that a lady once objected to the novel as "morbid," and retorts huffily that "no Latin temperament would have perceived anything morbid in the acute consciousness of lost honour" (ix). The ideal of honor, as Conrad here implies, tends to be Latin,[23] Catholic, and communal, rather than Germanic, Protestant, and individual; it is also distinctively masculine, noble, and secular; all these are values to which Conrad had been predisposed by his nationality, his family tradition, and his experience of life. It can, indeed, be argued that Conrad's emphasis on solidarity essentially derives from an older chivalric tradition of honor which had continued to animate the Polish nobility long after it had been replaced or transformed elsewhere.

Lord Jim, in fact, presents an obscure but continuous confrontation between honor on the one hand, and the more modern and more widely applicable, but much less definite, set of communal values represented by solidarity on the other. In that conflict Conrad found himself siding more and more with his ancestral inheritance, and its more absolute and peremptory allegiance to the ideal of individual honor; though fated to isolation and failure in the modern world, it nevertheless possessed an unmediated directness of personal application, and a heroic resonance, which Marlow's conception of solidarity was found to lack.

Lord Jim was André Gide's favorite among Conrad's novels, and it was its "despairing nobility" that he particularly singled out for admiration. This gives added significance to a letter in which Gide told Conrad that if he were ever to write an article about him it would be to Alfred de Vigny, and "to him alone, that I would wish to establish your kinship."[24] Like Conrad, Alfred de Vigny was a nobleman, a stoic, and a disillusioned romantic; both men combined deeply isolated natures with an emphasis on a collective ethic which had its roots in their early careers of professional service — in Vigny's case as an officer of the infantry rather than of the merchant navy. In the peroration of his *Souvenirs de servitude et grandeur militaires* (1835), Vigny wrote that honor was the only lamp still left "which keeps its vigil in us like the last lamp in a devastated temple."[25] The devastation was that caused by modern unbelief; but being a "purely human virtue that seems born from the earth," honor had outlasted all other creeds.

In some form, honor, and its corresponding human and literary style, nobility, are timeless and indispensable values, values which continue to find exemplars or admirers even in the most relativist and sceptical climates of thought. As Wallace Stevens once observed, "there is no element more conspicuously absent from contemporary poetry than nobility."[26] If the statement were extended to modern fiction, Conrad, and especially *Lord Jim*, would be conspicuous exceptions. Jim does something which no other hero of a great twentieth-century novel has done: he dies for his honor. His action implicitly embodies Stein's dispiriting truth that "one thing alone can us from being ourselves cure!" (212); still, in his mode of being cured Jim is surely sending a message to our impeccable world:

man is not a masterpiece, but his refusal to settle for less can make him amazing.

Notes

1. *Lord Jim*, Dent Collected Edition (London, 1946), pp. 336, 272. Later page references are to this edition; where no reference is given for subsequent quotations, they are from the same page, or those immediately before or after.

2. Albert Guerard, *Conrad the Novelist* (Cambridge, Mass.: Harvard University Press, 1958), p. 129. (Later cited by page number only in the text after the abbreviation *G*.) Guerard writes that "the novel . . . asks us to decide whether Jim . . . is truly redeemed."

3. The term is used by Robert E. Kuehn, in his introduction to *Twentieth-Century Interpretations of Lord Jim: A Collection of Critical Essays* (Englewood Cliffs, N.J.: Prentice-Hall 1969), p. 12.

4. Tony Tanner, in what is otherwise a most illuminating study (*Conrad: Lord Jim* [London, 1963], p. 48; later cited in text after the abbreviation *TT*).

5. Passages from the holograph of *Lord Jim* are quoted by permission of The Philip H. and A. S. W. Rosenbach Foundation, and the trustees of The Joseph Conrad Estate.

6. Dorothy Van Ghent, *The English Novel: Form and Function* (New York; Rinehart, 1953), p. 236. (Later cited by page number in the text after the abbreviation *VG*).

7. See Jerome Hamilton Buckley, *Seasons of Youth: The Bildungsroman from Dickens to Golding* (Cambridge, Mass.: Harvard University Press, 1974), p. 18.

8. By Tony Tanner, for instance (p. 47).

9. See, for instance, Bernard C. Meyer, *Joseph Conrad* (Princeton: Princeton University Press, 1967), pp. 159–62.

10. Gustav Morf, *The Polish Heritage of Joseph Conrad* (London: Sampson Low, Marston, 1930), pp. 157–58.

11. Gerhart Piers and Milton B. Singer, *Shame and Guilt: A Psychoanalytic and a Cultural Study* (Springfield, Ill.: C. C. Thomas, 1953), p. 11. I am indebted to Helen Merrill Lynd's *On Shame and the Search for Identity* (New York, 1958), whose second chapter, "The Nature of Shame," gives a richly documented survey of literary as well as psychological views of shame.

12. Max Scheler, *La Pudeur*, trans. M. Dupuy (Paris, 1952), pp. 10–12. In the manuscript Marlow comments that Stein "generously refus[ed] to fasten upon the obvious guilt" in his diagnosis of Jim, and chose instead to speak about the "as it were, abstract cause of suffering" (p. 426).

13. This is the only sense of the nine uses of "guilt" and "guilty" listed in James W. Parins *et al.*, *A Concordance to Conrad's "Lord Jim"* (New York: Garland, 1976).

14. *Vivants piliers: le Roman anglo-saxon et les symboles* (Paris, 1960), p. 127.

15. F. R. Leavis, *The Great Tradition* (London: Chatto and Windus, 1948), p. 190.

16. "Introduction," Rinehart edition of *Lord Jim* (New York, 1957), p. xxiii.

17. *The World as Will and Representation*, trans. Payne, I, 252–54. Stein's dream simile presumably starts from Calderon's title, *Life is a Dream*. Conrad used the couplet as the epigraph to *An Outcast of the Islands*.

18. There are, of course, several differences between Unamuno's sense of the tragic and Conrad's in *Lord Jim*; but there are also a good many similarities, beginning with the general idea of a specifically Catholic kind of "transcendental pessimism" in the face of the conflict, exemplified in Don Quixote, between reason and nature on the one hand, and feeling and imagination on the other. The conclusion of Unamuno's first formulation of the tragic sense of

life recalls both Stein's view of Jim, and the frequent burden of Conrad's own letters: "Man, by the very fact of . . . possessing consciousness, is . . . a diseased animal. Consciousness is a disease." (Miguel de Unamuno, *The Tragic Sense of Life in Men and in Peoples*, 1912, trans. J. E. Crawford Flitch [London: Macmillan, 1921], pp. 17–18, 130–131, 294. See also p. 323).

19. See Giambattista Pigna, *Il Duello* (Venezia, 1554), discussed in F. R. Bryson, *The Point of Honor in Sixteenth Century Italy* (New York: Columbia University Press, 1935), p. 11. I am indebted to Zdzislaw Najder's "*Lord Jim*: A Romantic Tragedy of Honour" (*Conradiana*, I [1968], 1–7), for this reference, as for much else.

20. There is a schematic historical summary of philosophical attitudes to honor in L. Jeudon, *La Morale de l'honneur* (Paris, 1911), pp. 5–72.

21. Hannah Arendt, *The Origins of Totalitarianism* (New York: Harcourt, Brace, 1958), p. 211.

22. Joseph Conrad, *Tales of Hearsay and Last Essays*, Dent Collected Edition (London, 1955), p. 123.

23. The soundness of Conrad's view is documented in an interesting collection of recent studies, *Honor and Shame: The Values of Mediterranean Society*, ed. J. G. Peristiany (London, 1966). In his "Conrad and the Idea of Honor," Najder discusses Conrad's general attitude to honor (*Joseph Conrad: Theory and World Fiction* [Lubbock, Texas: Texas Tech Press, 1974], pp. 103–14.

24. Ivo Vidan, "Thirteen Letters of André Gide to Joseph Conrad," *Studia Romanica et Anglica Zagrabiensia*, 24 (1967), 163. The friendship of Conrad and Gide is analyzed in Frederick Karl's "Conrad and Gide: A Relationship and a Correspondence," *Comparative Literature*, 39 (1977), 148–71.

25. *Oeuvres complètes* (Paris: Gallimard, 1948), II, 677.

26. "The Noble Rider and the Sound of Words," *The Necessary Angel: Essays on Reality and the Imagination* (New York: Random, 1951), p. 35.

Narrative Presence: The Illusion of Language in *Heart of Darkness*   Jerry Wasserman*

> Words, groups of words, words standing alone, are symbols of life, have the power in their sound or their aspect to present the very thing you wish to hold up before the mental vision of your readers. The things "as they are" exist in words. . . .
>
> — Conrad, *Letters*

> To render a crucial point of feelings in terms of human speech is really an impossible task. Written words can only form a sort of translation.
> — Conrad, "Author's Note," *Within the Tides*

Conrad's ambivalence towards the powers of language is nowhere more evident than in *Heart of Darkness*. If the function of narrative language is to present things "as they are," stripped of illusion, Marlow's experience quickly reveals its limitations. He finds that words are often

*Reprinted with permission from *Studies in the Novel* 6 (1974):327–39.

unable to cut through to the truthful heart of things, and that language itself may be nothing more than an outer form. In the case of his meeting with the Intended, language assumes the very characteristics of illusion it is meant to explode. And if words can cloak truth and feelings as well as reveal them, then the task of verbally communicating crucial experiences may become, as Conrad said, impossible.

To overcome these inherent difficulties Conrad looked to a style that would embody linguistic meaning in a concrete form capable of eliciting the vision he always sought in his readers. "I am haunted," he wrote Edward Garnett in March, 1898, "mercilessly haunted, by the *necessity* of style. . . . My story is there in a fluid — in an evading shape. I can't get hold of it. It is all there — to bursting, yet I can't get hold of it, any more than you can grasp a handful of water."[1] His solution in *Heart of Darkness* was Marlow; not just as character and narrator, but as the visual focus of the novel. Sitting before his audience and trying to recount his experience through words, Marlow himself embodies his experience. His physical presence both compensates for the limitations of language and helps explain them. He is literally and objectively the meaning of his own narrative. Only by seeing Marlow can his auditors ever hope to understand what he has been trying to tell them, and their ultimate failure is another triumph of the darkness. But the characters' failures are Conrad's successes. He was able to "get hold of" his story by making the physical immediacy of Marlow's narration the single most important aspect of his style. The form of Marlow's tale embodies not only his own experiences but Kurtz's as well, and in a sense the potential experiences of his audience, whose reactions confirm his meaning. Thus the style is the theme, in coherent and concrete form.

Ever since critics began responding to F. R. Leavis's attack on Conrad's "adjectival insistence upon inexpressible and incomprehensible mystery" in *Heart of Darkness*, it has become increasingly clear that the problems of language in the novel are not only stylistic but also thematic.[2] But the language theme is even more centrally important than has generally been recognized. It operates on two distinct levels which continually converge and intersect. On one level language is a metaphor or a function of civilization. If the Congo is the heart of darkness, it is also the heart of silence, and the white European brings not only light but speech. Language is an important psychological element of the imperialist conquest. Names, labels, categories should help bring order out of chaos; to name something is ostensibly to control and possess its very essence. But like the "light" the white men bring, the language they attempt to impose is a falsification and is ultimately as ineffectual. At the same time, Marlow's narrative includes a commentary on his own apparently futile attempt to reconstruct in words the experiences that he and Kurtz have undergone. What results is an aesthetic of which Marlow is only partially aware but in which he plays the essential part. In both his roles, as character and narrator, he reveals the basic quality of language to be its superficiality — as an index and tool of civilization, as well as an agent of discovery and revelation.

Marlow's experience in the Congo is one of conflicting loyalties, principles, and desires. There is a dualism in his nature which leaves him torn between an intellectual allegiance to duty, hard work, fidelity, and society; and an emotional attraction to a kind of romantic individualism bordering on anarchy. In *Heart of Darkness* the pull toward the darkness of the jungle and its kind is accelerated by his repulsion from the men and institutions of Europe. Nevertheless, Marlow inevitably affirms his allegiance to the latter. He is first attracted to Kurtz by his apparent ability to sustain this kind of dualism. And it is no coincidence that Kurtz's primary attribute is his "eloquence," for Marlow's ambivalence towards language and civilization becomes crystallized in his attitude toward Kurtz.

Early in his Congo experience, Marlow's respective attraction to the wild and repulsion from the civilized find expression in terms of language. As the French steamer cruised along the African coast, "we passed various places — trading places — with names like Gran' Bassam, Little Popo; names that seemed to belong to some sordid farce acted in front of a sinister back-cloth." On the other hand, the "voice of the surf heard now and then was a positive pleasure, like the speech of a brother. It was something natural, that had its reason, that had a meaning" (p. 61). This is an antithesis which Marlow consistently recognizes. Names, words, language in general, the province of the Europeans, are artificial, farcical, or absurd. They are fictions: as J. Hillis Miller puts it, "part of the human lie"; whereas "one way to define the darkness is to say that it is incompatible with language."[3] For Marlow the great silence of the wilderness is natural, profound, and full of meaning. So, too, is its voiced expression — the sound of surf, the rhythm of drums, the howls and cries of the natives.

Examples of this dichotomy are pervasive. Marlow finds the "definitions" given to the Africans — "enemies, criminals, workers . . . rebels" — laughable (p. 132). And the name "Kurtz," he observes, a word meaning *short* in German, is ridiculously unsuited to its bearer. The communicative function of language is practically nonexistent. Marlow's "speech in English with gestures" to his native carriers is eminently unsuccessful (p. 71). Only by nonverbal means, blowing the whistle on his steamer, does he ever get natives to respond to him. He himself mistakes Russian words for cipher, the Russian does not understand the dialect of the tribe with which he and Kurtz are living, and Marlow and the Intended, who speak the same language and use the same words, understand completely different meanings in their discussion of Kurtz. Perhaps the most successful communication in Marlow's entire Congo experience is the "amazing tale" of Kurtz which the Russian relates to him, "not so much told as suggested to me in desolate exclamations, completed by shrugs, in interrupted phrases, in hints ending in deep sighs" (p. 129).

Its resemblance to the mode of expression of the wilderness is not fortuitous, for it is there that Marlow finds significance. The sound of drums to him seems to have "as profound a meaning as the sound of bells in a Christian country" (p. 71). A wild native cry gives him "an irresistible impression of sorrow" (p. 107), and the dying glance of his native helmsman is one of "intimate profundity" (p. 119). There is also the silent eloquence of the native girl's farewell to Kurtz. But it is most of all the profound silence of the wilderness itself that reveals to Marlow the poverty of human speech. At the station, "the word 'ivory' rang in the air, was whispered, was sighed," but was "unreal"; while "outside, the silent wilderness surrounding this cleared speck on the earth struck me as something great and invincible, like evil or truth . . ." (p. 76). Listening to the brickmaker, Marlow notes "the silence of the land . . . its mystery, its greatness, the amazing reality of its concealed life. . . . All this was great, expectant, mute, while the man jabbered about himself" (pp. 80–81).

However much Marlow is attracted to this "reality," he never quite allows himself to yield to it. Physical work is the primary restraint through which he is able to immerse himself in "the mere incidents of the surface" which hide "the inner truth" (p. 93). But he also comes to realize that language is another restraint, and that it, too, may be merely a surface. Words, in the face of the wilderness, may seem as ridiculous as the costume of the chief accountant, but both serve their purposes. Language is the psychic dress of civilized man. In *Lord Jim* Marlow talks of his "conception of existence . . . that shelter each of us makes for himself to creep under in moments of danger"; and he concludes that "words also belong to the sheltering conception of light and order which is our refuge" (*Lord Jim*, p. 313). To reject language as a facade or a fiction is to open oneself to the possibility of understanding the true mysteries of the heart of darkness. But it is also to invite a kind of madness, as Marlow realizes when he comes upon the natives: "cursing us, praying to us, welcoming us — who could tell? . . . we glided past like phantoms, wondering and secretly appalled, as sane men would be before an enthusiastic outbreak in a madhouse. We could not understand . . ." (p. 96). As long as the white men maintain their shelter of language, they remain "sane." But, Marlow sees, it is sanity at the expense of truth. Nevertheless he again rejects that truth and maintains the surface forms. He will not divest himself of his "pretty rags," his language, his sanity. He does not "go ashore for a howl and a dance" (p. 97).

Kurtz, however, did, and he first appears to Marlow to have survived the experience and remained civilized. He is the quintessence of civilization, its ultimate product — pure eloquence. For Marlow he is a disembodied voice. The only quality of his "that carried with it a sense of real presence, was his ability to talk, his words" (p. 113). Almost every reference Marlow makes to him concerns his mastery of and identification with language. It is thus fitting that Kurtz should have been assigned to write a report for the International Society for the Suppression of Savage Customs, to oppose the savage silence with "the noble burning words" of Western culture. But his postscript reveals that he has not successfully survived. His communion with the wilderness has driven him insane and revealed to him hidden "in the magnificent folds of eloquence the barren darkness of his heart" (p. 147). He was all language, eloquence, and therefore all facade: "hollow at the core" (p. 131). Stripping himself of the accoutrements of civilization to communicate with the silent wilderness left him nothing but his own inner darkness. And the lesson of Kurtz's experience is not lost on Marlow.

Kurtz's final words are an expression of his self-revelation, but for Marlow they have additional significance. If "the horror" is a recognition of what lies beyond the pale of civilization, it emphasizes the importance of the tenuous civilized veneer separating the individual consciousness from the darkness. Even before Marlow begins his narrative, Conrad's narrator has suggested that there is not much preventing London from once again becoming "one of the dark places of the earth." Five times in the first four pages he alludes to a "mournful gloom, brooding" over the city, as if in wait to reassert itself (pp. 45–48). Marlow knows from his own experience the attraction of the wilderness and the ease with which it can overcome one's saving illusions. This is one reason why he understands Kurtz's cry as "an affirmation, a moral victory" (p. 151). To recognize that the darkness is horrible is at once an affirmation of that which keeps us from it, and a moral victory over the temptation to yield to it.

Consequently, Marlow sees Kurtz's cry as an affirmation of language itself, the foremost expression of civilization. Comparing his own illness and struggle with death to Kurtz's, he concludes that in the face of the final darkness, "I would have nothing to say. This is the reason why I affirm that Kurtz was a remarkable man. He had something to say. He said it" (p. 151). To say something is to hold back the darkness, to affirm the possibilities of community, solidarity, and order which are the necessary components of civilized society. The difficult task of the artist, as Conrad phrased it in his preface to *The Nigger of the "Narcissus,"* was to "awaken in the hearts of the beholders that feeling of unavoidable solidarity. . . ." This is performed on the most elementary level by the simple act of speech. In *Typhoon,* for example, only the voice of MacWhirr prevents the great wind, which "isolates one from one's kind," from causing the psychic disintegration of Jukes (*Typhoon,* p. 40). Although it carries only meaningless fragments of sentences to Jukes's ears, human speech alone is enough to reestablish his sense of fellowship and identity. In seeing the very act of speech as a moral victory, Marlow affirms all those aspects of civilization which language has come to represent for him in the course of his voyage.

Finally for Marlow, "the horror" is a recognition that the basis of European man's life is an illusion, a lie; yet one that must be maintained as the only viable alternative to the greater horror of the darkness, the truth with which he and Kurtz had come face to face. This is why Kurtz is his "choice of nightmares." The linguistic habits Marlow found absurd or inappropriate at the start of his voyage are no less absurd or inappropriate at its end. They must, however, be maintained. In refusing to respond to the savage voices of the wilderness, Marlow had confirmed his solidarity with Kurtz by telling his auditors, "I have a voice, too, and for good or evil mine is the speech that cannot be silenced" (p. 97). But behind these bracing words reverberates "the horror."

Thus the agonizing final scene with the Intended affirms the illusion that is civilization. In a tomblike room in the "sepulchral city" Marlow, for whom lies have "a taint of death" (p. 82), tells a deliberate lie. Faced with a conversation about words in which words have lost all objective validity, Marlow once more affirms the validity of Kurtz's words. He has no choice but to grant the Intended her illusions and take cover behind them himself. To refuse to do so would have been a "triumph for the wilderness" (p. 156). The final scene is thus another "moral victory" — and another manifestation of the horror. As the Intended says, "His words, at least, have not died" (p. 160).

In his role as narrator Marlow has the same kinds of problems with language that he has as a character. Its reality rarely corresponds with the humanistic assumptions according to which it is used. He can hardly make language even approximate the experiences he has undergone. Words are inherently unequal to the task of reproducing and communicating experience, but since Marlow is a story-*teller* they must necessarily be his medium. Further compounding Marlow's narrative difficulty is the danger that his audience will hear what it wants, as the Intended does, rather than what he really means. In a despairing letter written a year before he wrote *Heart of Darkness*, Conrad expressed the same feelings: "Half the words we use have no meaning whatever and of the other half each man understands each word after the fashion of his own folly and conceit" (*LL*, I, 222). In *Heart of Darkness* Conrad attempted to come to terms with this problem by embodying the communicable experience in the person of Marlow rather than in his speech. Conrad's medium is language, and Marlow is just a construct of language. But within the fictive world of the novel whatever success Marlow achieves by his narrative is due to his physical presence.

Phenomenologically, the narrative device of Marlow functions much as words do. M. Merleau-Ponty writes that "the meaning of words must be finally induced by the words themselves, or more exactly, their conceptual meaning must be formed by a kind of deduction from a *gestural meaning*, which is immanent in speech." Similarly, there is "an immanent or incipient significance in the living body," such that "in order to express it, the body must in the last analysis become the thought or intention that it signifies for us. It is the body which points out, and which speaks. . . ." Thus communication may take place by means of the interaction of one's visual consciousness and another's bodily expression of the "sediments" left behind by the objects of his previous perceptual experiences. "No sooner has my gaze fallen upon a living body in the process of acting than . . . the other body has ceased to be a mere fragment of the world, and become the theatre of a certain process of elaboration, and, as it were, a certain 'view' of the world."[4] The meaning of Marlow's experience is immanent as "gestural meaning" in both his physical presence and his words. Yet except at one crucial point, Marlow himself is never fully aware of the possibilities for communication implicit in his physical proximity to his audience. He continues to rely mainly on his linguistic abilities.

The impediments that he must overcome if he is to do this are severe. His greatest difficulty lies in the nature of his experience, which is simply not susceptible to apprehension by the means at his disposal. The Congo itself is so alien to the white European that not only language but the modes of thought at the basis of language are irrelevant to it. That it cannot be ordered to fit linguistic categories is best illustrated by Marlow's attempt to understand why the cannibals did not make a meal of him and his passengers. In the course of his voyage he has become aware of the white man's fallacious imposition of labels on the inchoate wilderness. Nevertheless, he tries to file the behavior of the cannibals under "restraint," as its linguistic equivalent. But all logic, all he knows about restraint and hunger tells him that it could not possibly be "restraint." The same with "superstition, disgust, patience, fear . . . honour." The words do not suit the circumstances. "But," he confirms, "there was the fact facing me—" (p. 105), the fact that they had not yielded to their hunger, the fact that makes a mockery of all his logic and his words. In addition Marlow's experience is of an inner nature. "The changes take place inside," the doctor tells him (p. 58), and words seem able to treat only surfaces. "I've been telling you what we said," Marlow explains to his friends, "repeating the phrases we pronounced—but what's the good? They were common everyday words—" (p. 144).

Obviously Marlow is aware of the limitations of his medium throughout the narrative. And he is aware at the same time that his function ought to be to make his audience "see." The improbability of achieving this kind of vision solely through language is evident to him from his own experience of Kurtz. "He was just a word for me," he tells his auditors. "I did not see the man in the name any more than you do" (p. 82). Still, though he seems to despair of ever adequately reconstructing his experience, he maintains a rhetorical pressure on his audience, as if the sheer weight of words could somehow make them see. "Do you see him? Do you see the story? Do you see anything?" he implores (p. 82). Kurtz, the supreme word-artist, had this ability. "He made me see things — things," the Russian tells Marlow. But the circumstances of this incident and the imagery in which Marlow relates it are significant: "They had come together unavoidably, like two ships becalmed near each other, and lay rubbing sides at last" (p. 127). Although Kurtz talked, the physical immediacy of his presence, alone with the Russian across a jungle campfire, may finally have been more evocative than his words.

So Marlow realizes that he can only hope to make his friends "see" anything by presenting himself before their eyes as the product of the experience he is trying to describe:

> He paused again as if reflecting, then added —
> "Of course in this you fellows see more than I could then.
> You see me, whom you know . . ." (p. 83).

But in fact they cannot see him at this moment because, as Conrad's narrator tells us, "it had become so pitch dark that we listeners could hardly see one another. For a long time already he, sitting apart, had been no more to us than a voice" (p. 83). The moment is a perfect microcosm of the novel. The darkness isolates each individual from the human community and sets its disintegrative power to work on him. Besides "the bond of the sea" holding these friends together (p. 45), the human voice alone bridges the void. But there is no real communication, no coherent transmission of experience. Marlow appears to his audience as Kurtz had first appeared to him — a disembodied voice in the darkness and silence. Only after coming face to face with Kurtz was Marlow able to go beyond the voice and the words to discover the truth of Kurtz's nightmare and then live it out as his own.

The listeners, however, remain literally and figuratively in the dark. Three of them are conceivably asleep at this point, and remain apathetic throughout the rest of the narration. And the fourth, the frame-narrator, can only conceive of understanding Marlow's meaning by listening to his words, though the irony is explicit even in his own description of the moment: "I listened, *I listened on the watch* for the sentence, for the word, that would give me the clue . . ." (p. 83, italics mine). He cannot visualize this narrative by merely listening. He does not catch the clue, and the momentary illumination sparked by Marlow's insight is quenched by the darkness. He does, of course, go on to retell the story as narrator of the novel. Like Marlow, he is strongly affected by his experience and feels that it must contain some profound meaning. But while his "faint uneasiness" (p. 83) is somewhat intensified by the end of the novel, his final statement suggests that he has not grasped the full extent of Marlow's revelation: "the tranquil waterway leading to the uttermost ends of the earth flowed sombre under an overcast sky — seemed to lead into the heart of an immense darkness" (p. 162). The darkness is still *out there* somewhere.[5] He remains safely sheltered behind the very illusions Marlow tried so hard to expose.

To what extent, though, has Marlow himself consciously chosen the narrative strategy to which he has reverted here? The problem is to reconcile his intentional use of the word "see," in its visual sense, with the little faith he has professed to have in the appearances that for him conceal inner truth. "I don't like work—no man does—but I like what is in the work,—the chance to find yourself. Your own reality—for yourself, not for others—what no other man can ever know. They can only see the mere show, and never can tell what it really means" (p. 85). On the other hand so much of his experience has contradicted this conviction. He has learned that surfaces can have their own legitimate reality. Various modes of work have positive "surface-truth" (p. 97), similar to the kind Conrad describes in a letter to Galsworthy, praising his "fidelity to the surface of life, to the surface of events,—to the surface of things and ideas." The justification for this kind of art is that "most things and most natures have nothing but surface" (*LL*, I, 224). Even where Marlow has discovered both surface and depth, however, he has found that surfaces can reveal as well as conceal. It was only by virtue of Kurtz's "show" that Marlow was able to see beyond it to the reality. And the cannibals' "restraint" appears to Marlow as a surface truth which suggests its own profundity: "the fact dazzling, to be seen, like the foam on the depths of the sea, like a ripple on an unfathomable enigma" (p. 105). Here is an analogue to the phsyical presence of Marlow during his narrative—the fact of his being there, to be seen, as a surface indicating the depth of experience he has undergone.

Furthermore, we have been told at the beginning of the novel that he indeed conceives of externals as phenomenologically significant: "to him the meaning of an episode was not inside like a kernel but outside, enveloping the tale which brought it out only as a glow brings out a haze . . ." (p. 48). In spite of the characteristic vagueness of the language, the aesthetic implied by this description demands a mode of narration which can present reality in an outwardly objective form. Thus Marlow is not only aware of these problems but has apparently dealt with them before in the course of previous narratives. Telling his friends that they can understand more of the story because they can see him follows logically, as well, from his discovering the paucity of language and the eloquence of silence.

In any event Conrad means *us* to see that the meaning of Marlow's tale is to be found in Marlow himself. Marlow begins his narrative by minimizing the importance of "what happened to me personally," as opposed to "the effect of it on me," which is what he wants his audience to understand (p. 51). Still, only by knowing what happens to him can we understand Kurtz: "It is his extremity that I seem to have lived through," Marlow concludes (p. 151). But it is not just his relationship with Kurtz that explains Kurtz; it is the sum of Marlow's experiences. Brussels, the

French ship bombarding the shore, the Swede who hung himself, the grove of death, Marlow's "baptism" in the native helmsman's blood — these all contribute to our understanding of Kurtz's response to the Congo. "The horror," after all, is only a verbal approximation of Kurtz's experience just as "restraint" inadequately approximates the cannibals' behavior. "The horror" becomes concrete and specific for us only in terms of Marlow's experience and his condition as he tells the story.

In short Marlow is the objective correlative of his own tale — objective in the sense that he is an object of perception in the dramatic context of the novel, one of "the external facts," in Eliot's formulation, "which must terminate in sensory experience."[6] His audience must read him as we read the words on the page. But we too must "see" Marlow to fully understand his narrative. This is suggested early in the novel through the image of Marlow in the poses of the Buddha. William Bysshe Stein has discussed how the particular posture in which Marlow is first described represents iconographically "a divine truth which is incommunicable in words," and the doctrine "that verbal communication between human beings is ultimately futile."[7] The second posture, however, has more specific implications for Marlow's narrative role. Conrad's narrator describes Marlow "lifting one arm from the elbow, the palm of the hand outwards, so that, with his legs folded before him, he had the pose of a Buddha preaching in European clothes and without a lotus-flower" (p. 50). Zen teaches that language belongs to *maya*, the illusion that we can apprehend the world through classification or definition, and that words are therefore incapable of transmitting profound experience, of grasping "the fluid forms of nature in [their] mesh of fixed classes." But it is possible to communicate what cannot be conveyed linguistically, through some nonverbal method of "direct pointing." In a well-known episode in Zen tradition the Buddha transmits the experience of supreme awakening to his chief disciple by silently holding up a lotus flower before him.[8] The last phrase of the narrator's description seems to allude to this tradition, which uses the flower as an archetypal objective correlative. But Marlow is without a lotus because the experience he is trying to convey has a different meaning. Its perfect expression is *himself* as he sits before his disciples. "In European clothes," especially, since the illusions and realities of European man's life are the substance of his experience, Marlow holds himself up as the embodiment of all he is about to try to tell. The ability of physical presence to express a reality beyond itself is illustrated by the Russian, who seemed to Marlow "to have consumed all thought of self so completely, that even while he was talking to you, you forgot that it was he — *the man before your eyes* — who had gone through these things" (pp. 126–27, italics mine). It is in this sense that Marlow would deny the importance of "what happened to me personally."

Thus, when understood as inclusive of Marlow's narration, Conrad's style is both a function of and a response to the problems of language in

the novel. The abundance of abstract, imprecise adjectives reflects the
verbally inexpressible nature of the darkness as well as the tentative nature
of language itself, which comes to represent the major barrier between
ourselves and that darkness. The Buddha image that begins the novel tells
us to watch Marlow for its meaning, and Marlow's frequent insistence
upon the inadequacy of words keeps reminding us to do so. Finally,
Marlow illustrates the theme of his tale by continuing to tell it, by opting
for language in spite of its failings. Style does not merely imitate content;
it objectively represents it. The signified is absorbed in the signifier.

Though we must not overlook the fact that we, unlike the fictive
audience, "see" Marlow only as a result of Conrad's words, our visual
experience of Marlow and the silence of his presence are equally significant. For if we cannot see him, we are left with his voice and eloquence as
our only means of comprehending his tale. And we have had substantial
evidence of the illusory nature of verbal eloquence. But language in *Heart
of Darkness* is a paradoxical medium. It comes to be defined as that which
conceals, and at the same time that which reveals itself as that which
conceals. Conrad's language makes us "see" Marlow, the embodiment of
an experience whose conclusion is that language is a lie. The success of the
novel, then, is finally a result of Conrad's ability to turn the struggle with
his medium to an advantage. By submitting himself to the paradoxical
nature of language, taking his own visual metaphor literally, and concret-
izing style in the person of Marlow, Conrad reversed the usual function of
the dramatized narrator in a unique way. "Telling as showing," in Wayne
Booth's phrase, has literally become showing as telling.[9]

Notes

1. G. Jean-Aubry, *Joseph Conrad: Life and Letters* (Garden City, N.Y.: Doubleday,
Page, 1927), I, 232. Subsequent references to this edition will be indicated in my text as *LL*.
All other citations of Conrad will refer to the Doubleday, Page edition of his works (1923–27).
Heart of Darkness, contained in the volume, *Youth: A Narrative, and Two Other Stories*, is
noted by page numbers.

2. F. R. Leavis, *The Great Tradition* (London: Chatto & Windus, 1948), p. 177. For
the range of critical responses to Leavis's argument, see W. Y. Tindall, "Apology for Marlow,"
From Jane Austen to Joseph Conrad, ed. Robert C. Rathburn and Martin Steinmann, Jr.
(Minneapolis: Univ. of Minnesota Press, 1958), p. 280; John Oliver Perry, "Action, Vision, or
Voice: The Moral Dilemmas in Conrad's Tale-Telling," *MFS*, 10 (1964), 3–14; and James
Guetti, *The Limits of Metaphor: A Study of Melville, Conrad, and Faulkner* (Ithaca, N.Y.:
Cornell Univ. Press, 1967), pp. 46–68.

3. *Poets of Reality: Six Twentieth Century Writers* (Cambridge: Harvard Univ. Press,
1966), p. 36.

4. M. Merleau-Ponty, *Phenomenology of Perception*, trans. Colin Smith (London:
Routlege & Kegan Paul, 1962), pp. 179, 197, 215, 353.

5. See George Walton Williams, "The Turn of the Tide in *Heart of Darkness*," *MFS*, 9
(1963), 172.

6. T. S. Eliot, "Hamlet and His Problems," *Selected Essays*, new ed. (New York: Harcourt, Brace & World, 1964), pp. 124–25.

7. "*The Heart of Darkness*: A Bodhisattva Scenario," *Conradiana*, 2 (Winter 1969–70), 42–43.

8. Alan W. Watts, *The Way of Zen* (1957; rpt. New York: Knopf, Vintage Books, n.d.), pp. 39–45.

9. Commenting on " 'nihilisms' in fiction, [like] Conrad's heart of darkness," Booth notes that, "since nothingness cannot be described in itself, let alone shown dramatically, *something* or *someone* must always be shown doing *something* . . ." (*The Rhetoric of Fiction* [Chicago: Univ. of Chicago Press, 1961], pp. 297–98).

The Semiotics of Description in Conrad's *Nostromo*
Leonard Orr*

Readers and reviewers have always considered Conrad to be an unusually descriptive author, but there was never any certainty about whether Conrad's descriptive plenitude helps his novels or ruins them. There is not even any agreement on the question of whether Conrad writes descriptions or passages which look like descriptions but which function in some extraordinary manner. Ford Madox Ford, about eight years after the publication of *Nostromo*, noted that "We can most of us describe, some of us can get atmospheres—but it is only the very great writer who can so interpenetrate his characters with seas and skies, or the houses, fabrics, and ornaments that surround them. For that is what Conrad seems to do. It is not what he actually does—actually he sends through all the seas and skies the very beings of the men who look upon them. For a descriptive writer—or rather a writer known for his descriptions—he describes very little" (Sherry 248). Yet a 1915 reviewer of *Victory* sees that Conrad "is here no more a character-delineator (in the sense in which Thackeray is, say, or Meredith) than Turner was a portrait-painter. As in Turner, the human figures are pathetic against lurid and fuliginous spaces. The profoundest things in *Victory* are generalisations and descriptions" (Sherry 300). It is certainly an interesting question to ask how it is possible that "generalisations and descriptions" can be the "profoundest things" in a novel. We are so used to seeing description always as background, as something ancillary to narration, and certainly as an inferior element of the novel (compared to character and plot).

We can see a completely different approach to Conrad's descriptive oddity in a 1920 review of *The Rescue* which in the same sentence draws attention to the descriptions and then denies that the descriptions have been noticed: "Mr. Conrad is an acknowledged master of description; but

*This essay was written specifically for this volume and is published here with the permission of the author.

the pictures of which this book is full, exquisite as they are, never once obtrude on the eye" (Sherry 344). Description is expected to be transparent, in place and functioning but in some way not seen, not calling attention to itself. But Conrad's descriptions are highly visible and stand out from the surrounding text. A reviewer of *The Rover*, in 1923, claims that "Conrad's real strength . . . lies in the unsurpassed vividness of some of his descriptions, both of persons and of scenes, and in the highly charged atmosphere of fatality with which he envelops them" (Sherry 359).

I have been quoting reviewers because literary critics have for the most part been prejudiced against description, and hope only for its brevity and verisimilitude. Roland Barthes, in *The Pleasure of the Text*, finds that "our very avidity for knowledge impels us to skim or to skip certain passages (anticipated as 'boring') in order to get more quickly to the warmer parts of the anecdote (which are always its articulations: whatever furthers the solutions of the riddle, the revelation of fate): we boldly skip (no one is watching) descriptions, explanations, analyses, conversations. . . ." In fact, the skimmable, skippable content of the novel provides the grounds for the reading pleasure: "it is the very rhythm of what is read and what is not read that creates the pleasure of the great narratives: has anyone ever read Proust, Balzac, *War and Peace*, word for word?" (Barthes 11). There is no great amount of jargon or technical study of narrative description; description is not even treated as a literary term in most specialized literary dictionaries.

It is not surprising, then, that those who wish to praise Conrad for his evocative descriptions, who speak in terms of vividness and atmosphere, connect Conrad with literary impressionism. Ford Madox Ford argued this as early as 1935, and since then, many others (Ian Watt, Eloise Knapp Hay, etc.) have found Conrad to be impressionistic in his techniques. Impressionism is, however, a misapplied analogy. It implies a lack of concern for detail or clarity and instead an interest in bringing out "atmosphere." This is the notion which led F. R. Leavis and others to complain loudly about Conrad's murky "adjectival insistence" in *Heart of Darkness*:

> Hadn't he, we find ourselves asking, overworked "inscrutable," "inconceivable," "unspeakable" and that kind of word already?—yet still they recur. Is anything added to the oppressive mysteriousness of the Congo by such sentences as: "It was the stillness of an implacable force brooding over an inscrutable intention"? The same vocabulary, the same adjectival insistence upon inexpressible and incomprehensible mystery, is applied to the evocation of human profundities and spiritual horrors; to magnifying a thrilled sense of the unspeakable potentialities of the human soul. The actual effect is not to magnify but rather to muffle. (Leavis 216)

If this were an accurate picture of Conrad's descriptive style, it would indeed be unfortunate. Leavis' opinion has been widely disseminated and, until recently, it has been taken as a critical donnée. By its very name impressionism emphasizes that what is presented in the artwork is some one particular observer's impression of the scene depicted, thus tone, atmosphere, murkiness again. Jacques Berthoud has attempted to dissociate Conrad from impressionism because of these connotations: " 'Impressionism' in what sense? In *Nostromo* Conrad's elementary purpose is to bring to full actuality the life of an imaginary republic. To organize the novel conventionally — for instance, by providing a preliminary historical survey — would be self-defeating. Instead, he presents Costaguana as if (like the London of *The Secret Agent*) it already possessed an independent historical existence, to be acquired by readers incidentally and piecemeal, rather like the citizens of the country itself. This method of verisimilitude (rather than 'impressionism') is perfectly compatible with consistency of detail" (Berthoud 97). Recently critics have considered the spatial and temporal qualities of impressionism. It would seem that literary impressionism takes a rapid series of single moments and may or may not rearrange these moments chronologically, or may more or less fragment such moments, presenting and re-presenting what H. Peter Stowell calls "privileged moments of spatialized presentness" (Stowell 18; see also Kronegger; Gibbs; Muller).

This concept seems almost inevitably to intersect with Joseph Frank's argument about the spatialization of time in modern fiction, much refined and commented on in the last forty years (see Smitten and Daghistany). For if the reader is presented with numerous fragments which repeat some scenes while other scenes remain unique and discontinuous, these scenes and fragments are nevertheless formed into a satisfactory unity by the reader who reads necessarily temporally (as opposed to the spatializing analogy of impressionism). This has been widely misunderstood, beginning with the critical tag of *ut pictura poesis* and continuing to the present. William York Tindall, contrasting the effects of *Heart of Darkness* and *A Portrait of the Artist as a Young Man*, claimed that in Joyce's work, "narrative, attended by images that enlarge it, is central; in Conrad's book, narrative and subordinate details are centered in image. Tied to narrative, Joyce's images develop thematically in time, whereas Conrad's organization, more nearly static, is spatial in effect. If metaphors of other arts can help, Joyce's arrangement is musical and Conrad's is sculptural" (Tindall 91). This is rhetorically neat but quite untenable.

It is doubtful that Conrad's novels, which are for the most part heavily framed and discontinuous, so much so that many critics have decided that chronology is not recoverable, function in ways that can be accounted for either by impressionism or spatialization. I would place against Leavis' "adjectival insistence" a certain temporal insistence, especially in the longer fiction. *Nostromo* is, in most critical accounts, a novel of action, of politics, of heroism and cowardice, of imperialism; it is treated as a conventional novel and analyzed through its plot and characters. But the novel's fragmentation and its extended use of description work against narrative. Instead of "privileged moments of spatialized time," we always have another moment or scene or event juxtaposed and often contradicting the first account. Sometimes in *Nostromo* the juxtaposed moment is brought into contact proleptically with an earlier moment, thus removing the reading-motive of suspense we find in conventional fiction. Sometimes an analeptic description, informing readers of the characters' earlier failures or failings, is juxtaposed with a moment of a character's heroism or planning for the future but in this way is already predictive of future failure.

It is necessary to reconsider the functions of description in *Nostromo*. A recent critic, following Leavis' criticism of Conrad's apparently unwarranted obscurity, has noted that Conrad's fiction "deploys a variety of figures which combine to imply that the narrative is only a hint or clue to some immense secret enclosed within it. The tragic gloom which hangs listlessly over so many of the stories can be related both to the threatening proximity of this transcendent symbolic realm, and the lack of any possibility of locating it" (White 109). It is easy to find impatience with Conrad's extended descriptions in *Nostromo* among narrative-oriented critics, who are seeking the narrative codes within the descriptions and ignore the rest (thus declaring the remainder of the description superfluous). Astute critics of Conrad such as Albert Guerard may be found arguing, when dealing with descriptions in *Nostromo*, that "Certain descriptions in an older manner are frankly 'written'; the blocks are piled wearily into place, the eye is rather deperately on the object. And even where there is an attempt to suggest very informal narrative . . . the details may accumulate too rapidly" (Guerard 179). According to Guerard, it would be "inaccurate and even absurd to suggest that all of *Nostromo*'s numerous digressions exist to authenticate the country and the narrative" (182).

In a similar manner, Helen Reiselbach believes that the first chapter of *Nostromo* is a standard sort of nineteenth-century exposition which gives us physical background and indicates the moral lesson of the novel. The second chapter "hints at the attitude we are to take toward the story with Captain Mitchell's capsule history of Costaguanan politics. . . . Here, as often in the novel, the important detail is buried among other details and impressions . . ." (13). Actually, it is impossible to choose "the important detail" from among the unimportant ones. The descriptive passages, especially the repeated scenes or episodes, are complex while the narrative itself is rather simple and melodramatic, once the sequence of events and the dates are determined. Here again, plot-oriented critics are at a loss because of the fragmentation of events. Guerard confesses that it "has been my sad experience, each time I have tried to disentangle the time-scheme of *Nostromo*, to come up with a different result" (211). This is a common experience for readers of *Tristram Shandy*, Joyce, or Faulkner as well; Berthoud (98–100) provides the clearest disentanglement of the time-scheme of *Nostromo*. It is, in fact, largely unnecessary to the reading experience of the novel. To attempt to chart out the time-scheme and sequences of events is to attempt to rewrite the book into a conventional, chronological novel without first trying to understand why the novel was structured as it was and how exactly it functions.

Since the time-scheme of the novel is so disorienting (for we are often out of the presence of the main characters, such as Nostromo and the Goulds) the book is held together in other ways. Here, I am suggesting, is the importance of the placement and repetition of the descriptions. Repeated descriptions apply to all named characters, that is, all the major and minor characters but not usually momentary agents of action who appear only once (particular rioters, messengers, guards, etc.); this is true of all novels. We accumulate our understanding of the characters, settings, buildings, mannerisms, politics, and so on, through such temporally received information.

In *Nostromo* the descriptions are more complex than this. First, we have certain permanent objects which are treated in a highly changeable manner as they are viewed by different characters under different circumstances. In this case, the objects remain the same and the description of them is fairly consistent, but the meaning of the objects change constantly depending on the context. In this case, the descriptions do not function by accumulation but instead comment reflexively on the surrounding action or characters. Second, we have descriptions, especially of characters, which stand out because they do not reflect the present circumstances (and therefore seem unrealistic, following our normal codes of vraisemblance) or the material with which they are juxtaposed. Instead, these descriptions are constantly looking either back through time and reflect historical circumstances (these backwards-referring descriptions we will designate as *anaphoric descriptions* or *anaphora*), or forward through the novel's time-scheme and so reflect the future (such forwards-referring descriptions we will call *cataphoric descriptions* or *cataphora*). In order to demonstrate this in a limited space, I will concentrate on two well-known descriptive series in *Nostromo*: the mountain Higuerota, which dominates the landscape in the province, and the much-described but problematic Señor Hirsch, the hide merchant from Esmeralda.

The Occidental Province is isolated from the rest of Costaguana, bounded on the one side by the Golfo Placido, a blank horizontal frame, and on the other side by a mountain range (the Cordillera) which is itself dominated by the Higuerota, a threatening vertical frame. One or the other is always present within sight of the characters. These two vast, blank, mysterious areas, of changeable but never very clear and detailed appearance, contain the poles of the novel's action. The Golfo Placido contains the Three Isabels, and the Higuerota is the location of the Gould Concession. The mountain barrier is the main obstacle for deposed and fleeing dictators and officials or to invading armies, while the barrier of the windless gulf is the main obstacle to be crossed by Nostromo and Decoud in their attempt to remove the silver before Sotillo's troops arrive in Sulaco. According to Benita Parry, the "frontiers made by gulf and mountain define the pristine landscape on which successive cultures had acted and which it is the ambition and vocation of imperialism to destroy . . ." (121).

The characters of *Nostromo* (and the significant material interests, the shipping company and the mine) are arrayed between these two axes and in opposition to both. William Bonney notes that such places in Conrad's fiction "usually signal areas of semiotic overdetermination that threaten to annul language itself" (199–200). The vagueness and obscurity, the repetition of adjectives of darkness and mystery, which turn up so frequently in critical discussions of Conrad's style represent precisely the inability of the characters to domesticate or completely control the environment. Here the more obvious examples appear in *Heart of Darkness* with the rusted tracks and overturned locomotive, or the French warship, rusted and with a disease-ridden crew, which has for some time been firing the ship's guns, to no apparent effect, into a certain distant spot in the jungle. Typically, in the late Victorian and Edwardian novel, "nature" is gazed at or discussed by tourists; it is bought, divided, inherited, or exploited. In Conrad's work, and in *Nostromo* in particular, the turning away of the ironic narrator from the characters to the permanent objects of nature (the gulf and the mountain) is always to the disadvantage of the characters. The turning aside to the mountain serves to shrink the human figures and to trivialize their concerns, relationships, politics, ideals, wars, and acts of heroism or greed.

Jacques Berthoud has recently pointed out that the "entire novel, from its opening description of the gulf of which darkness is said to be impenetrable to 'the eye of God himself' to its closing return to the same august and sombre setting, is filled with evocations of the sublime aloofness of an untouched nature" (108). This is what Philip Weinstein calls the "Higuerota perspective": "The mountain stands . . . as an impressively mute and alien witness to the sordid turmoil in its midst. . . . Viewed from far enough away, normal sized-throats become 'tiny' and their death cries faint. The physical activity depicted here, wholly ungraced by spirit, verges upon the absurd" (Weinstein 172). The mountain cannot be thought of merely as a large feature in the landscape. Edward Said reminds us that Arnold Bennett saw Higuerota as the principal personage of *Nostromo* (Said 123). It is incorrect to consider the mountain symbolic, which implies either a culturally conventionalized (stable) meaning for a given sign or, at the very least, a consistent one-for-one signification (in the case of some private mythopoetic symbol). Higuerota figures much more actively and changeably than this in *Nostromo*, becoming almost an ironic chorus. Said, using for evidence Conrad's biography and letters, argues that Higuerota's solidity gives the novel "a specific spatial perspective," but that the mountain is actually emblematic of Conrad's "desperate search in his personal life for Higuerota's positive qualities of consistency, power, and unity" (Said 123).

The mountain literally and figuratively rises "majestically upon the blue" with its "smooth dome," its "white head" of snow above the treeline, the mining stations, and the "serrated" Cordillera. We can see the typical verbal collocations in the very first detailed description of the mountain which is worth quoting fully:

> Then, as the midday sun withdraws from the gulf the shadow of the mountains, the clouds begin to roll out of the lower valleys. They swathe in sombre tatters the naked crags of precipices above the wooded slopes, hide the peaks, smoke in stormy trails across the snows of Higuerota. The Cordillera is gone from you as if it had dissolved itself into great piles of grey and black vapours that travel out slowly to seaward and vanish into thin air all along the front before the blazing heat of the day. The wasting edge of the cloud-bank always strives for, but seldom wins, the middle of the gulf. The sub — as sailors say — is eating it up. Unless perchance a sombre thunder-head breaks away from the main body to career all over the gulf till it escapes into the offing beyond Azuera, where it burst suddenly into flame and crashes like a sinister [*sic*] pirate-ship of the air, hove-to above the horizon, engaging the sea. (*Nostromo* 6; hereafter abbreviated as *N*)

We note the prevalence of disappearances: the shadows are replaced by clouds, they swathe the crags, *hide, is gone from you, had dissolved itself, vanish into thin air, wasting edge, eating it up, till it escapes*. There is menace and destruction: *sombre tatters, crags of precipices, stormy trails, blazing heat, always strives for, but seldom wins, sombre thunder-head, breaks away from the main body to career all over the gulf, it bursts suddenly into flames and crashes like a sinister pirate-ship*. (The description of the gulf which follows this [*N* 6–7] follows exactly the same pattern.) And the insubstantial or intangible is made concrete: *great piles of grey and black vapours*. The movement of clouds, shadows, sun, smoke, vapors, and so on lend movements to the mountain. William Bonney correctly notes that in *Nostromo* "land can be liquified and all substantiality liquidated" (198). Reiselbach generalizes that "the landscape itself has an illusory, almost supernatural aspect. . . . Things (and people) in *Nostromo* appear and disappear mysteriously. We cannot always trust our perceptions, nor can we put complete faith in continuity or predictability" (12).

By either descriptive juxtaposition or direct comparison, the Garibaldino is often compared with Higuerota; he frequently is seen looking up at it, and Conrad usually places in close connection the white dome of the mountain and the white hair of Giorgio Viola (*N* 26). Giorgio is compared to Higuerota just before he indicates to Decoud his lack of interest and involvement in the current military preparations (166–67). In fact the Garibaldino is the character who most frequently takes on the Higuerota perspective:

> On this memorable day of the riots his arms were not folded on his chest. His hand grasped the barrel of the gun grounded on the threshold; he did not look up once at the white dome of Higuerota, whose cool purity seemed to hold itself aloof from a hot earth. His eyes examined the plain curiously. . . . Knots of men ran headlong; others made a stand; and the irregular rattle of firearms came rippling to his ears in the fiery, still air. Single figures on foot raced desperately. Horsemen galloped towards each other, wheeled round together, separated at speed. Giorgio saw one fall, rider and horse disappearing as if they had galloped into a chasm, and the movements of the animated scene were like the passages of a violent game played upon the plain by dwarfs mounted and on foot, yelling with tiny throats, under a mountain that seemed a colossal embodiment of silence. (*N* 26–27)

Giorgio doesn't look at the mountain, but what he sees and how he reacts is framed by the mountain in this description and it is from that perspective that he reacts. And the image of men as noisy, violent dwarfs, contrasted with the mountain as a "colossal embodiment of silence," is continuous. Shortly after this scene, we have a description of Sir John's visit to the mining engineers' camp above the mountain range's tree line but still below the dome of Higuerota. Here the engineers even live like dwarfs or fairies "in a stone hut like a cubical boulder." When Sir John speaks with the chief engineer about the railroad tracks to be laid, the engineer cries out, "We can't move mountains!" and "Sir John, raising his head to follow the pointing gesture, felt the full force of the words. The white Higuerota soared out of the shadows of rock and earth like a frozen bubble under the moon." The engineer argues that "tunnelling under Higuerota would have been a colossal undertaking" (40–41). And Don Pépé, merely "insect-like going to and fro upon the face of the rock" (395), is awaiting word to blow up the mine, but Higuerota dwarfs all of the activity, all the attempts to build on or transform the mountain through man-made paths or other signs; describing the mountain at sunset, the mine and its protectors are barely noticeable:

> . . . the precipitous range of the Cordillera, immense and motionless, emerging from the billows of the lower forests like the barren coast of a land of giants. The sunset rays striking the snow-slope of Higuerota from afar gave it an air of rosy youth, while the serrated mass of distant peaks remained black, as if calcined in the fiery radiance. . . . From the plain the stamp sheds and the houses of the mine appeared dark and small,

high up, like the nests of birds clustered on the ledges of a cliff. The zigzag paths resembled faint tracings scratched on the wall of a cyclopean blockhouse. (*N* 394)

As Bonney has commented, ostensibly "the narrative voice is describing the appearance of the landscape near Sulaco at sunset; but it is also concocting an ontological commentary by means of the bewildering rhetorical devices that are incorporated into the description. . . . the narrative opens with a citation of descending shadows, a chirascuro landscape, and ends clinging to chromatic glories that futilely and anachronistically lend 'an air of rosy youth' as the evening sun declines" (see Bonney 198–99).

The Goulds make important incursions against Higuerota, of course. Doña Emilia is frequently spoken of having "gone 'up to the mountain.' " We see the effect of this again in terms of disappearances, rather than appearances. A waterfall "existed no longer. The tree-ferns that had luxuriated in its spray had died around the dried-up pool, and the high ravine was only a big trench half filled up with the refuse of excavations and tailings. . . . Only the memory of the waterfall, with its amazing fernery, . . . was preserved in Mrs. Gould's watercolour sketch" (106).

However, it is mainly the permanence and continuity of the mountain that is mentioned in the descriptions: "Through good and evil report . . . , the Gould Concession, 'Imperium in Imperio,' had gone on working: the square mountain had gone on pouring its treasure down the wooden shoots. . . . All the fighting took place on the other side of that mighty wall of serrated peaks lorded over by the white dome of Higuerota and as yet unbreached by the railway . . ." (135). This "lording over" by the mountain creates different responses in the characters who regard it.

When Pedrito Montero is crudely attempting to bribe Charles Gould by offering him a title (" 'Eh, Don Carlos? No! What do you say? Conde de Sulaco — Eh? — or marquis . . .' "), the juxtaposed presence of the enormous distant mountain indicates the improbable nature of the proposal: "And above the roofs, next to the perpendicular lines of the cathedral towers the snowy curve of Higuerota blocked a large space of darkening blue sky before the windows of the Intendencia. After a time Pedrito Montero, thrusting his hand in the bosom of his coat, bowed his head with slow dignity. The audience was over" (405–06). Similarly, a few pages later we see Dr. Monygham, in one of the most selfless acts of courage in the novel, walking to the Custom House to purposely mislead the desperate Sotillo about the location of the silver; the description of Higuerota reflects his isolation and strength. "The doctor walked briskly. A darkling shadow seemed to fall upon him from the zenith. The sun had set. For a time the snows of Higuerota continued to glow with the reflected glory of the west. The doctor, holding a straight course for the Custom House, appeared lonely, hopping amongst the dark bushes like a tall bird with a broken wing" (410–11). Here we note *zenith, continued to glow, reflected glory, straight course*. On the same page and at the same time Nostromo wakes up in his hiding place at the moment of the sun's disappearance:

> At last the conflagration of sea and sky, lying embraced and still in a flaming contact upon the edge of the world, went out. The red sparks in the water vanished together with the stains of blood in the black mantle draping the sombre head of the Placid Gulf; a sudden breeze sprang up and died out after rustling heavily the growth of bushes on the ruined earthwork of the fort . . . He stood . . . with the lost air of a man just born into the world. (*N* 411)

Shortly after this, "The Capataz de Cargadores, on a revulsion of subjectiveness, exasperated almost to insanity, beheld all his world without faith and courage. He had been betrayed! . . . With the boundless shadows of the sea behind him, out of his silence and immobility, facing the lofty shapes of the lower peaks crowded around the white misty sheen of Higuerota, Nostromo laughed aloud again, sprang abruptly to his feet, and stood still" (417–18).

As we can see, Conrad's descriptions in *Nostromo* are not murky or impressionistic; quite the contrary, they are, if anything, overdetermined and referentially redundant.

One of the oddest figures in *Nostromo* is Señor Hirsch. Indeed, he appears with such ubiquity through the middle section of the book (after p. 200) that many critics find this a baffling flaw of construction in the novel. Why is so much attention devoted to the hide merchant from Esmeralda in a book about Nostromo and the Goulds and silver? Hirsch's strange role is to be a victim, only a victim, to be tortured and killed; he is to die and then to be seen dying, then to be seen frightened, and then to be tortured, and then to be dead once more, and then almost to metamorphose into something unhuman and even transcendent. Hirsch's role is unattractive and thankless, but it certainly is a powerful force in the descriptions in the latter part of the book.

Albert Guerard believes that "Conrad's imaginative concern with the death of Hirsch is obsessive, even sadistic" (207n.). Rieselbach also notes that "Hirsch's corpse broods over the scene between Nostromo and the doctor — a memento mori further confirming Nostromo's distrust of Monygham . . ." (Reiselbach 31), and Berthoud, speaking of the same scene, refers to the hanged Señor Hirsch as "the macabre object that casts its shadow over the entire encounter. . . . For Monygham, it is a clue to Sotillo's nature, which must be unravelled if his purposes are to succeed. For Nostromo, it is a symbol of his own predicament, a 'terrible example of neglect' confirming Monygham's pitiless disregard of men no longer useful to him" (Berthoud 122). The fullest analysis of the significance of Hirsch has been by Weinstein, who shows that it is part of a significant related structure throughout *Nostromo*:

> *Nostromo* is so constructed as to present the collapse scene before the celebration scene. (Weinstein 169).

> More gruesomely, Decoud is memorialized before we see him die, and Hirsch is hanged and resurrected several times. (169n.)

> The structure of *Nostromo* makes Decoud's death doubly appalling, by 'resurrecting' him, as it were, after the societal commemoration of his death, and then making him die again, this time in bodily isolation and nihilistic despair. Conrad's most malignantly manipulated figure, though — the man whose terrified body, now dead, now alive, is dragged through 150 pages — is not Decoud but Hirsch. (177; see 177–79)

At one point after the death of Hirsch, Nostromo calls the corpse, "You man of fear!" (*N* 461). This is in fact the dominating characteristic of Hirsch. When we first meet Señor Hirsch, the hide merchant from Esmeralda (200), he has come to Sulaco to receive assurances from Gould that he might *now* conduct and expand his business in safety. Apparently up to this point he had been too frightened by conditions in the country to carry on his business properly.

Hirsch always abjectly seeks safety, asking in a cringing whine for security and freedom from those who might harm him. He is always seen (when he is not unconscious, dead, swooned, or stunned) in a state of generalized panic or hysteria. Gould promises nothing ("He seemed to beg Charles Gould for a confirmatory nod, a grunt of assent, a simple nod even," 201), and Hirsch immediately jumps to a particular instance to explain to the blank Gould why he is fearful. "His alarm increased, and in the pauses he would dart here and there; then, loth to give up, he would branch off into feeling allusion [*sic*] to the dangers of his journey" (201). He had mistaken Nostromo on the road for a highwayman, the "audacious Hernandez," and thought he would be killed. Gould briefly dismisses Hirsch's fears and then withdraws communication with Hirsch; he "gave not a sign, made no sound. The impenetrability of the embodied Gould Concession had its surface shades" (203). Hirsch's fear of being killed on the way back to Esmeralda is what keeps from leaving Sulaco (381); this disastrous fear leads to his eventual capture and torture by Sotillo. His identification of Nostromo as an audacious robber forecasts Nostromo's taking of the silver and becoming rich slowly.

The second time we see Hirsch, sixty pages later, he is on board the ill-fated lighter of silver with Nostromo and Decoud. Ironically, he has stowed away in the darkness because he was fearful of the fighting in the city. Hirsch is invisible in the darkness of the gulf. He is first discovered when Nostromo says, "If it were possible I would think that I, too, have dozed off. I have a strange notion somehow of having dreamt that there was a sound of blubbering, a sound a sorrowing man could make, somewhere near this boat. Something between a sigh and a sob" (262). Feeling their way across the boat they discover Hirsch, who is prophetically described:

> . . . their hands came upon the limbs of a man, who remained as silent
> as death. Too startled themselves to make a sound, they dragged him aft
> by one arm and the collar of his coat. He was limp — lifeless.
>   . . . The thick lips were slightly parted, but the eyes remained
> closed. Decoud, to his immense astonishment, recognized Señor Hirsch,
> the hide merchant from Esmeralda. Nostromo, too, had recognized
> him. And they gazed at each other across the body, lying with its naked
> feet higher than its head, in an absurd pretence of sleep, faintness, or
> death. (270)

Coming some 200 pages before Hirsch actually dies, we see him again and
again in his deathly aspect (*limp, lifeless, silent as death*); his body is
treated as a corpse and dehumanized (*its naked feet, its head*). We can also
see how inappropriate it is to constantly identify fully this lifeless figure as
"Señor Hirsch, the hide merchant from Esmeralda." This is a technique
Said mentions, "Conrad's excessive use of appositional phrases. . . . A
source of constant ironic shocks, excessive in its jocularity and courtesy, the
technique is Dickensian." Although Said does not discuss this technique
with reference to Señor Hirsch, it seems accurate enough when Said notes
that repeated appositional phrases "cannot be developed; hence they serve
to remind us of the character's beginning authority" (Said 127).

Dickens might use the technique for such characters as Jaggers or
Barkus or Micawber; it has quite a different impact when used with
Hirsch whose death is forecast and then anaphorically described so
frequently that we always associate the name with torture and death.
Further, Hirsch lacks beginning authority; if we remember the earliest
scenes with Hirsch, we remember his fears.

The forecasting is obvious enough (though not on a first reading since
we are not watching out for Hirsch's reappearances). When Hirsch
attempts to sneak past the guards onto Nostromo's lighter, in an anaphora
presented after the scene in which Nostromo discovers him on the lighter
in the middle of the dark gulf, a guard calls out " 'Quien vive?' There were
more dead men lying about and he flattened himself down at once by the
side of a cold corpse. He [Hirsch] heard a voice saying, 'Here is one of those
wounded rascals crawling about. Shall I go and finish him?' " (272).
Nostromo tells Decoud after the collision that Hirsch, who was actually
pulled aboard Sotillo's ship, was "knocked overboard and drowned" (301).
Hirsch is taken away from Sotillo's interrogation "more dead than alive"
(342). Hirsch trips in the darkness while trying to go to the forward part of
the dark lighter and afterwards "all was still in the fore-part of the lighter
as though he had killed himself in his headlong tumble" (272); later we are
informed anaphorically that at the time he fell, Hirsch had "given himself
up for dead" (293). Nostromo thinks of ways to quietly kill the hysterical
Hirsch before they get too close to Sotillo's ship.

Hirsch's final torture is cataphorically indicated. Nostromo orders
Hirsch forward and we are told that "Hirsch was one of those men whom

fear lashes like a whip . . ." (273). Decoud "thought that it was a thousand pities the wretch had not died of fright"; the fate of Hirsch "remained suspended" (274, 275). On Sotillo's ship "Señor Hirsch" was "beaten a little for telling lies," but "he was beaten only a little" (294). Sotillo's men hear Hirsch's screams while he is being given the *estrapado* in the Custom House, but this too is forecast. Nostromo and Decoud fear Hirsch screaming out in terror (283); his "piercing shriek for help" signals the collision with Sotillo's ship (291). Decoud anaphorically thinks of this first shriek and then the continuing but increasingly distant screams of Hirsch, inadvertently pulled away by the ship (292); then we are told again about the first scream, now more specifically " 'Save me!' " (293), and about how instinctively at the moment of the collision the terrified Hirsch had wrapped his arms and legs around the flukes of the ship's anchor and was suspended from the side of the ship (just as his fate remained suspended and he is suspended during his torture).

Hirsch's terrible suffering is attributed to a "certain kind of imagination," "that sort of imagination which adds the blind terror of bodily suffering and of death, envisaged as an accident to the body alone, strictly — to all the other apprehensions on which the sense of one's existence is based" (338). Certainly, too, Hirsch seems predestined for his role because of his peculiar otherness. While there are many Europeans in Sulaco, they are in groups (English, Italian); Hirsch is alone. Hirsch is from Esmeralda rather than Sulaco. Hirsch has a Germanic name, and Sotillo always refers to Hirsch as a Jew; he believes that Hirsch is involved with keeping him from the silver and attributes this to Hirsch's "Jewish cunning" (330; see also 448, 451).

Hirsch's corpse, finally, is found by Nostromo and Monygham before we are told how Hirsch died, which is described about twenty pages later; Nostromo, of course, did not know that Hirsch had survived the collision. When Nostromo first makes his way to the Customs House, the first figure he encounters is the unidentifiable shadow of Hirsch. Nostromo "had seen within the shadow of a man cast upon one of the walls. It was a shapeless, high-shouldered shadow of somebody standing still, with lowered head, out of his line of sight." Nostromo meets Monygham while rushing away from the shadow of the corpse (425), then confronts the corpse directly and realizes the man has been tortured (427). It is only when Dr. Monygham is examining the corpse that Nostromo recognizes (long after the reader) that it is Hirsch (428). Then the two men discuss for several pages the torture and death by shooting of Hirsch.

Hirsch's death fascinates and confuses Monygham, who studies the corpse for clues about Sotillo's mentality. Hirsch's corpse is shattering to the heroic mission he had taken upon himself out of love for Emilia Gould: ". . . the risk, deadly enough, to which he exposed himself, had a sustaining and comforting effect. To that spiritual state the fate of Hirsch presented itself as part of the general atrocity of things" (439). At this point, the reader knows no more than Monygham about the reason Sotillo finally killed Hirsch.

We are given an extended anaphoric description of Sotillo's final interrogation and torture of Hirsch (still called "Señor Hirsch" by the narrator [446–47]), and Sotillo's impulsive shooting. The actual killing of Hirsch is further intriguing because what occurred is so out of keeping with the image of Hirsch that we had built up so far.

> . . . And as Sotillo, staying his raised hand, waited for him to speak, with the sudden flash of a grin and straining forward of the wrenched shoulders, he spat violently into his face.
>
> The uplifted whip fell, and the colonel sprang back with a low cry of dismay, as if aspersed by a jet of deadly venom. Quick as thought he snatched up his revolver, and fired twice. (449).

What occurred is clearly described, but the motivations behind the actions are not clear. Was Hirsch's grin a real grin or was it a grimace? Was he happily defiant or was he grinning because he knew Sotillo would finally kill him and so release him from further pain? Did Sotillo feel dismay because he had lost control of his victim, or because he knew he would not be able to stop himself from immediately killing Hirsch without discovering anything more about the treasure? For immediately upon firing the shots, Sotillo knows it is a mistake, that the Monterist army and Pedrito Montero in particular would never forgive this loss of control. The fear is transferred from Hirsch to Sotillo who thinks at once of "headlong flight" or even "the craven and absurd notion of hiding under the table" (449). Shortly after this, the corpse of the "late Señor Hirsch, merchant from Esmeralda" is left hanging and his shadow can be seen, the shadow seen by Nostromo later in time but earlier in the novel.

In descriptions of Hirsch after his death is finally told, he seems to be either unhuman or transcendent, transformed or apotheosized into a sign of the failure of the Monterist movement, or the success of the mine and material interests: "The light of the two candles burning before the perpendicular and breathless immobility of the late Señor Hirsch threw a gleam afar over land and water, like a signal in the night" (451). He is left like this because the soldiers ordered to burn his corpse failed to get the fire started correctly; this failure makes it seem as if now Hirsch is invulnerable, having passed through the severe tests set for him. Still later a frightened and anguished Nostromo seems to react against this inhuman or superhuman Hirsch: "He laughed wildly and turned in the doorway towards the body of the late Señor Hirsch, an opaque long blotch in the semi-transparent obscurity of the room between the two tall parallelograms of the windows full of stars" (461). Hirsch and his fate are a warning against violent action, against fear, but Nostromo disregards this "signal in the night" (as a lighthouse warns sailors). "Behind them the late Señor Hirsch preserved the immobility of a *disregarded* man" (458; italics mine). Nostromo's end is cataphorically described through his identification with Hirsch; when he again believes he is betrayed, he cries out "with a violent movement, as shadowy to the doctor's eyes as the persistent immobility of the late Señor Hirsch" (454).

Numerous other objects and figure descriptions function in *Nostromo* in the same manner as Higuerota and Hirsch. Close attention to the descriptions reveal them to be far more systematic (and clear) than is usually thought by Conrad's critics, and quite sophisticated compared to many of Conrad's contemporaries. This essay is too brief to do more than indicate how such analyses might be conducted, and necessarily omits a vast array of technical tools developed by narrative semioticians (see especially Hamon; Bal; Riffaterre; Blanchard; Sternberg).

Works Cited

Bal, Mieke. "Theorie de la description: L'Exemple *Madame Bovary*." Ed. P. M. Wetherill, *Flaubert: La dimension du texte* (Manchester: Univ. of Manchester Press, 1982): 175–236.

—————. *Narratology: Introduction to the Theory of Narrative*. Tr. Christine van Boheemen (Toronto: Univ. of Toronto Press, 1985).

Barthes, Roland. *The Pleasure of the Text*. Tr. Richard Miller (NY: Hill & Wang, 1975).

Berthoud, Jacques. *Joseph Conrad: The Major Phase* (Cambridge: Cambridge Univ. Press, 1978).

Blanchard, Marc Eli. *Description: Sign, Self, Desire* (The Hague: Mouton, 1980).

Bonney, William S. *Thorns and Arabesques: Contexts for Conrad's Fiction* (Baltimore: Johns Hopkins Univ. Press, 1980).

Conrad, Joseph. *Nostromo: A Tale of the Seaboard* (Garden City: Doubleday, Doran & Co., 1930).

Ford, Ford Madox. "Techniques," *Southern Review*, 1 (July, 1935): 20–35.

Gibbs, Beverly Jean. "Impressionism as a Literary Movement." *MLJ*, 36 (1952): 175–83.

Guerard, Albert J. *Conrad the Novelist* (NY: Atheneum, 1967).

Hamon, Philippe, "Rhetorical Status of the Descriptive," *Yale French Studies*, 61 (1981): 1–26.

—————, "What is a Description?" *French Literary Theory Today*. Ed. Tzvetan Todorov (Cambridge: Cambridge Univ. Press/Paris: Editions de la Maison des Sciences de l'Homme, 1982).

Hawthorne, Jeremy. *Joseph Conrad: Language and Fictional Self-Consciousness* (Lincoln: Univ. of Nebraska Press, 1979).

Kronegger, M. E. *Literary Impressionism* (New Haven: College and Univ. Press, 1973).

Leavis, F. R. *The Great Tradition* (Garden City: Doubleday / Anchor, 1954).

Muller, Herbert J. "Impressionism in Fiction: Prism vs. Mirror." *The American Scholar*, 7 (1938): 355–67.

Parry, Benita. *Conrad and Imperialism: Ideological Boundaries and Visionary Frontiers* (London: Macmillan, 1983).

Reiselbach, Helen Funk. *Conrad's Rebels: The Psychology of Revolution in the Novels from Nostromo to Victory* (Ann Arbor: UMI Research Press, 1985).

Riffaterre, Michael. "Descriptive Imagery," *Yale French Studies*, 61 (1981): 145–61.

Said, Edward W. *Beginnings: Intention and Method* (Baltimore: Johns Hopkins Univ. Press, 1975).

Sherry, Norman, ed. *Conrad: The Critical Heritage* (London: Routledge & Kegan Paul, 1973).

Smitten, Jeffrey R. and Ann Daghistany, eds. *Spatial Form in Narrative* (Ithaca: Cornell Univ. Press, 1981).

Sternberg, Meir. "Ordering the Unordered: Time, Space, and Descriptive Coherence." *Yale French Studies*, 61 (1981): 60–88.

Stowell, H. Peter. *Literary Impressionism, James and Chekhov* (Athens: Univ. of Georgia Press, 1980).

Tindall, William York. *The Literary Symbol* (Bloomington: Indiana Univ. Press, 1965).

Weinstein, Philip M. *The Semantics of Desire: Changing Models of Identity from Dickens to Joyce* (Princeton: Princeton Univ. Press, 1984).

White, Allon. *The Uses of Obscurity: The Fiction of Early Modernism* (London: Routledge & Kegan Paul, 1981).

Narrative Perspective in *Victory*: The Thematic Relevance

William W. Bonney*

I

Much of the critical resistance that has been directed at *Victory* for its supposedly inept use of point of view seems due to readers' failure properly to understand both the novel's thematic statement and its ontology; and this inadequacy has consequently prevented satisfactory responses to the artistic function of the novel's narrative perspective, which employs conventions and confirms a thematic content of which many remain unaware.

Typical of the most outspoken critics of the use of narrative perspective in *Victory* is Albert Guerard:

> *Victory* begins with an unidentified crude jocular narrator who presently calls in the no less commonplace Davidson. The narrative difficulties, once Heyst reaches his island, are theoretically insoluable. . . . But this is only in theory, and the pretense of a narrator is soon dropped. The limited view gives way abruptly to standard omniscient narrative with Heyst as the usual post of observation. . . . The improbable appearance of Davidson at the end could be accepted with amused tolerance had it granted Conrad the detachment he needed. So far as the reader is concerned, there is no reason for Davidson to appear. The omniscient and certainly uninhibited narrator of the heart of the book could have described the holocaust just as well.[1]

*Reprinted with permission from *Journal of Narrative Technique* 5 (1975):24–39.

Guerard finds no aesthetic value in the unnamed speaker, who narrates the first section of the novel, or in Davidson, whose official report ends it; to him *Victory* only "offers a dullard within a dullard, Davidson within the 'I.' "[2] One of the few lonely voices of dissent belongs to John Palmer, who asserts, in a uniquely complimentary response, that "it is probable that both the structure and point of view of *Victory*, Davidson included, are the best that Conrad might have devised for his special artistic purposes."[3] Palmer's judgment anticipates the manner in which current critical theory has recently decided in favor of the device of narrative discontinuity,[4] and the task of critics of fiction is no longer to attempt merely to validate such modes, but rather to explore their aesthetic merits by means of rigorous inquiry into the function of discontinuous point of view in specific works. Accordingly, I wish to suggest that a positive analytic evaluation of the narrative perspective which Conrad employs in *Victory* will not only demonstrate that it is a pointedly successful artistic tool, but also that such an evaluation necessarily makes accessible a new understanding of the novel's theme and unity.

II

The traditional view of *Victory* regards the novel as a moral treatise which condemns detachment and recommends a supposedly redemptive involvement such as that exemplified by Lena's "victory" of causing Heyst to commit himself to his vision of her.[5] I regard this approach as untenable simply because there can be no victory in terms of the phenomenal world if an individual's conduct is disastrous. In a universe devoid of supernatural compensation or moral absolutes, Lena's deluded obsession, which leads to the ugly deaths of five people, including herself, cannot be regarded as a triumph; and repeatedly Conrad's novels and letters clearly deny both the existence of a transcendental realm and the value of a philosophy which persuades its advocates to believe in the existence of such a realm.[6] I am convinced that Conrad, by means of the title, the "Author's Note," and the use of conventionally admirable sentiments like love and religion, has contrived the novel to mislead both those readers whose ontological assumptions are akin to those of Lena and those who would assert that in the face of a godless universe the naive gesture of "getting involved," of committing oneself, is inherently valuable and praiseworthy, even if ultimately disastrous.

It is a critical commonplace to claim that Conrad regards "loyalty and service as the central virtues of his world," and that his supreme test of a character's moral fiber is basically involved with determining "whether or not he is faithful to the community."[7] This is all quite true when it is applied to characters who first willingly engage with a situation which will demand to an excruciating degree their fidelity and service; individuals, that is, who consciously involve themselves in situations which will rigorously test the strength of a commitment that includes the voluntary acceptance of responsibility for the welfare of other human beings. Persons like Donkin or Jim are treated with irony because, in spite of the fact that the demands of their jobs should have been apparent to them before the contract was made, these men accepted a burden with which they could not cope. Conrad's scorn is levelled at people who entertain naive and exaggerated concepts of their own adequacy, and who, because of their lack of awareness, become threats to the lives of those for whose welfare they are responsible. However, it does not necessarily follow that Conrad disapproves of those dissenting, enlightened characters who choose not to accept a contract of responsibility or to engage with the human community; and neither the aesthetic merits nor the thematic statement of *Victory* can be understood as long as the mistaken idea persists that the novel is attacking the detachment recommended by Axel Heyst's father and practiced in its purest and consequently most successful form by Wang, the Chinese coolie, and the nameless narrator, whose voice opens the book.

Conrad is a pessimist in the sense that the world as he envisions it is without inherent order and value. Intelligible pattern must be imposed by human beings, but this order is always illusory insofar as it is subjective, always an inadequate manner of dealing with chaos, and often a source of destructive psychological entrapment. In the words of J. Hillis Miller, to Conrad "All human ideals, even the ideal of fidelity, are lies. They are lies in the sense that they are human fabrications. They derive from man himself and are supported by nothing outside him."[8] Accordingly, generalizations about Conrad's metaphysics which identify him with a specific code of behavior are questionable. From novel to novel Conrad continually experiments with and explores different, often opposing, mental states, levels of awareness, and life styles; and, if in a given novel one character's "way" is successful, there is usually another character in the Conrad canon (at times within the same work) whose "way" is equally successful, but diametrically opposed to the first individual's code of conduct. For every Marlow there is a Captain MacWhirr or, indeed, another far different Marlow.[9] The tragedy inherent in Conrad's vision is that there is ultimately no life style which is capable of redeeming the human condition, for all eventually prove to be inadequate. Even the position of complete withdrawal, although it is to be recommended in *Victory* in preference to all others, fails because it cannot be maintained with sufficient austerity; the mentality "of even the most detached and far-seeing man is still oriented toward the world, watching it, dwelling within it, open to its solicitations, subject to its glare and garish rattling."[10] The tragedy of *Victory* is not that Axel Heyst cannot commit himself, but rather that Axel Heyst cannot preserve his pose of detachment.

Throughout the novel characters are arranged on a continuum with reference to their proximity to the detached attitudes recommended by

Old Heyst, and it is safe to over-simplify and assert that they live or die insofar as they preserve their psychic discretion and avoid obsessive values or aversions. Jones and Heyst both die because they "get involved" in the sense that they permit their behavior to be governed by private, subjective, irrational needs, and therefore lose sight of the void which waits to engulf prematurely those who drop their guard. Compare, for instance, the manners in which those who indulge in commitment die with the death of Old Heyst: the former end their lives in a frantically deluded and violent way, whereas Old Heyst dies peacefully in bed. Moreover, Wang, who builds fences even on an island to keep others away, and whose life style most closely approximates that recommended by Old Heyst, continues to live, inheriting the island after cleansing it with his pistol of the final vestige of emotional bondage—Pedro, who worships Jones for saving his life in an echo both of Morrison's and Lena's attitudes toward Heyst, and of Heyst's, Schomberg's, and Ricardo's attitudes toward Lena. Most relevant to the purposes of this paper, however, is the fact that the unnamed speaker and Davidson belong on this continuum, too; and it is possible to define their mental positions relative to the option of detachment by examining the attitudes implicit in their uses of language and in their few overt acts.

III

The authorial point of view employed by Conrad in his lengthy "Author's Note" to *Victory* provides an indication of precisely how consistently and viciously ironic the novel is; and a detailed consideration of the attitudinal content of this prefatory essay is a necessary prelude to an adequate response to the later use of narrative perspective throughout the work. The author immediately establishes a tension between his attitudes toward detachment and involvement. He mocks those who continually meddle with profound issues like "the Last Judgment," and praises the man who is made of "wonderfully adaptable cloth" due to "his power of endurance and . . . his capacity for detachment." The detached man, "with perfect propriety," will not worry about things that do not concern him personally or which he cannot remedy. Far from opposing detachment and attacking the critical mode of perception in his prefatory remarks, Conrad uses the critic as an example of the mental stance which he is praising: in the face of "the lightning of wrath," ". . . the critic will go on criticizing with that faculty of infinite littleness and which is yet the only faculty that seems to assimilate man to the immortal gods."[11] Significantly, "the Last Judgment," "the lightning of wrath," is inescapable in Conrad's cosmos. His use of Christian terminology is a further example of his ironic pose, for in Conrad's works these ideas are synonymous with inevitable destruction and are stripped of consoling theological connotations.

Conrad goes on to describe the dangerous kind of situation that can seduce "even the best representative of the race . . . to lose his detachment." The aloof man is only in danger when he encounters a situation into which he is able to project himself because "the catastrophe [of the situation] matches the natural obscurity of [his] fate" (p. x). In other words, it is the gesture of getting enmeshed which is dangerous. It may be countered, of course, that all involvement is obviously perilous since the ultimate effects of all action are unknowable; but this applies equally well to the act of deciding to detach oneself, an act which within the aesthetic framework of *Victory* Conrad lauds, while specifically opposing involvement, saying "There should [be] a remedy for that sort of thing" (p. x). Both Heyst and Ricardo destructively commit themselves to Lena precisely because they are able to project themselves into a situation or onto another character; and it is clear that Conrad is defining in the "Author's Note" just what sort of attitude to take toward such involvement.

Conrad's apparent criticism of Heyst's "fine detachment" and "habit of profound reflection" also needs to be clarified. Plainly, in the "Author's Note" to *Victory* Conrad is not totally opposing detachment. Detachment is bad in terms of the character of Axel Heyst in that it causes him to lose the ability to assert himself. But this is a criticism specifically limited to Heyst, for Wang is even more thoroughly detached than Heyst, yet he appropriates Heyst's revolver and retains the power to act. What Conrad implicitly defines as harmful is not the attitude of detachment leading to "profound reflection"; the truly damaging mental event is the formation of a habit, whatever its specific manifestation, for "all the habits formed by civilized man" are, implicitly, "pernicious" (p. xi).

Perhaps the most perplexing aspect of Conrad's "Author's Note" is his tongue-in-cheek protestations of good will for his characters. Readers have never found it difficult to dislike Axel Heyst, but few have ever remarked about the discrepancy between their interpretations of the negative attitude the novel fosters toward Heyst and Conrad's insistence that "I wouldn't be suspected even remotely of making fun of Axel Heyst" (p. xi). Of course, the novel often directs caustic irony at Heyst, and in this instance it is plain that Conrad is tricking the gullible reader in his prefatory remarks. The case of Lena is more delicate, however. The existence of irony is always difficult to prove because, by definition, it remains unstated. I submit, nevertheless, that Conrad's naive and optimistic tone, which he adopts when discussing Lena's fate, is meant to be ironic in the most merciless way. Although the rhetorical question puts the burden of cold-blooded awareness upon the reader, there is no way I can take Conrad's generalization about Lena's "end" at face value: ". . . in view of her triumphant end what more could I have done for her rehabilitation and her happiness?" (p. xvii). If Conrad had simply called her demise a "triumph" there would be little ground for claiming an ironic intent, but to ask what more could have been done "for her rehabilitation and her happiness" in view of her absurd and tragic death is outrageous, and I am convinced Conrad meant it to be so.

But Conrad does not limit his craftsmanship to the caustic implications of his generously optimistic rhetorical questions. He develops his own personality at some length almost like a character in a novel, describing in detail the subjective impressions which caused him wrongly to regard the person after whom Lena was fashioned as adequate. Blurring the boundaries between biography and fiction, Conrad describes himself witnessing the girl leave him "for her meeting with Heyst," and tells us that he remained reticent at her departure because, due to his own subjective illusions at the time, he conceived of her as being able to handle any situation: "It was my perfect idleness that had invested the girl with a peculiar charm, and I did not want to destroy it by any superfluous exertion. The receptivity of my indolence made the impression so permanent that when the moment came for her meeting with Heyst I felt she would be heroically equal to every demand of the risky and uncertain future" (p. xvii). Conrad realizes such an impression is wrong, of course,[12] and he further undercuts the seriousness of the encounter of "Lena" with "Heyst" as described in the "Author's Note" by naming their trysting place the "Place de la Comedie." Only by means of a sustained application of the sort of bleakly harsh perspective developed by the author in his prefatory remarks can the aesthetic subtleties of the narrative in *Victory* be appreciated.

IV

The novel opens with the voice of an anonymous persona whose presence perpetuates the authorial recommendations which were established in the prefatory essay. The speaker does not exist as a person who is intimately involved with the people and events he describes, and whose personality is altered by his experiences. On the contrary, he remains a static, detached, ironic voice, gathering most of his information at second hand, who seems to use the subject matter of his narrative as a buffer between himself and his world. He can commit himself, so to speak, only to a tale told by someone else, which he modifies by adding his own details, and then relates again, all the while engaging in a minimum of intimate and revealing personal contact. We finally know very little about the speaker's innermost feelings, for he keeps himself hidden. All we can discover about him is that his attitude toward a life style of ironic detachment is positive, and perhaps this is all that is necessary for the artistic purposes of the novel. The speaker embodies a placid model of Old Heyst, who, like the speaker, also kept a cushion of public statements around himself; moreover, both these characters are equally one-dimensional, functioning essentially as attitudinal norms which reinforce the successful, early behavioral mode of Axel Heyst, from which he later deviates due to his infatuation with Lena's voice.

The speaker preserves his detachment from his tale by toying with words, so that the resultant irony becomes an amusing and epistemologically definitive end in itself, distracting both the teller and listener, and preventing thereby the mental entrapment consequent upon a projection of self into events and characters. He describes, for instance, how talk of "these coal-outcrops begin to crop up" (p. 6) in Heyst's conversations. When a drunk to whom Heyst suggested " 'Come along and quench your thirst,' " calls Heyst " 'a . . . utopist,' " the speaker responds with the sarcastic hypothesis that anyone "who could propose, even playfully, to quench old McNab's thirst must have been a utopist . . ." (p. 8). The speaker's downright indifference to emotive responses is revealed when he describes with cold amusement the moving scene in which Morrison and Heyst share confidences ("It must have been funny, because they were very serious about it" [p. 18]), and when he intolerantly criticizes Mrs. Schomberg for smiling vapidly, and calls her "an It — an automaton, a very plain dummy, with an arrangement for bowing the head at times . . ." (p. 39). When word reaches him that Heyst "must be starving on his island" with Lena, the speaker callously suggests that Heyst may have to resort to cannibalism: "he may end yet by eating her . . ." (p. 44). This sort of irreverence toward the idea of death is indicative of still another dimension of the speaker's means of diversion within the narrative: a continual manipulation of biblical references for the sake of creating preposterous contexts. For instance, echoing a famous parable of Christ (see Matthew 6:28), the persona describes Heyst's secretive way of making a living as that of a man "who didn't toil or spin visibly" (p. 15). In the Bible this state of being is a sign of God's favor to the beasts and plants, but the speaker uses the idea as a way to undercut Morrison's view that Heyst was sent by God to lend aid: to the narrator, Heyst seems "the very last person to be the agent of Providence in an affair concerned with money" (p. 15). Another example of a ludicrous application of a biblical allusion can be seen in the speaker's deprecatory description of the omnipresence of the topic of Heyst at Schomberg's hotel due to Schomberg's obsession: "Whenever three people came together in his hotel, he took good care that Heyst should be with them" (p. 25; see Matthew 18:20).

From his vantage point of ironic detachment the nameless persona can understand the limitations inherent in Heyst's essentially congruent life style. He is quick to note that Heyst's problems seem to develop because of his inability to achieve total isolation: "his detachment from the world was not complete. And incompleteness of any sort leads to trouble" (p. 30). The narrator does not mean to imply that the proper degree of detachment is necessarily only to be achieved on an island, at complete physical remove from the bustling mainland, so to speak. Indeed, in Heyst's case physical withdrawal only increases the intensity of Heyst's psychic entanglement with his vision of Lena, whereas, in marked contrast, the narrator and Old Heyst are examples of detachment which

are as pure as any in the Conrad canon, and these individuals have
attained their mental aloofness while remaining physically connected to
their respective social orders, successfully resisting the "romantic" tendencies of Axel Heyst who vulnerably colors "the world to the hue of [his] own
temperament" (p. 49).

V

Soon after the theft of Lena the narrative perspective modulates to a
third-person omniscient point of view, probably because no first-person
narrator could logically have been present on Samburan, since the novel's
thematically appropriate conclusion dictates that every member of Heyst's
intimate circle who might be used as the voice through which to describe
events on the island be killed. More important, however, is the fact that a
major concern of the remainder of the novel is a detailed exploration of
Heyst's and Lena's respective psychic contents and the revelation that the
two lovers do not remotely understand one another; and an omniscient
narrative voice is the only aesthetic convention by means of which access
can properly be provided to interior characterological subjectivity. This
narrative technique lends an objective quality to the novel which was
pointedly lacking in the section dominated by the persona, where an
entirely subjective view of Heyst was presented in terms of both vague
rumors and specific tales told by identifiable characters, depending highly
upon spatial and temporal discontinuity to sketch the "impermanent
dweller amongst changing scenes" (p. 87).

The third-person narrative voice of *Victory* is usually an omniscient
voice which attacks one character after another with its ironic, perceptive
analysis of respective illusory causes of involvement; but it is not obtrusive,
and enters the novel in an ontologically definitive manner only occasionally. Moreover, it is necessary to qualify the omniscience of the narrative
voice, and modify thereby the traditional concept of this artistic device,
because there are instances in *Victory* when this voice chooses to evade
absolute resolutions of characters' motives. This occurs most markedly in
relationship to the topic of Heyst's past, which was left nebulous by the
nameless persona, and which the narrative voice also pointedly fails to
clarify. For example, in the following passage the subjunctive is used to
avoid a conclusive definition of Heyst's response to his dead father's
belongings: "It seemed as if in his conception of a world not worth
touching, and perhaps not substantial enough to grasp, these objects
familiar to his childhood and his youth and associated with the memory of
an old man, were the only realities, something having an absolute
existence" (p. 166). After his abortive involvement with Morrison, Heyst
realizes that he has abandoned the way of life suggested by his father. The
narrative voice hints that it was the influence of his father's belongings,
vestiges of a lost faith, that caused Heyst to remain on the island after the

economic failure of the Tropical Belt Coal Company; but, again, flat statements of fact are avoided: "The manager of the Tropical Belt Coal Company, unpacking them on the verandah in the shade besieged by a fierce sunshine, must have felt like a remorseful apostate before these relics. He handled them tenderly; and it was perhaps their presence there which attached him to the island when he woke up to the failure of his apostasy. Whatever the decisive reason, Heyst had remained where another would have been glad to be off" (p. 167). These lapses in the narrative voice's omniscience are strange, but perhaps there is a reason for them. Conrad prevents the third-person voice from contradicting the first-person speaker by causing both points of view to be unclear about the precise, personal motives that conditioned Heyst's past. Unlike the technique used in *The Nigger of the "Narcissus,"* in which the omniscient third-person voice functions as a means of de-mythologizing the world presented by the anonymous narrator who sailed as a crewman on the "Narcissus,"[13] the accuracy of the first-person narrator in *Victory* is not challenged. The nameless speaker in the latter novel is meant to function as a normative character and not as an individual in whose opinions we are to be interested because they are fallible due to the limitations of human subjectivity. This is not to say that we are required to embrace the persona's tale as valid the way we are implicitly compelled to trust the information made available by the omniscient narrative voice; but it is to say that Conrad's interest does not lie in dramatizing the limitations of his speaker. Rather, he paradoxically qualifies the awareness of his third-person narrative voice at times so that the persona's vague tale of Heyst's past will not be cancelled to the detriment of the synthesizing human source.

Major functions of the narrative voice in *Victory* include the presentation of crucial generalizations about human psychology and the place of man in the novel's universe. For instance, the extent of Conrad's commitment to his own ontology in *Victory* can be seen when he chooses to present his ideas through his narrative voice, which describes them as a human instinct. Conrad is to some extent a universalist, for his characters all ultimately share the same problems and limitations: the need to project an invalid, and often irrelevant, structure of order and value onto external chaos. For a character like Heyst to succumb to the siren call of excessive subjectivism in spite of his awareness of the illusory nature of human values supports Conrad's idea that such a dilemma is a limitation analogous to an instinct. The narrative voice observes that "all the world . . . had instinctively rejected [Old Heyst's] wisdom" (p. 88); this instinct is shared by all members of the human race, and is properly called "the oldest voice in the world":

> Heyst meditated in simple terms on the mystery of his actions; and he answered himself with the honest reflection:

"There must be a lot of the original Adam in me, after all."

He reflected, too, with the sense of making a discovery, that this primeval ancestor is not easily suppressed. The oldest voice in the world is just the one that never ceases to speak. If anybody could have silenced its imperative echoes, it should have been Heyst's father, with his contemptuous, inflexible negation of all effort; but apparently he could not. There was in the son a lot more of the first ancestor who, as soon as he could uplift his muddy frame from the celestial mould, started inspecting and naming the animals of that paradise which he was so soon to lose. (pp. 163–164)

Heyst is engaged in a struggle which pits his physical and philosophical father against the primeval, instinctual "father," Adam, standing for the need of all men to partake of the illusory order which ultimately causes their "fall" to destruction. Significantly, the one example of all Adam's acts which is chosen to function as an analogue to Heyst's involvement is the imposition of order on the world by speaking and giving objects names. The echo of Heyst's entanglement with Morrison and Lena through the spoken word is clear. Conrad pointedly avoids talking about a "fall" by means of the act of "eating the fruit," and the fact that the innocent, instinctual, and necessary act of naming things, ordering one's surroundings, should be seen as analogous to a collapse forces a confrontation with Conrad's idea that the prerequisite of sane life is also the source of the psychic trap which causes confusion and death.

Proper understanding of the relevance of the "original Adam" to the manner in which the very act of perception becomes a snare in *Victory* also clarifies that dimension of the novel's narrative technique which has given rise to mistaken critical judgments that the work is written in an allegorical mode.[14] A reading of *Victory* which suggests that the thematic concerns center around a simple dichotomy involving a negative Mr. Jones and a positive Lena must ignore completely the manner in which the narrative connects satanic terms and death imagery with almost every character in the novel. Lena, for instance, is seen as a "phantom-like apparition," "white and spectral" (pp. 80,82). To Schomberg, Heyst is "the devil" (p. 30), and Ricardo suspects that Heyst may be "in league with the devil himself" (p. 224); to Lena, Schomberg is a "horrible red-faced beast," the Zangiacomo woman is a "devil-woman" (p. 195), and Ricardo is "the embodied evil of the world" (p. 279); to Heyst action is "devilish" (p. 52), and Wang's smiling face looks like a "conceited death's head" (p. 326), which is exactly the way Heyst had regarded Jones's face earlier in the novel (see p. 217); women are almost synonymous with the devil to Jones (see pp 109–110); and to Schomberg the trio appears as a "spectre, a cat, an ape" (p. 140), and Jones especially looks like "a corpse," which seems to imply some sort of "menace from beyond the grave" (p. 107). The import of all this imagery is plain: each character applies satanic tags to whomever or whatever is alien to his experience, terrifies him, or seems to stand opposed to his respective values. Much of what superficially appears like an allegory with "Christian elements"[15] in the novel is the result of the characters' deluded, pseudo-allegorical manners of regarding one another in terms of a simplistic moral dichotomy. There is no justification whatsoever to assert that Lena's delusion that Ricardo embodies "the evil of the world" (p. 279) is to be taken as an absolute moral judgment, while denying the relevance of similar remarks voiced by other characters just because these characters are conventionally villainous. Moral touchstones dissolve in the novel beneath the corrosive effect of Conrad's third-person narrative voice as it juggles traditional semantic functions while presenting the ghoulish associations of the major characters and demonstrating thereby the self-confounding nature of human values.

VI

Yet, in spite of the importance of the narrative voice, Conrad does not use it to end his novel; and this decision is significant. The innocuous Davidson is permitted to relate the details of the resolution of the conflict on Samburan, an artistic choice which Moser feels only contributes to a "preposterous" ending (p. 108); and if the value of Davidson's appearance must rest upon his significance as a character, as F. R. Leavis thinks,[16] Conrad's decision to use him as a means of ending a complex novel may be questionable, for Davidson's character is never developed at any length, and his mind is quite uncomplicated, devoid of abstract insight into the events which he witnesses. But perhaps the discrepancy between the philosophical and thematic implications of the tale Davidson relates and his own pedestrian understanding of his experiences is precisely what Conrad wishes to establish when he permits Davidson to preside over the final pages. It is entirely appropriate to the novel's ironic narrative mode, for instance, that Heyst's oft-cited "woe to" statement[17] be presented from a perspective of invincible dullness; and it is only by reading the work from a similar perceptual nadir that one can embrace Heyst's remark as conclusive support for a thematic content which supposedly lauds the success of Lena ". . . in extricating from Heyst at least a posthumous expression of his love. This is a victory, indeed. . . . She shakes Heyst out of his accustomed mold and almost reconciles him to the world."[18] If Lena has indeed caused Heyst to decide that detachment is wrong, his decision must be regarded simply as another sign of the degree to which he has strayed both from his father's prescribed way of life, and from the aloofness which is cited in the "Author's Note" as "the only faculty that seems to assimilate man to the immortal gods" (p. x). Apart from Heyst's inaccessible conscious understanding of his own meaning, however, the statement functions most significantly on a thematic level, for it is an echo semantically of the narrative voice's earlier assertion that acute perception, by permitting freedom from much illusion, causes a profound unhappiness; to be one of the "clear-sighted" is to be "unhappy in a way unknown to mediocre souls" (pp. 89, 88). Anyone who escapes the "blessed, warm mental fog" (p. 89) of hope, love, and "trust in life" (p. 383) is plagued by "woe"; but this clearly is not to say that such a mental state is necessarily detrimental. As he presents his summary of the destructive events on Samburan, Davidson's voice can remain "placid" because his superficial intellect has prevented him from being abstractly "unhappy in a way unknown to mediocre souls" (p. 88); and the simple man no doubt finds it difficult, consequently, to be troubled when, after all, there is " 'nothing to be done' " (p. 384) anyway.

Like the other characters in *Victory*, Davidson's behavior must be evaluated primarily in terms of the previously mentioned hierarchy of detachment and involvement, which ranks Old Heyst at the top; although we learn very little about Davidson as a complex entity, we are given sufficient information to understand him in these terms. He is the obese captain of the "Sissie" (compromising details, surely), a transport ship which puts in at island ports along the Java Sea approximately once a month. His occupation insures his physical remove from the human community, and also forces a certain psychological detachment, for he is employed by "a Chinese firm," and, since he only hauls foreigners, "he never had any sort of company on board" (p. 31). Davidson's aloofness is also prompted by his own very discreet personality, which prevents him from imposing upon others, and therefore keeps him from making acquaintances. As the narrator remarks, "He was the most delicate man that ever took a small steamer to and fro amongst the islands" (p. 50). Yet Davidson, like Heyst, is a very considerate, humane person, and Heyst is touched by the Captain's concern expressed by his monthly patrol of Heyst's island.

Although they are far different mental types, Davidson's manner of observation parallels that of the anonymous narrator, for both of them remain emotionally apart without totally detaching themselves physically from their society. The narrator's remove is static, however—he only gets interested in stories, which he passes on while offering ironic commentary. Davidson, on the other hand, because of his potentially destructive humane urges, moves from the isolation surrounding himself initially, to a dangerous involvement with Heyst, and back again to an essentially detached position after Heyst's death; thus, the character of Davidson, fluctuating between detachment and commitment, serves as a measure of both the ironic narrator and the tragically entrapped Heyst. Due to his discreet sympathy, Davidson is more conventionally admirable than the rather nasty speaker, but it is precisely due to this capacity for sympathy that Davidson is drawn ever deeper into the threatening situation developing around Heyst. This is why Davidson appears illogically at the moment of greatest threat on Samburan; his involvement with Heyst has led him through parallel paths to the same situation as Heyst's involvement with Morrison and Lena, and Davidson, too, must consequently risk death.

Because Davidson's commitment to Heyst is qualified by the Captain's exaggerated sense of delicacy, and because the masculine relationship does not involve the bewitching erotic potential that captivates Heyst, Davidson is able to disengage himself from the situation even when he witnesses the death of the individual whose welfare has come to be valuable to him, unlike Heyst, who destroys himself soon after Lena's demise. Davidson is redeemed from disastrous commitment by the chance annihilation of the persons with whom he would align himself, and he ends the novel with only renewed aloofness, the sole articulate survivor of the deadly confrontations on Samburan, presenting his tale in the form of an official report immaculate in its detached narrative.[19]

VII

The disparate modes of narrative perspective in *Victory* serve definite, though often highly specialized, aesthetic functions. Throughout the novel, by skillfully manipulating an inconsistent narrative technique which contains two human personalities and an omniscient narrative voice, Conrad establishes the bleak ontology in terms of which *Victory* must be read, and validates the detachment of the human narrators by causing their aloof positions to be congruent with that recommended by the narrative voice and Old Heyst. Moreover, the catastrophic events of the final pages confirm what the various points of view have implied throughout, that, indeed, "he who forms a tie is lost" (p. 188); and the novel ends with a futile human attempt to articulate negation which actually can be accomplished only "at the point where the final sentence dissolves into the blackness of the margin . . . in the silence which follows the last words"[20] as the narrative perspective utterly disintegrates.

Notes

1. *Conrad the Novelist* (Cambridge, Mass., 1958), pp. 273–274.

2. Guerard, p. 259.

3. *Joseph Conrad's Fiction* (Ithaca, N.Y., 1968), p. 183.

4. See, e.g., Morse Peckham, *Man's Rage for Chaos: Biology, Behavior, and the Arts* (Philadelphia, 1965), *Art and Pornography* (New York, 1969), and *The Triumph of Romanticism: Collected Essays by Morse Peckham* (Columbia, S.C., 1970); *Aspects of Narrative: Selected Papers from the English Institute*, ed. J. Hillis Miller (New York, 1971); William W. Bonney, "Semantic and Structural Indeterminacy in *The Nigger of the 'Narcissus'*: An Experiment in Reading," *ELH*, 40, 4 (Winter, 1973), 564–583.

5. See, e.g., Thomas Moser, *Joseph Conrad: Achievement and Decline* (Cambridge, Mass., 1957), p. 145; Guerard, p. 272; M. C. Bradbrook, *Joseph Conrad: Poland's English*

Genius (Cambridge, 1941), p. 67; Leo Gurko, *Joseph Conrad: Giant in Exile* (New York, 1962), p. 212.

6. One of Conrad's favorite analogues for the universe is a self perpetuating knitting machine; and "the most withering thought is that the infamous thing has made itself: made itself without thought, without conscience, without foresight, without eyes, without heart. It is a tragic accident, — and it has happened . . . and it is indestructible." In the same letter, Conrad goes on to state quite explicitly that the universe is devoid of morality and meaning: "It knits us in and it knits us out. It has knitted time, space, pain, death, corruption, despair and all the illusions, — and nothing matters" (Georges Jean-Aubry, *Joseph Conrad: Life and Letters* [Garden City, N.Y., 1927], I, 216).

7. Moser, p. 14.

8. *Poets of Reality* (Cambridge, Mass., 1965), p. 17.

9. In the words of E. W. Said, Conrad describes human experience by means of only two possible opposing psychological extremes: his "view of experience . . . allows *either* a surrender to chaos *or* a comparably frightful surrender to egoistic order. There is no middle way, and there is no other method of putting the issues" (*Joseph Conrad and the Fiction of Autobiography* [Cambridge, Mass., 1966], p. 13). As Conrad himself put it, "I am no slave to prejudices and formulas, and I never shall be. My attitude to subjects and expressions, the angles of vision, my methods of composition will, within limits, be always changing — not because I am unstable or unprincipled but because I am free" (*Life and Letters*, II, 204).

10. J. Hillis Miller, *Thomas Hardy: Distance and Desire* (Cambridge, Mass., 1970), p. 23.

11. P. x; all references to the text of *Victory* have been taken from the Modern Library edition (New York, 1921).

12. Lena's inadequacy is quite clearly emphasized by the narrative voice when it informs the reader that Lena is incapable of understanding or coping with the situation into which Heyst has led her: "She had no general conception of the conditions of the existence he had offered to her. Drawn into its peculiar stagnation she remained unrelated to it because of her ignorance" (p. 233).

13. See Bonney, "Joseph Conrad and the Discontinuous Point of View," *JNT*, II, ii (May, 1972), p. 102.

14. See Palmer, pp. 168–178.

15. *Ibid.*

16. See *The Great Tradition* (New York, 1948), p. 209.

17. Davidson reports that "practically the last words he [Heyst] said to me . . . were: 'Ah, Davidson, woe to the man whose heart has not learned while young to hope, to love — and to put its trust in life!' " (pp. 382–383).

18. Gurko, pp. 214–215.

19. James Joyce, of course, uses the same device of an official report in "A Painful Case," a story which is concerned with problems of human experience similar to those encountered in *Victory*.

20. Royal Roussel, *The Metaphysics of Darkness* (Baltimore, 1971), pp. 188–189.

Metafiction: The Double
Narration in *Under Western Eyes*   Penn R. Szittya*

Of the reflexive and often self-doubting qualities of contemporary art, Christopher Ricks has recently remarked that "A principled distrust of the imagination is nothing new. One triumph of the imagination is that it can be aware of the perils of the imagination, the aggrandizements, covert indulgences, and specious claims which it may incite. Great art is often about the limits of what we should hope for even from the greatest of art."[1] Joseph Conrad's distrust of imagination was perhaps less principled than insecure, but he was nonetheless aware of its perils and limits, as his letters amply testify. His art, however, the art of adventure on the Arabian Sea, of jungle horrors in the Congo, of political intrigue around the Golfo Placido, seems often to dwell on the surfaces of events and to turn but little toward itself, its artistic indulgences and specious claims. From few of Conrad's novels do the limits of imagination seem more remote than from *Under Western Eyes*, whose reputation as a political novel, perhaps Conrad's best, seems secure.[2] Its paramount concerns are with revolutionary politics and with what Conrad called the "mind" of Russia, together with the more personal and familiar themes of isolation and self-betrayal. Without denying the priority of any of these in *Under Western Eyes*, I want to focus attention on a neglected feature of its narrative form that makes the perils of fiction obliquely its concern as well and so gives artistic witness to the distrust of imagination evident on other grounds in Conrad's life. The novel is only covertly and obliquely about fiction, but its very obliqueness is an indication of the insecurity about fiction that informs it, and a sign of the paradoxical triumph of the imagination of which Ricks speaks.[3]

Like most first-person fictions, *Under Western Eyes* is in form a narrative masquerade, perpetrated by a novelist pretending to be a character, telling a "true" story he has invented. "To begin with," he says in the first sentence of the novel, "I wish to disclaim the possession of those high gifts of imagination and expression which would have enabled my pen to create for the reader [that is, to invent] the personality of the man who called himself, after the Russian custom, Cyril son of Isidor—Kirylo Sidorovitch—Razumov" (1).[4] In this pose as faithful if unimaginative historian, Conrad is writing in a familiar tradition. But there is an unusual feature of the novel's form which distinguishes it from most other novels and narrative masquerades, including Conrad's own: namely, that a masquerade or pose also happens to be its subject, in this case, Razumov's, whose betrayal of Haldin propels him into a fiction of his own identity. Furthermore, Conrad has so contrived the novel that the protagonist's mask reflects and calls attention to the author's, in such a way that

*Reprinted with permission from *English Literary History* 48 (1981):817–40.

the narration becomes mirrored in its own subject. These two kinds of concentric fictions, an outer and an inner, the novel and the hero's pose within it, are not precisely identical in either function or tone. Razumov's serious disguise derives from his spying mission in Geneva and is necessary to preserve his life. Conrad's disguise is comic, part of the artistic game played between author and reader in all fiction. But the language of the novel, with its insistent characterization of Razumov as a writer, for example, suggests that the two fictions are analogous in ways that defy their differences. Author and hero each pretends to be someone he is not; each undermines his pretense by flaunting his masquerade; each consequently speaks a language which is predominantly ironic; each because of his mask poses hermeneutic difficulties for the characters or for the reader who reads about them. If *Under Western Eyes* is a novel of concentric fictions, its subject embraces more than the shadowy politics of the East. The novel is what Robert Scholes has called in another context metafiction — fiction about fiction, and especially about itself.[5] Its concerns are with the sufficiency of fictions as bases for life; with the possibility of interpretation; and ultimately with the insecurity of the novelist's work, which as Conrad was uneasily aware, was to live, even while he wrote about the truth, within an invented world.

As the major theme of the novel is duplicity, the characteristic feature of its construction is doubleness or duplication. Razumov's masquerade fractures him into a double man who speaks in two voices: one to the revolutionaries, one to himself; a voice that comes to us through what the language teacher heard, a voice from Razumov's diary. Our information about Razumov then manifests itself in a double narration, by the language teacher on the one hand, by Razumov on the other. This is the most important of several doublings which give the novel its texture. Hence it is not accidental that the novel is filled with images of doubling: mirrors, masks, shadows, echoes, phantoms. Events, places, people unsettlingly recur: the dark mist of Geneva reduplicates the dark snowstorm of St. Petersburg; Natalia reincarnates Haldin; the beating of Ziemianitch is atoned for in the beating of Razumov; Razumov's confrontation with snow-covered Russia — "sullen and tragic mother" (26) — is recapitulated in another with Mother Haldin, "silent, quiet, white-haired figure of sorrow" (287); Haldin's prostrate form on Razumov's bed, hands over his eyes, reappears as the phantom in the snow and then as Razumov himself, "lying here like that man" (18, 29, 58); Haldin's pale figure drawn asunder on the rack becomes an image of Razumov's suffering brain (73); the events of the fateful day opening the novel are replayed in a compulsive ritual in which Razumov takes Haldin's part (253–54); and in a similar ritual, the night of the confession plays out again the night of the betrayal, as "the facts and the words of a certain evening in his past were timing his [Razumov's] conduct in the present" (305). Doubleness, duplication, duplicity are the signatures in the novel's genetic code.[6]

One doubling is particularly important because it affects the narration: Razumov is a double of the first person narrator. Psychologically this seems unlikely because their differences are so striking: age as against youth; a rationalist as against a mystic tendency; Western as opposed to Eastern eyes; a predisposition toward outward as against inward analysis. And yet Conrad subtly and insistently suggests an affinity between them throughout the novel. The narrator is conspicuously the only Englishman in a novel otherwise populated by Russians, but early in the book Razumov's mysterious reserve is strangely described as "frigid English manner" (12) and Haldin calls him "a regular Englishman" (16). The narrator's reserve, like Razumov's, "inspires confidence" and results in his close alliance with Natalia Haldin. Both men are bachelors, solitaries, seemingly without kin or "anyone to turn to." One is a professor; the other wants to be a "celebrated old professor" (10). Both are political moderates, ultimately sympathetic with neither autocracy nor revolution. These superficial similarities seem to be signposts for a deeper psychological affinity.[7] That he retells the story is itself an indication that the language teacher is obsessed with Razumov, even while he tries to distance himself from him at every unsettling turn in the narrative. Unwittingly Razumov is to the narrator what Haldin is to Razumov: a frightening figure who seems to correspond to a side of himself that he has been unwilling or unable to recognize, let alone understand. Such narrator-hero doubling is not unusual in Conrad's first person narratives, notably "Heart of Darkness" (Marlow-Kurtz), *Lord Jim* (Marlow-Lord Jim), and "The Secret Sharer" (the captain-Leggatt). Indeed it is common in first-person narratives generally, as recently pointed out by Thomas F. Walsh: "almost any story which seems to be 'about' one character (as the title often suggests) and is narrated by another character is a story of the double in which the subject character is the double of the narrator."[8] Examples might include Melville's "Bartleby the Scrivener," Poe's "William Wilson," Nabokov's *Lolita*, or Hesse's *Demian*.

Razumov, however, is the narrator's double in another, less psychological sense which is lacking in Conrad's other first-person narrations. He is the narrator's literary double, that is, he duplicates some of the latter's literary functions in the story. Both are writers, the one ostensibly of the novel itself, the other of the diary which is (ostensibly) the novel's main source; both are narrators; both are ultimately figures of the novelist in general and, as I will try to demonstrate at the end of the essay, of Conrad in particular. This narrator-hero duplication is all the more striking because Razumov is not a writer by profession, but Conrad nevertheless takes pains to associate him with writing throughout the novel.[9] Razumov is "a man who had read, thought, lived, pen in hand" (301). At the beginning of the novel, his greatest desire is to achieve success and recognition through writing, and all his obsessions are focused on the essay which will win him the Silver Medal. When Haldin enters Razumov's room, he destroys all opportunity that the essay might have opened for him. After Haldin departs to certain death and the clock strikes its explosive "One!" Razumov drags himself to a table and sits down to write as before. But he finds he cannot take up life, or writing, where he left off. As if to signify, even his handwriting is changed:

> He took a pen brusquely and dipped it with a vague notion of going on with the writing of his essay — but his pen remained poised over the sheet. It hung there for some time before it came down and formed long scrawly letters.
>
> Still-faced and his lips set hard, Razumov began to write. When he wrote a large hand his neat writing lost its character altogether — became unsteady, almost childish. He wrote five lines one under the other.

The five lines turn out to be his "political confession of faith" (82) and are the first indication that writing will henceforward serve as a vehicle not to success but to a new and as yet uncertain identity. During the next days, as we learn later, Razumov isolates himself in his room and writes furiously, obsessively, from early morning till far in the night, for nearly a week (253). Just what he is writing we are never told, but we can be sure that this is the period during which the diary is begun (see p. 72), and comes to replace the Silver Medal essay as Razumov's primary written occupation. The diary is a symbolic counterpoint to the essay: one is public, the other private; Haldin destroys the writing of the one, but generates the writing of the other; the first was to have been the key to material success, the other becomes the key to spiritual truth.[10] And most important this writing is a vehicle by which Razumov comes to understand himself; and when he does, he can at last address his self-confession to someone else — Natalia — and makes his confession public at Laspara's. When he finishes the diary, Razumov flings his pen away into a distant corner (305). His writing is at an end, as he says to Laspara just before his public revelation: "I have written already all I shall ever write" (307). Thus the terminal points of Razumov's career in the novel, and symbolically his understanding of himself, are defined by the act of writing.

But Razumov is more than just a writer; he is also a narrator. *Under Western Eyes* actually consists of two narrations, one contained by the other. One is the novel as a whole, told by the old language teacher, and the other is Razumov's diary, which is quoted at length within the primary narration as an authoritative document that helps to explain the strangeness of unfolding events. Novel and diary share some conspicuous features. Both are personal records; both tell the same story, though diversely refracted through Eastern or Western eyes; both are first person narrations. Hence as the diary is quoted and molded into the tale, Razumov becomes a narrator in his own right, the voice for the inner story as the language teacher is for the outer. This narrative doubling gives to *Under*

Western Eyes a schizoid character, in effect dividing the reader between two narrators, two stories, two points of view, two chronologies, two styles.

It will be pertinent to my later discussion of Conrad himself that this narrative doubling was a relatively late development in the progress of the novel and seemed to help resolve an impasse in the writing. From Conrad's letter to Galsworthy on 6 January 1908, we know that the novel was first conceived as a short story whose title was to be *Razumov*.[11] But before Conrad finished — twenty-five months later — it had grown into a full scale novel with two entirely new sections (II and III) and a somewhat different ending. For the most part, however, the plot remained as outlined to Galsworthy. The crucial addition was the new narrator, who changed dramatically the thrust of the story, as the new title signified: no longer *Razumov*, but *Under Western Eyes*. Razumov was displaced not only in the title but in the narrative, which now became, involutedly, not Razumov's story, but the language teacher's story of Razumov's story: a diary of a diary.

This displacement of the original narration has several literary advantages which are apparent on every page: aesthetic distance; a concomitant decrease in the intensity of the story; a necessarily more meditative reader; complex doubling in point of view, with two perspectives juxtaposed and commenting upon each other silently, dialectically, ironically.[12] However, in the Author's Note added in 1920 Conrad claimed the chief advantage of the new narrator was validation of the narrative. As an eyewitness and as the custodian of Razumov's diary, he provided a credible occasion for the telling of the story. Thus says Conrad: "In my desire to produce the effect of actuality it seemed to me indispensible to have an eyewitness of the transactions in Geneva," (ix). Despite this retrospective claim, it seems to me that the major effect of this particular narrator is authorial retreat: from direct involvement with the hero and his suffering; from revealing too much of himself in his story; from taking a clear position in judgment or in sympathy toward his hero. Conrad takes refuge behind the comic and ill-fitting mask of the old language teacher, whose judgments (as we can see from Razumov's diary) are often wrong and whose most consistent attitude toward his story is incomprehension: "I have no comprehension of the Russian character" (2); "what sort of peace Kirylo Sidorovitch Razumov expected to find in the writing up of his record it passeth my understanding to guess" (3); "I suppose one must be a Russian to understand Russian simplicity" (88); "her sayings seemed always to me to have enigmatical prolongations vanishing somewhere beyond my reach" (99); "vague they [Razumov's words] were to my Western mind and to my Western sentiment . . . once more I had the sense of being out of it . . . on another plane whence I could only watch her from afar" (143); "this story too I received without comment in my character of a mute witness of things Russian, unrolling their Eastern logic under my Western eyes" (321).

At the end of this essay I want to explore the psychological dimension of Conrad's retreat behind this mask of incomprehension. But there is an aesthetic dimension as well. Every reader, even if he knows little about Conrad, readily perceives that the narrator is not the author as he claims but rather a mask through which the author speaks. The art of the narrative itself belies the narrator's authorial claims, because it reveals the presence of an author who is everything the narrator denies about himself: artist, contriver, verbal craftsman, serious man of imagination, constructing out of the inventions of his own brain the tapestry of Razumov's life.

> In the conduct of an invented story there are, no doubt, certain proprieties to be observed for the sake of clearness and effect. A man of imagination, however inexperienced in the art of narrative, has his instinct to guide him in the choice of his words, and in the development of the action. A grain of talent excuses many mistakes. But this is not a work of the imagination; I have no talent; my excuse for this undertaking lies not in its art, but in its artlessness. Aware of my limitations and strong in the sincerity of my purpose, I would not try (were I able) to invent anything. I push my scruples so far that I would not even invent a transition.   (84)

Transitions aside, this passage can hardly fail to evoke a smile from the reader, aroused partly by the narrator's gratuitous nervousness that he might be thought to have invented his story, or worse yet, to be a novelist. But the reader is of course reminded by these very words that he reads them within a novel whose prominent inventions include the narrator himself. The old language teacher is a patent masquerade by an author pretending loudly to be someone he is not. All novels, especially naive first-person narrations, are masquerades or counterfeits in this sense, but *Under Western Eyes* pushes the masquerade into the foreground more insistently than most by all sorts of techniques of language like irony or reflexive reference to itself: by the narrator's denials of any sort of art or contrivance at some of the most artistic and contrived points in the narration; by his insistence on the historicity of all his knowledge (witness his comments on Madame de S— — above) in juxtaposition with his possession of knowledge he could not possibly have acquired (the scene in which Razumov is injured by the trolley) as well as his sympathetic entry into the minds of certain of his characters; by his contrived vacillation between an omniscient and a limited point of view; and most of all by the novel's repeated claims, in various voices, not to be a fiction. Razumov, for example, once says testily: "I am not a young man in a novel" (156). Such statements are short circuits: they explode the circle of illusion because they remind us precisely that the young man *is* in a novel. They expose the authorial masquerade of telling a true story, just as the narrator's repeated claims that he is not a novelist expose the novelist behind him.

Razumov then is a double of the narrator in a more complicated sense, which must take in the author. Not only does he duplicate some of the narrator's literary functions as writer and as narrator of his own story, but his own masking in certain limited ways is a pattern of the masking of the author as narrator. Both the hero masquerading as a revolutionary and the author masquerading as the old language teacher are schizoid figures, duplicitous in the etymological as well as the received sense of the word. Behind the face and voice which Razumov presents to the Geneva circle, behind the voice they think is that of a political idealist, a heavy-hearted intimate of the martyr, Haldin, the reader is privileged to hear that other inner voice in which Razumov curses Haldin, writhes in his guilt, fends off phantoms, struggles in a vortex of hate and despair. The author's doubleness in the novel is ostensibly playful, part of the game of fiction, but like Razumov he speaks to the reader in two voices: a public one, noisy and slightly tedious, the one we hear almost constantly, which comes from the old language teacher; and a private one, mysterious and quiet, which we may suppose is Conrad's own, which can speak to us only through the language teacher but manages through contrivance to communicate judgments quite different in tenor and tone. Thus the hero's duplicity, his doubleness, is a paradigm of the author's.

Both duplicities are insecure; the mask threatens to slip aside, the circle of illusion to be broken. The fragility of their masquerades occasions the dominant tone of their speech and hence of the novel: irony. Irony, indeed, is the tonal correlative of structural doubleness and verbal duplicity: double talk. Razumov's sometimes crazy double talk reveals his increasing inability to bear the tension between what he appears to be (Haldin's disciple) and what he knows he is (a Judas). His ironic utterances explode that tension and become a compulsive form of release. Indeed the compulsion is so strong that irony often comes palpably close to madness, and threatens to strip away his disguise. Dark allusions to his betrayal of Haldin slip from him involuntarily, sometimes hysterically, as in this bit of nervous babble to Haldin himself, who is the man he alludes to in the last sentence:

> "The most unlikely things have a secret power over one's thoughts—the grey whiskers of a particular person [Prince K— —]—, the goggle eyes of another [General T— —]."
> Razumov's forehead was moist. He took a turn or two in the room, his head low and smiling to himself viciously.
> "Have you ever reflected on the power of goggle eyes and grey whiskers? Excuse me. You seem to think I must be crazy to talk in this vein at such a time. But I am not talking lightly. I have seen instances. It has happened to me once to be talking to a man whose fate was affected by physical facts of that kind. And the man did not know it."   (49)

Or as in this to Madame de S— —, who claims she can see into Razumov's soul: " 'What is it you see? Anything resembling me? . . . Some sort of phantom in my image? . . . For I suppose, a soul when it is seen is just that. A vain thing. There are phantoms of the living as well as of the dead. . . . I myself have had an experience,' he stammered out, as if compelled. 'I've seen a phantom once.' " (189). Or this to Peter Ivanovitch, who thinks Razumov has been sent to him by revolutionists: " 'What else has drawn me near you, do you think? It is not what all the world knows of you surely. It's precisely what the world at large does not know. I was irresistibly drawn—let us say impelled, yes, impelled; or, rather, compelled, driven—driven,' repeated Razumov loudly, and ceased, as if startled by the hollow reverberations of the word 'driven' along two bare corridors and in the great empty hall" (192). Or to Natalia, who says to him:

> "I can at any rate, thank you for not dismissing me from your mind as a weak, emotional girl. No doubt I want sustaining. I am very ignorant. But I can be trusted. Indeed I can!"
> "You are ignorant," he repeated thoughtfully.   (152)

Or to the narrator, who queries him as to whether he might not have something consoling to report to the Haldin ladies:

> The twitching of his lips before he spoke was curious.
> "What if it is not worth telling?"
> "Not worth—from what point of view? I don't understand."
> "From every point of view."   (161)

All of these utterances are full of double and hidden meanings which echo like the word "driven" down the corridors of the novel: phantom, ignorant, not worth telling, instances, the man whose fate was affected by goggle eyes and grey whiskers. There are contradictory impulses in most of them: self-incrimination, guilt, the compulsion to confess and so be absolved on the one hand; on the other a note of scornful mockery—"the man did not know it"—toward those who naively believe fictions about him and cannot sense the truth. Razumov thus flaunts his fiction but simultaneously wants it shattered. The insecurity of his masquerade reflects the uncertainty of his conception of himself.

If Razumov's ironic speech threatens to explode his mask—the short circuit again—authorial irony does so no less to the author's mask, although in a more playful mood: "Wonder may be expressed at a man in the position of a teacher of languages knowing all this with such definiteness. A novelist says this and that of his personages, and if only he knows how to say it earnestly enough he may not be questioned upon the inventions of his own brain in which his own belief is made sufficiently manifest by a telling phrase, a poetic image, the accent of emotion. Art is great! But I have no art, and not having invented Madame de S— —, I feel bound to explain how I came to know so much about her" (156). The very first sentence of the novel, in fact, initiates this mode of authorial double talk:

> To begin with I wish to disclaim the possession of those high gifts of imagination and expression which would have enabled my pen to create for the reader the personality of the man who called himself, after the Russian custom, Cyril son of Isidor—Kirylo Sidorovitch—Razumov. . . . I could not have observed Mr. Razumov or guessed at his reality by the force of insight, much less have imagined him as he was. Even to invent the mere bald facts of his life would have been utterly beyond my powers. But I think that without this declaration the readers of these pages will be able to detect in the story the marks of documentary evidence. And that is perfectly correct. It is based on a document; all I have brought to it is my knowledge of the Russian language, which is sufficient for what is attempted here.   (1)

"I have no art"; "not having invented Madame de S— —"; "could not have guessed"; "much less have imagined"; "even to invent"; "based on a document": these are the correlatives of Razumov's ironic "driven," "ignorant," "phantom." The irony is of course the author's, not the narrator's, and its effect depends, like Razumov's, upon a secret which the reader shares to the exclusion of other characters in the story. Like the hero, the author seems to be laughing at his mask. Although his mood is more comic, his laughter suggests, like Razumov's nervous laugh, that it would be even more laughable if anyone actually believed in the masquerade.

There is something else that they share. In many of the narrator's comments about his narration, where authorial irony appears most clearly, there is an undercurrent of suspicion and doubt about fiction itself. The language teacher ostensibly praises art ("art is great!") but his language here and elsewhere reveals a profound distrust of imagination. A novelist, he says, concocts "inventions of his own brain" which he can pass off if he writes "earnestly enough," with a "telling phrase, a poetic image, the accent of emotion." Imagination and art the narrator sets in opposition to truth and sincerity. He says he has no art because he has no talent, but one tends to think that he really feels he needs no art because his story is true. Art for him is contrivance; writing the manipulation of words; words "the foes of reality" (1). Hence his unflattering consignment of the childish and the crude to works of the imagination: "All ideas of political plots and conspiracies seem childish, crude inventions for the theatre or novel" (92). The same disparagement appears in Razumov's angry "I am not a young man in a novel" (156), which in its context is a way of denying that he is a foolish romantic. How are we to interpret this self-conscious skepticism about fiction? Perhaps it is merely an insider's joke between author and reader. After all, the characters may distrust fictions all they like, but they are *in* one, as Conrad implicitly reminds us every time they mention novels. And yet, this is a novelist who says he felt it necessary, in order to achieve the "effect of actuality," to disguise his novel as a documentary history, a "true story." And a similar skepticism about fiction, though fiction in life rather than in books, pervades the diary of the hero of the novel: that fictions — in his case, of identity — may be a deluding and hence dangerous way to try to gain control over the vicissitudes of life.

The parallels so far developed between author and hero — as writers, as narrators, as masters of double talk, as simultaneous creators and destroyers of obscuring masks, as skeptical makers of fictions they doubt — all suggest that Razumov may be an oblique figure of the novelist. The obliqueness of the figuration needs to be stressed, because there are obvious differences between a man narrating a novel and one living a life under an assumed identity. For Conrad, however, the distance between them is not as great as it might seem, insofar as he felt his own life as an English novelist, as a man "without country and language," to be a life lived under an assumed identity, masking a real Conrad, a Slav, an adventurer, who had been abandoned — betrayed, said some of his fellow Poles — some years back.[13] There are in fact many similarities between Conrad and Razumov, as there are between Conrad and the other writer in the story, the old language teacher who serves as his narrative mask. The refraction of Conrad into these two writers and narrators is the subject of the final section of this paper and need not be dwelt on here. But the close relationship between Conrad and Razumov suggests that Razumov's life, among the other things it shows, reveals in shadow some of the paradoxes and insecurities of the novelist's life, particularly of a novelist named Joseph Conrad. Indeed his story can be read on one level as a parable of the dangers of fiction. With the arrival of "crazy fate" in the form of Haldin's shadowy figure in his room, Razumov's life disintegrates into chaos, his freedom lost, his hopes, plans, daily life thrown into uncertainty and fear. To regain some control he creates a mask to live out a fiction, a fiction which in some measure enables him to avenge himself upon the forces of chaos. Fiction is his response to his destiny; it is his defiance of determinism. Razumov's plight is in that respect like that described in John Barth's metafiction, "Lost in the Funhouse": a frightened boy who is "lost in a funhouse," a figure of the artist trapped in life, regains control by *imagining* himself in a funhouse.[14] Likewise Razumov, whose life is thrown into chaos when he is thought by all sorts of people to be a revolutionary, restores his equilibrium by pretending to be a revolutionary. By creating a fiction to live in, he regains control over the world which he had lost — but at the same time nearly loses himself. To his horror he comes to recognize that the mask makes him into a phantom like the man he had betrayed, unreal not only to the world but also to himself. Living within a fiction of identity makes him into a moral cripple, unable to experience human pleasures, debilitated, weak, deaf to the voices of truth and love, and so he ends his story by casting off the mask and confessing. He recovers himself, but because chaos (in the form of the man nicknamed "Necator") descends on him again, he ends physically weak, deaf, crippled—an emblem not just of the dangers of counterrevolutionary espionage but of the peril of living in a fiction that is not true to oneself.

Hence the pervasive aura of unreality and unstable illusion that envelops Razumov's developing fiction like a mist. As his fiction begins, with his simulated flight from Russia and the charade of receiving help from madcap Kostia, Razumov thinks "it was like a game of make-believe" (265). Or "it's a dream . . . nobody does such things." The whole trip out of Russia is described as like a dream, in which Razumov watches himself with extreme attention, a dream "wearing one into harsh laughter, to fury, to death—with the fear of awakening at the end" (266). The dream is not only the fiction into which Razumov enters here but an emblem of life itself. "Perhaps life is just that," reflects Razumov, "a dream and a fear [of waking]" (266). Razumov's life, the novel's life, our own life—all these, Conrad suggests, are in varying degrees, make-believe. That is why fiction, and especially fiction about fiction, can speak to us at all.

What it bespeaks, what it "means," is another matter. All these doublings I have been speaking of—the double fictions, the double talk of irony, the double narration and double narrators, even the psychological doubles connected with the hero—pose unusual difficulties for interpreting the novel. This is so not only because of the contradiction and ambiguity we might expect, but also because in such a novel the act of interpretation always doubles back upon itself.

If the novel is about fiction, it is also about interpretation. Everyone who comes into contact with Razumov has to struggle with the difficulty of interpreting him and almost everyone fails: Haldin, Natalia, all of the revolutionists, Mikulin, and most important, the narrator himself. Those who believe in him as a counterrevolutionary spy find their interpretation insufficiently complex. The novel is consequently suffused with the language of interpretive failure—the mysterious, imperceptible, inconceivable, incomprehensible, mystical, strange, dark, obscure. Indeed Conrad's sense of reality in all his writings seems heavily involved with our inability to understand: "The part of the inexplicable," he says of himself, but the remark could apply equally well to Razumov, "should be allowed for in appraising the conduct of men in a world where no explanation is final."[15] And misinterpretations are not confined to the subject of Razumov alone: the revolutionists misconstrue Ziemianitch's death, Madame de S——'s intentions concerning her fortune, Nikita's allegiances, Peter Ivanovitch's capacity for simple love. The narrator, who in Geneva produced some of the most remarkable misinterpretations of Razumov—as Razumov is about to wrench forth his tortured confession to Natalia in the anteroom, the narrator anticipates a love scene—this same narrator stands before us now and confesses himself frankly baffled by the whole bizarre and, to him, "foreign" affair. The novel is a chronicle of interpretive failures; its epigraph might well be Razumov's complaint to Mikulin, "I begin to think there is something about me which people don't seem to be able to make out" (81).

Swept into this widening circle of interpretive failure, we find, of course, ourselves, the readers. We find in fact images of ourselves reading, failing, throughout the novel, chiefly in the verbose, prosaic form of the narrator, who attempts to be "critic" and interpreter of his document, attempts but fails to evolve a hermeneutics that can explain the mystery that is embodied in the pages of Razumov's diary. That the narrator is in some measure a comic image of the reader is perhaps hinted in the title, whose Western eyes belong to the squinting narrator, but also to the Western, and especially English, reader of this English novel. The title too confirms that for Conrad the central concern of the book was not the story of Razumov, but the interpretation of the story of Razumov; or what one might call the story of the story of Razumov. The plot is only apparently the center of interest; there is another "plot" in the dramatic relationship between author and reader through the medium of the narration. In *Under Western Eyes*, the duplicity of the medium itself is the message.

If so, the problem of interpretation in the novel is also the solution. Several years ago in an essay entitled "Metacommentary," Fredric Jameson observed: "In matters of art, and particularly of artistic perception . . . it is wrong to want to *decide*, to want to *resolve* a difficulty: what is wanted is a kind of mental procedure which suddenly shifts gears, which throws everything in an inextricable tangle one floor higher, and turns the very problem itself (the obscurity of this sentence) into its own solution (the varieties of Obscurity) by widening its frame in such a way that it now takes in its own mental processes as well as the object of those processes."[16] This seems to be precisely what happened when Conrad widened his frame from *Razumov* to *Under Western Eyes* and so created a fiction about a fiction. It is also what happens perforce to a reader who recognizes the metafictive circuit in the novel. If the novel is about itself, we cannot interpret it without watching ourselves in the act of interpretation. And what we see in the characters is what we see in ourselves seeing them: that is, the difficulty of interpreting a fiction, a falsehood that is also true. That is among the highest "meanings" the novel conveys: not a message but an experience of baffling duplicity and duality in the medium itself.[17] This is not at all to say the novel is meaningless. Our experience in reading is, we recognize from its reflection in the novel, a metaphor for what we experience in life. Razumov's story is of the difficult, ambiguous, and sometimes dangerous relationship between fiction and reality, between the true and the imagined, between a vision and a waking dream. His problem, and that of his peers, is the problem of interpretation: "How can you tell truth from lies?" (158). What do we know? On what basis do we act? Where does fiction end? And these are also the problems of reader and artist, especially in the modern world.

The problems of fiction and interpretation existed as much in Conrad's life as in his books. Although I have so far tried to avoid discussing Conrad personally, one can hardly speak of Razumov as an oblique figure of the novelist without speaking of Joseph Conrad, who resembles his hero in certain psychological qualities as well as in aesthetic function. Their mutual obsessions with identity and their roles as writers are closely allied. Hence it is possible by way of conclusion, to reinforce on psychological grounds the argument made so far on artistic grounds, that on one level this fiction is involved with the problems of fiction.

Like many of his major novels after 1898, *Under Western Eyes* gave Conrad immense difficulties in the writing. Its composition covered an unusually long period—from December of 1907 until January of 1910— especially prolonged for a man who wrote for an income and whose family needed money desperately at the time. Both his young son Borys and the baby had been violently ill, and Borys almost died near the time Conrad began the story; Jessie Conrad was virtually crippled by her leg; Conrad himself had painful gout intermittently all during the writing of the novel.[18] His letters of this period are filled with depression and despair at the crazy fate which like Razumov's had appeared in his room: "All this is ghastly. I seem to move, talk, write in a sort of quiet nightmare that goes on and on."[19]

The prolonged nightmare, especially the gout, made it extremely difficult for him to write, and he began to doubt his own capacities. His letters speak of "a lump of slack mud" in his head, of ill-omened doubts that are fatal for an imaginative man, of his "clogged pen," of horror and dread, horrible depression, sheer despair of ever writing a line.[20] That he had turned fifty in 1908 only exacerbated his feeling of incapacity. The problems Conrad had with *Under Western Eyes*, however, were not solely due to the bleak reality that surrounded him. Reading the letters one senses that there was something mysteriously problematic about the novel itself, as there had been with several earlier novels, that made it so difficult for him to write. The subject, he confesses, had long "haunted" him, but he is unable to write it; it is "a bone sticking in my gizzard," keeping him in agonies.[21] Writing the novel is "like working in Hell."[22] Most intriguing of all are circumstances surrounding the completion of the novel. Finishing was apparently quite a triumph, if the small celebration at the end of the manuscript is any indication: "End," wrote Conrad with a flourish, "22 Jan. 1910. J.C." But he had no sooner flung away the pen than he became seriously ill—partly with gout but also with what Jesse Conrad characterized in a letter as "a complete nervous breakdown" which lasted for almost four months. Meanwhile, she said, the manuscript, which was due for revisions and then printing in book form, "lays at his foot of his bed and he lives mixed up in scenes and holds converse with the characters."[23] In May he was almost well, but finishing the revision again put him on his back: "For the next 24 hours I lay supine but not so broken up as I feared."[24] So ended Conrad's long struggle with *Under Western Eyes*.

To students of Conrad's other works, these agonies are not unfamiliar. The same anxieties and doubts couched in a similar language of nightmare can be found during the periods Conrad was working on *Lord Jim* (1898–1900), *Nostromo* (1902–1904), *The Secret Agent* (1905–1907), and especially *The Rescue*, ironically titled, which threatened to take Conrad under whenever he returned to the writing of it from 1898 until practically the end of his life. Conrad's best work seemed to come on the brink of breakdown, mental, physical, and financial; indeed Frederick Karl suggests that such chaos was necessary to, or at least closely connected with, the working of his literary imagination.[25] Why this should be so is at heart a personal and creative mystery; but it seems clear from studies of Conrad over the last fifty years that a major source of difficulty with many of the novels was that they were in an oblique way about himself, and less about his historical self than about his tortured and dimly understood emotional life. Conrad in a famous passage put it aptly, perhaps better than he knew: "I know that a novelist lives in his work. He stands there, the only reality in an invented world, among imaginary things, happenings, and people. Writing about them, he is only writing about himself. But the disclosure is not complete. He remains to a certain extent, a figure behind the veil; a suspected rather than a seen presence — a movement and a voice behind the draperies of fiction."[26]

Writing about the invented world of *Under Western Eyes*, with its double narration and conflicting points of view, Conrad was at least in part writing about himself behind the veil of fiction. As is now well-known, he was a man of violently contradictory history and temperament. There was on the one hand the Josef Teodor Konrad Korzeniowski of the past, born in Russian-occupied Poland, a man of ardent Slavic temperament and loyalties; and on the other, the Joseph Conrad of the present, English citizen, reserved in demeanor, political moderate, family man, spokesman of order. There had been the young sailor, explorer, exotic adventurer, passionate man of action; now there was the mature writer, the contemplative, the intellectual, brooding from his vantage point of the present upon those utterly different experiences of the past. Conrad called himself "homo duplex," as first sailor and then author, leading "a double life, one of them peopled only by shadows growing more precious as the years pass."[27]

Conrad took up his "double life" of writing because (among other reasons) he felt a need to rescue his earlier experiences (and perhaps himself) from chaos and the oblivion of time. But ironically, self-conscious fiction only made him discover and objectify a deeper, more frightening chaos in himself. He speaks of it over and over in his letters, nowhere so grimly as in this from 1899: "The fright is growing on me. My fortitude is shaken by the view of the monster. It does not move; its eyes are baleful; it is as still as death itself — and it will devour me. Its state has eaten into my soul already deep, deep. I am alone with it in a chasm with perpendicular sides of black basalt. Never were sides so perpendicular and smooth, and high."[28] Readers of Conrad's early work can recognize that same darkness in the novels themselves. But Edward Said argues convincingly in his *Joseph Conrad and the Fiction of Autobiography* that Conrad did not want it thought by the reading public that such monsters, frights, chasms were part of his own experience.[29] After a few literary successes and a modest reputation, he began — around 1903, according to Said — to construct an elaborate public *persona*, a contrived identity for public consumption which differed markedly from the despairing, uncertain, sometimes terrified Conrad one finds in the letters. This *persona* pops up in prefaces, in letters to strangers and businessmen, in the somewhat autobiographical *Mirror of the Sea*, but most important for my purpose, in *A Personal Record*, which was written in 1908 and 1909 in between Conrad's fitful attempts at *Under Western Eyes*. *A Personal Record* claims to be autobiography but is almost frank in its fictional aim, the construction of a satisfactory *persona*: "[These reminiscences] have their hope and their aim. The hope that from the reading of these pages there may emerge at last the vision of a personality; the man behind the books so fundamentally dissimilar as, for instance, "Almayer's Folly" and "The Secret Agent," and yet a coherent, justifiable personality both in its origin and in its action. This is the hope."[30] Thus the publically expressed hope is to reconcile for a confused public the seemingly conflicting interests and personal traits of a *homo duplex*, sailor and writer, adventurer and intellectual. But the effect was to help create another kind of *homo duplex*, a public and private Conrad. The public man was in large part facade, camouflage for the incertitude of the private man. It was a pose, of the rationalist, optimist, adventurer, and romantic idealist mellowing with dignity as he approached fifty — a composed man. The public Conrad was a spokesman of light rather than darkness; he cast his allegiance with Marlow rather than Kurtz, with language teachers rather than spies.

To a reader unfamiliar with Conrad's habitual ways of working, it is startling to realize that *A Personal Record*, the cornerstone in the architecture of this new *persona*, with its calm retrospective examination of the emergence of the English writer from the Polish sailor, was written precisely in the midst of what Conrad called the "nightmare" of the composition of *Under Western Eyes*, in 1908 and 1909. It is startling not only because of the almost schizophrenic difference between the light self-portrait of the *Record* and the dark one of the private letters of the same period, but also because that "schizophrenia" is precisely what appears in *Under Western Eyes* with its two narrators, two voices, two points of view. The language of Conrad's private letters about himself — the language of nightmares, fatality, dread, portents, agonies, phantoms, Hell — is the language of Razumov. The language of Conrad's public *persona* — of the right word, of truth of a modest sort, of sincerity, of piety, of serenity and resignation — is the language of his narrator, the teacher of languages.

One notices other faintly recognizable similarities between Conrad and his two narrators. The narrator like Conrad in 1908 is in his fifties; is an Englishman in a foreign land; speaks many languages; makes his living from words, and distrusts their ability to convey reality. Likewise, as many critics have noticed, there is a great deal of Conrad in Razumov: the Slav with English characteristics; the vulnerable solitary; the young man without parentage (Conrad was orphaned at eleven); the political moderate, cynical about both autocracy and revolution; the patriot; a man accused of betrayal.[31] We might seek out with some success other echoes of the historical Conrad in his two narrators. However, to demonstrate a historical resemblance is not my purpose here. The point is rather structural: that the artistic dialectic of the two narrators is of the same nature as the dialectic within Conrad himself between a public *persona* and a private self. Psychologists call this phenomenon decomposition, or doubling, when a mind gives an internal conflict form by projecting it into an embodied dramatic conflict which may appear in dreams, or in hallucinations, or psychoses.[32] This is not to say that the novel is about Conrad himself, nor that Razumov and the narrator are, or even represent, Conrad, as if personality were a static object that could be objectified. Rather the energies that characterize the novel characterize the man; the aesthetic double structure I have been describing throughout this paper is an image and a product of a doubleness in Conrad's own life and mind.

This pattern of conflict between the public and the private Conrad has recently been traced by Edward Said in *Nostromo*, a novel that anticipates a great deal in *Under Western Eyes*.[33] Its hero's double life, with his attempt to author a public version of his history, says Said, reflects the author's. The personal and artistic crisis Conrad had reached by 1903 has its analogue in the historical crisis in Costaguana; the new Conrad that emerged, publicly replacing the tortured figure of the preceding twelve years, is mirrored in the "new" Nostromo, who is successful because of Decoud's timely death, which recapitulates the suppression of the private Conrad. These smiling public men, Conrad and his Nostromo, both achieve a new identity based on deliberate fraud, which the novel implicitly condemns. Separated by only four years, *Nostromo* (finished 1904) and *Under Western Eyes* (begun 1908) are shaped by similar conflicts of public and private selves. *Under Western Eyes*, however, is significantly closer to radically self-conscious novels like Gide's *Les faux monnayeurs*, largely because of narrative features that *Nostromo* lacks: double and concentric narrations, both in the first person, both by figures who are masquerading as someone else and whose parallels are emphasized repeatedly when the reader is reminded that their masks are false, their authority therefore suspect. Whereas the relationship between Nostromo and Conrad is psychological and outside the text, the relationship between Razumov and Conrad is both without and within, both psychological and aesthetic. Razumov is, like Nostromo, a figure of Conrad the man, but unlike him, a figure also of Conrad the author masquerading in *Under Western Eyes* as an aging, garrulous Englishman.

More explicitly than in *Nostromo*, the hero, the narrator, and the author-as-narrator in *Under Western Eyes* are all writers and fiction-makers, whose activities all have reference back to the fictions in the life and art of Conrad. In trying to construct a believable public *persona* in *A Personal Record* Conrad was engaged in approximately the same kind of fiction-making in the sphere of his own life as in the sphere of the novel he was working on at the same time. And in the novel, to come the full neurotic circle, he writes about the self-destruction of a Razumov who constructed for himself a public *persona* he knew was false. No wonder then that the novel was difficult to finish: writing about Razumov's lie, his lack of self-knowledge, his self-betrayal was to write about his own. To finish the novel honestly was to indict himself, and in a sense to pass sentence. Whereas finishing would of necessity bring about some sort of resolution of Razumov's contradictions, it would only point up Conrad's failure to resolve. Novels, as Frank Kermode has made us aware, have endings, but life has only an End.

The other fiction-maker in the novel is of course the old narrator, who refracts Conrad through yet another prism. He "makes" the novel, even while declaring it a true story, but as I mentioned earlier, either mistakenly interprets or confesses himself baffled by Razumov's strange history. His failure to understand is a comic analogue of the older Conrad's own inability to understand what happened to the younger, the Slav, the sailor, the adventurer, and of his incapacity to grapple with the terrors of the darkness he kept finding within. His strategy, like the narrator's, was retreat back into a public pose he could try to believe in, to construct like the narrator's story of Razumov, "a personal record." And so, if we view the novel psychologically rather than aesthetically, we come around again to the conclusion that interpretation fails, failed Conrad here as it does the narrator in the story. Conrad failed to interpret himself, and hence his narrator, who so obviously was intended as sprightly make-believe — the comic, over-fifty-garrulous technocrat of language, the writer whose imagination has dried up — is an accurate and to us sadly ironic portrait of Conrad himself, or at least of Conrad's fate. The fiction becomes the truth; the mask turns into the man.

As Razumov and the narrator are both fiction makers, they are both writers, of a diary on the one hand and of a story on the other. But their attitudes toward the tale they both write are vastly different. For Razumov the story is intensely personal and dangerous, and the diary is a way of interpreting, making sense of, himself. By writing, we are told, he is trying to find "some formula of peace." Conrad says almost the same thing of himself in a contemporary letter (17 February 1908): "It's an impossible existence, but I keep on writing—trying to catch the spectre, the flying shadow of peace."[34] For the language teacher who writes a documentary history, the story is only a story; it is—he wants to believe—outside himself; he is only the complacent if slightly puzzled conduit through which the story passes unchanged and, he would have us believe, uninterpreted because uninterpretable.[35] These two kinds of writing in the novel are closely analogous to the personal and "impersonal" books Conrad was simultaneously working on in 1908 and 1909: *A Personal Record* and *Under Western Eyes*. And yet, the distinction resists definition. As we've already seen, *A Personal Record* is to some degree fiction; and more important, the fiction of *Under Western Eyes* is, if not a personal record, at least a faithful mirror of Conrad's very real personal conflicts. These metafictive confusions tell us something very important about fiction. Neither Razumov or the old professor is a novelist, but together they express the novelist's (and Conrad's) double relation to his fiction: it both is and is not about himself; it is both a confession and a disguise; in Conrad's case, it arises from the personal terror, the danger, the formless darkness of experience, but demands cold and calculated craft in the telling. Psychologically the dialectic between Razumov and the language teacher is a pattern of Conrad's mind and of his writing. But in the broadest terms it is a metafictive paradigm of the seemingly impossible knot of tensions which is fiction, where formlessness is bound with form, feeling with thought, subject with object, emotional intensity with aesthetic space.

Notes

A shorter version of this paper was read at an MLA Seminar on the Double in Literature at Chicago, Dec. 1977.

1. The W. D. Thomas Memorial Lecture given at University College, Swansea, in February 1978, reprinted in *TLS*, 30 June 1978.

2. For political readings of the novel see especially Eloise Knapp Hay, *The Political Novels of Joseph Conrad* (Chicago: University of Chicago Press, 1963) and Avrom Fleishman, *Conrad's Politics* (Baltimore: Johns Hopkins Press, 1967). Also George Goodin, "The Personal and the Political in *Under Western Eyes*," *Nineteenth Century Fiction*, 25 (1970–71), 327–42; Irving Howe, *Politics and the Novel* (New York: Fawcett, 1957).

3. Only within the last three or four years have critics begun to speak of the concern of the novel with language, writing, and fiction, most notably Avrom Fleishman, "Speech and Writing in *Under Western Eyes*" in *Joseph Conrad: A Commemoration* (Papers from the 1974 International Conference on Conrad), ed. Norman Sherry (London: Macmillan, 1976), 119–28. Fleishman is the first so far as I know to describe the complex structure of writings which constitute the novel and to point to the self-referentiality that results. In his terms, the novel consists of three texts: the fiction written by Conrad; the document prepared by the narrator; and the collection of documents upon which the narrator bases his report—Razumov's notebook above all. Fleishmen stresses the consequences of this multiplicity of texts, that is, the concern of the novel with language: its multiple resonances, the difficulty of

attaining understanding or peace through words, the use of language for self-definition, the dialectic between the written and the spoken word. He stops short of concluding that the novel is "a declaration of ultimate despair of written language, and of the art of fiction along with it," but does not suggest that it expresses "the anxiety of every conscientious writer about the efficacy of his writing."

Jeffrey Berman in *Joseph Conrad: Writing as Rescue* (New York: Astra Books, 1977) suggests more directly that *Under Western Eyes* is "Conrad's most complicated study of artistic creation"; that Razumov is a "portrait of the artist"; and that while the confessional art he creates is at first a form of rescue from chaos and a means by which he regains himself, it ultimately results in the extinction of the artist.

4. All citations from *Under Western Eyes* are from the Anchor Books edition (New York: Doubleday, 1963).

5. Scholes, "Metafiction," *The Iowa Review*, 1 (1970), 100–15, later translated in *Poétique* as "Metaécrit," focusing on short fiction by Barth, Barthelme, Coover, and Gass. Scholes' is the first substantial comment on metafiction, although Gass uses the term in *Fiction and the Figures of Life* (New York: Knopf, 1970). Scholes treats the subject in more detail in his recent *Fabulation and Metafiction* (Chicago: University of Illinois Press, 1979). See also Neil Schmitz, "Robert Coover and the Hazards of Metafiction," *Novel*, 7 (1973–74), 210–19. There are also analogous terms: James L. Calderwood, *Shakespearean Metadrama* (Minneapolis: U. of Minnesota, 1971); Lionel Abel, *Metatheatre: A New View of Dramatic Form* (New York: Hill and Wang, 1963); metapoetry in Rene Wellek, "The poet as critic, the critic as poet, the poet-critic," in Frederick P. McDowell, ed., *The Poet as Critic* (Evanston, Ill.: Northwestern University Press, 1967), p. 98; Fredric Jameson, "Metacommentary," *PMLA*, 86 (1971), 9–18; and David Henry Lowenkron, "The Metanovel," *College English*, 38 (1976–77), 343–55.

6. Several critics have noted the Razumov-Haldin doubling. See especially Claire Rosenfield, *Paradise of Snakes* (Chicago: University of Chicago Press, 1967), 123–72; Frederick R. Karl, "The Rise and Fall of *Under Western Eyes*," *Nineteenth Century Fiction*, 13 (1958–59), 313–27. For the concept of psychological doubling and its bearing on literary doubling, see Robert Rogers, *A Psychoanalytic Study of the Double in Literature* (Detroit: Wayne State University Press, 1970); C. F. Keppler, *The Literature of the Second Self* (Tucson: University of Arizona Press, 1972); Otto Rank, "The Double as Immortal Self," in *Beyond Psychology* (New York: Dover, 1958), pp. 62–101.

7. The point is discussed by Rosenfield, *Paradise of Snakes*, pp. 161–66. See also Dwight Purdy, "Creature and Creator in *Under Western Eyes*," *Conradiana*, 8 (1976), 241–46; Ronald Schleifer, "Public and Private Narrative in *Under Western Eyes*," *Conradiana*, 9 (1977), 237–54; and Robert Secor, "The Function of the Narrator in *Under Western Eyes*," *Conradiana*, 3 (1971), 27–38.

8. "Teaching a Course on the Double," paper delivered at MLA Seminar on the Double, Dec. 1975.

9. Razumov's given name, Kirylo (Cyril), may be intended to emphasize his role as a writer. St. Cyril (826–69), the so-called "Apostle of the Slavs," was said to have invented an alphabet called Glagolithic (the ancient Slavonic alphabet), and so was considered the founder of Slavonic literature. See F. L. Cross, *The Oxford Dictionary of the Christian Church* (London: Oxford University Press, 1971), s.v. "Cyril."

10. Emily K. Izsak (Dalgarno), in "*Under Western Eyes* and the Problems of Serial Publication," *RES*, 23 (1973), 429–44, demonstrates among other things an even stronger association between diary and essay in the MS version of the novel; also a greater emphasis upon the diary as a "free and revolutionary act of self-discovery" (see especially pp. 438, 440).

11. "Listen to the theme. The Student Razumov (a natural son of Prince K.) gives up secretly to the police his fellow student, Haldin, who seeks refuge in his rooms after committing a political crime (supposed to be the murder of de Plehve). First movement in St. Petersburg. (Haldin is hanged of course).

"2d in Geneve. The student Razumov meeting abroad the mother and sister of Haldin falls in love with the last, marries her and, after a time, confesses to her the part he played in the arrest of her brother.

"The psychological developments leading to Razumov's betrayal of Haldin, to his confession of the fact to his wife and to the death of these people (brought about mainly by the resemblance of their child to the late Haldin) form the real subject of the story." G. Jean-Aubry, ed., *Joseph Conrad: Life and Letters* (Garden City, N.Y.: Doubleday, 1927), II, 64–5 (hereafter referred to as *LL*).

12. For an excellent study of the narrator and his effect upon the story, see Schleifer, "Public and Private Narrative."

13. See the letter to John Galsworthy, end of July 1908; *LL*, II, 70. Jocelyn Baines, *Joseph Conrad* (New York: McGraw-Hill, 1960), p. 352 ff. links Conrad's decision to leave Poland and his decision to leave sailing for writing as the most important events of Conrad's life, both clouded by feelings of betrayal. At the time he was writing the story of Razumov's self-betrayal in *Under Western Eyes*, Conrad was also writing about "a fugitive and vagabond on the earth" in "The Secret Sharer" and trying to justify his own desertion of Poland in *A Personal Record*.

14. See the discussion in Scholes' "Metafiction," pp. 110–111.

15. *A Personal Record* (Garden City, N.Y.: Doubleday, 1923), p. 35. See also Frank Kermode's comments on the novel, "The Structures of Fiction," *MLN*, 84 (1969), 905–15; and C. B. Cox, "Joseph Conrad and the Question of Suicide," *Bulletin of the John Rylands University Library*, 55 (1973), 295–97.

16. *PMLA*, 86 (1971), 9.

17. One of the best theoretical discussions of this kind of meaning is Stanley Fish's "Literature in the Reader: Affective Stylistics," *NLH*, 2 (1970–71), 123–62.

18. See Izsak (Dalgarno), "Problems of Serial Publication," pp. 429–37; also the letters of 1908 and 1909.

19. 6 June 1909; *LL* II, 51.

20. 6 May 1907, 6 Jan. 1908, end July 1908, 5 June 1909; *LL*, II, 47, 65, 70, 98.

21. 7 Jan. 1908, MS letter cited in Roderick Davis, "*Under Western Eyes*: 'The Most Deeply Meditated Novel,' " *Conradiana*, 9 (1977), 59; also 28 August 1908, 28 December 1908 in *LL*, II, 83, 93.

22. Letters of 15 Nov. 1909, 28 June 1910, in *LL*, II, 103, 113; and 19 Dec. 1909 to Perceval Gibbon, cited in Jocelyn Baines, *Joseph Conrad*, p. 359.

23. Letter by Jesse Conrad, 6 February 1910, in William Blackburn, ed., *Joseph Conrad: Letters to William Blackwood and David S. Meldrum* (Durham, N.C.: Duke University Press, 1958), p. 192.

24. 17 May 1910; *LL*, II, 107.

25. Frederick R. Karl, *Joseph Conrad: The Three Lives* (New York: Farrar, Straus, and Giroux, 1979), p. 527.

26. *A Personal Record*, p. xvii.

27. Conrad, *Lettres françaises* (Paris: Gallimard, 1929), p. 60, and letter of 7 Oct. 1907, C. T. Watts, ed., *Letters to R. B. Cunninghame Graham* (Cambridge: Cambridge University Press, 1969), p. 170.

28. Edward Garnett, ed., *Letters from Joseph Conrad, 1895–1924* (Indianapolis: Bobbs-Merrill, 1928), p. 153.

29. (Cambridge, Mass.: Harvard University Press, 1966), esp. Chaps. III, VII.

30. (Garden City, N.Y.: Doubleday, 1923), xxv.

31. See Davis, "Most Deeply Meditated Novel," p. 68ff., and Baines, *Joseph Conrad*, pp. 352–59. For a response to the latter, see Cox, "Question of Suicide," pp. 289–90.

32. For the psychological phenomenon, see the works by Rogers and Rank cited in n. 6.

33. In *Beginnings: Intention and Method* (New York: Basic Books, 1975), pp. 100–137.

34. Quoted in Intro., *LL*, II, 5.

35. For the narrator's struggle to avoid involvement with his story, see Schleifer, "Public and Private Narrative."

The Secret Agent: The Agon(ie)s of the Word
William Bysshe Stein*

I. ANARCHY AMONG THE MAD HATTERS

Under his hat, worn with a slight backward tilt, his hair had been carefully brushed into respectful sleekness.[1]
Tenniel's illustration of the Mad Hatter in Lewis Carroll's *Alice's Adventures in Wonderland* supplies Conrad with the model for Verloc's (and the other anarchists') dandyism, though not without his consciousness of the masculine fripperies in the fashionable circles of London. Appropriately, Verloc later morosely ponders his failure to dynamite the Greenwich Meridian Observatory in "the little parlour of the Cheshire Cheese" (SA, 191) as Conrad's reminder that the Cheshire Cat directs Alice to the Mad Tea-Party. Later he also salutes Humpty-Dumpty for his inspiration in molding the arbitrary word-worlds of his characters in the novel. Immediately the pun on "sleekness," to conceal, betrays the deceit of Verloc's respectability.

However, the Cheshire Cheese also directs attention to another facet of contemporary literary history. The name of a club in London, it headquartered the Rhymer's Club, founded by William Butler Yeats to promote the esthetic fantasies of Walter Pater. Verloc's dandyism, no doubt, accredits his trespass into this sanctum sanctorum of transcendental and alcoholic inspiration. Unfortunately not meeting Lionel Johnson or Ernest Dowson, Verloc deprives himself of the drink or three that might have at least protracted his life. Certainly Conrad could have assimilated such an incident into the narrative along with his less assimilated material. Wild! No, as the accumulated evidence below reveals.

The old terrorist [Yundt] . . . gave a swaggering tilt to a black felt sombrero. (SA, 54)
Conrad mixes up his nationalities. Rightly the Spanish sombrero belongs in the wardrobe of the Assistant Commissioner with "his accentuated features of an energetic Don Quixote" (SA, 103).

*Reprinted with permission from *boundary 2* 6 (1978):521–40.

A blue cap with a patent leather peak set well at the back of his yellow bush of hair gave him the aspect of a Norwegian soldier bored with the world after a thundering spree. (SA, 54)

Ossipon, "nicknamed the Doctor" (and never so referred to again [SA, 50]) takes on the identity of his hat, but Conrad in another analogical accolade endows Chief Inspector Heat with a "Norse rover's moustache" (SA, 103).

[Heat's] hat, tilted back, uncovered a good deal of forehead. (SA, 78)

This exhibition of baldness (and perhaps boneheadedness) anticipates the Chief Inspector's confrontation on a London Street with the menacing skullduggery of "The Perfect Anarchist" (SA, 246), the Professor. Considering his obsession with the destruction of the human race, the latter manifests a kinship with George Bernard Shaw's The Perfect Wagnerite, especially in terms of *Die Götterdämmerung.*

He sat down to consume [the supper], wearing his hat pushed far back on his head. It was not devotion to an outdoor life, but the frequentation of foreign cafes which was responsible for that habit. (SA, 149).

Conrad places too much faith in the reader's suspension of disbelief on this occasion. His explanations for the probable origins of Verloc's idiosyncrasy sound like captions to a cartoon in *Punch.*

He ate as if in a public place, his hat pushed off his forehead, the skirts of his heavy overcoat hanging in a triangle on each side of the chair. (SA, 154)

Verloc's fixation on his hat and overcoat tickles off any number of belly laughs. Here Conrad attires the obese anarchist in an outer garment strong enough to carry the weight of the symbolic triangle that he so promiscuously dumps everywhere. The only sign of Verloc's identity in the good old days of counterspying suffers a fall in secrecy and meaning, not to ignore status, in the ongoing action. Used by Conrad for a name tag in Stevie's overcoat and for a description of the area in front of Verloc's shop, the triangle eventually ceases to be even a sign. As vented by Verloc's overcoat, it evolves into mere verbal wind. But the overcoat still invites further comment. In the immediate surroundings where a fire blazes (SA, 156), it stirs an equal proportion of wonder and laughter, especially when later Verloc and Stevie go for a walk, apparelled in similar hats and coats (SA, 157). How the frail Stevie shoulders the burden of his greatcoat poses another mystery in the novel (SA, 155). However, Conrad dispels the necessity of probing too deeply into this incongruity earlier during the gathering of the anarchists in Verloc's parlor. By the by, only a writer of fantasy fiction would venture to crowd so many people into "the little parlor" which, "becom[ing] frightfully hot," forces Verloc to open "the door leading to the kitchen" (SA, 49). Yet when the meeting breaks up,

Conrad describes Verloc in a state compatible with neither a loyalty to the outdoor life nor to the outdoor cafe society: "Mr. Verloc saw his guests off the premises, attending them bareheaded, his heavy overcoat hanging open" (SA, 54). Surely, a suppressed guffaw lurks somewhere in this situation.

With troubled eyes [Michaelis] looked for his round hard hat, and put it on his round head. His round and obese body seemed to float low between the chairs under the sharp elbow of Karl Yundt. (SA, 54).

Conrad pricks the bubble of revolutionary babble on Yundt's elbow, even though Michaelis safely rides the hot air out of Verloc's parlor, comically emulating Alice in Wonderland. Unlike the rhetorical skirmish between Verloc and Vladimir, this context of insults among equals ends up in a stalemate. Nobody attends the speeches of anybody else, and the bloody wordshed affects only Stevie, who always literalizes language. Conrad's burlesque of roundness spins off Ossipon's obsession with "the cold glitter of the [Professor's] round spectacles" (SA, 67). Needless to say, Stevie's circle making, as rationally irrational as carving up the surface of the earth in imaginary meridians, noises Conrad's contempt for symbols, anticipating in clangor Wallace Stevens with his "cymbals crashing."

The triad of rounds, one of many such repetitions in the novel, solidly anchors the method of narration behind the looking glass. It illustrates the rule of three, the cachet of tale of a tub and of the nonsense creation. The thrice-said statement always takes on the authority of truth. A host of great writers attest this magical permutation of language: Rabelais, Sterne, Melville, Flaubert, and James.

COMMENT

THE FLOW OF ACTION IN *THE SECRET AGENT* ERODES IN MEANING UNDER THE INSIDIOUS COUNTERFLOW OF LANGUAGE. CHORICALLY SPEAKING, THE HAT CROTCHET ALWAYS WORKS AT CROSS-PURPOSES, ABORTING THE CONTAINING INCIDENTS OF THEIR SUSPENSE OR SERIOUSNESS. THE RECOURSE TO DETAIL, EITHER PATENTLY REDUNDANT, ABSURD, OXYMORONIC, OR SUPERFLUOUS, CONSTANTLY INVITES LAUGHTER IN THE MIDST OF SUPPOSEDLY PORTENTOUS PLOTTING AND COUNTERPLOTTING. THIS MANIPULATED INCONGRUITY, LIKE CONRAD'S PREPOSTEROUS AND IRRELEVANT CLASSICAL ALLUSIONS, SMACKS OF PARODY. THEN, IN THE INSTANCE ABOVE, CONRAD'S NOTORIOUS DISLIKE OF DOSTOEVSKY BELLOWS OUT IN MICHAELIS' GIRTH AND HIS IMPRISONMENT IN A "COLOSSAL MORTUARY FOR THE SOCIALLY DROWNED" (SA, 49), HIS "AUTOBIOGRAPHY OF A PRISONER" REPLICATING THE RUSSIAN'S *THE HOUSE OF THE DEAD*.

II. A LA MODE

Some of the last kind had the collars of their overcoats turned right up to their moustaches, and traces of mud on the bottom of their nether garments, which had the appearance of being much worn and not very valuable. And the legs inside of them did not, as a general rule, seem of much account either. (SA, 17)

The adult patrons of Verloc's junk shop (an incredible hoax on the part of Conrad from the standpoint of verisimilitude) slink in like disreputable shades of the dead (the pun on "nether" suggesting both Hades and the criminal underworld). Then Conrad's superfluous, if not ridiculous, appraisal of the soiled trousers tails off into a nonsensical depreciation of the contained limbs. This rhetorical attrition reduces the figures to scarecrows, mock vehicles of Conrad's scarecrow strategies.

The evening visitors — the men with turned up collars and soft hats rammed down — nodded familiarly to Mrs. Verloc. (SA, 19)

Conrad advertises the caricatural mannerism of a shady character in a hack mystery, capriciously of course. Even as her sense of aloneness after murdering her husband attests, Mrs. Verloc's intimate acquaintances comprise the revolutionaries who enact the Mad Hatter's skit, and only one of them wears the appropriate headgear. These visitors or, perhaps more accurately, visitants belong in a subplot that Conrad never develops.

[T]hen by a sudden inspiration [he] raised the collar of his jacket. This arrangement appeared to him commendable, and he completed it by giving an upward twist to the ends of his black moustache. (SA, 128)

The Assistant Commissioner confuses the roles of the criminal and the sleuth, or else Conrad refuses to take his characterization seriously. Evidence for this latter judgment accumulates in the hand-and-chin game that takes place during his conference with Chief Inspector Heat (SA, 128).

[H]e was tall and thin, and wore his moustaches twisted up. In fact, he gave the sharp points a twist just then. His long, bony face rose out of a turned up collar. (SA, 166)

Succumbing completely to the spell of his murky imaginary role, the Assistant Commissioner allows fiction to displace actuality, and Mrs. Verloc, beguiled by the illusion, takes him for a foreigner. Compared with the foreigners of her acquaintance, he ranks alone: he has no claim to existence in the world of flesh and blood people. Conrad's twisting of detail affirms the triumph of make-believe. And the framing rhetoric of the ensuing dialogue supports this judgment.

"Will you assume a disguise?" (SA, 124)

After learning of the Assistant Commissioner's scheme to conduct a secret investigation, Sir Ethelred associates its success with a scenario from a Sherlock Holmes thriller. Meanwhile Conrad converts his chagrin at the popularity of Sir Arthur Conan Doyle's potboilers into a sneer.

The lank man, with eyeglasses on a broad ribbon, pronounced mincingly the word "Grotesque," whose justness was appreciated by those standing near him. They smiled at each other. (SA, 99)

Conrad summons his lanky dandy from the illustrations of *Punch*. Deprecating Michaelis' obesity during a drawing room gathering at the residence of the great lady, he mistakes the cause of the laughter. The affected fussiness of his taste and expression puts him into the camp of decadents, and the knowing exchange of smiles cancels out any wild appreciation of his scornful epithet. Conrad's earlier description of this unnamed character anticipates the reversal: "a clean shaved individual with sunken cheeks, and dangling a gold-mounted eyeglass on a broad black ribbon with an old world, dandified effect" (SA, 98).

In front of the great doorway a dismal row of newspaper sellers standing clear of the pavement dealt out their wares from the gutter. It was a raw, gloomy day of the early spring; and the grimy sky, the mud of the streets, the rags of the dirty men harmonized excellently with the eruption of the damp, rubbishy sheets of paper soiled with printer's ink. (SA, 75)

Even on the lowest rung of the social ladder, Conrad adapts the clothes of his puppets to the season and the setting. Almost with a tailor's pride in his garment of words, "harmonized excellently," he transforms the sordid and squalid into sublime nonsense. As the resolution of the action affirms, a close affinity prevails between facts of fiction and the fiction of facts (journalism), and Conrad mercilessly subsumes this relationship under the rubric of garbage—the stench of printer's ink, the lies of language. For anyone who takes Conrad's treatment of Ossipon's remorse seriously, the *Angst* induced by the newspaper story, " '*An impenetrable mystery seems destined to hang for ever over this act of madness or despair*' " (SA, 249; italics mine), betrays a susceptibility to the influence of words that hardly requires hermeneutic analysis. Conrad simply elects Ossipon to dramatize the narcotic effects of ink on paper: they alladinize into gospel truth. In contriving this epilogue Conrad parodies Dostoevsky's *Crime and Punishment*, deliberately equating the needs of the mind and the body in a rhetoric that suits the word to the action: "*He had lately failed to keep several of these appointments [assignations], whose note used to be an unbounded trustfulness in the language of sentiment and manly tenderness. The confiding disposition of various classes of women satisfied the needs of his self-love, and put some material means into his hand. He needed it to live. It was there. But if he could no longer make use of it, he ran the risk of starving his ideals and his body*" (SA, 249–50).

COMMENT

BY ARTISTIC DESIGN *THE SECRET AGENT*, IN JEST AND EARNEST, PARASITI-CALLY FEEDS ON FICTIONAL STEREOTYPES, BOTH IN THEIR ORIGINAL FORMS AND IN THEIR PARODIC MUTATIONS IN THE HUMOR MAGAZINES. LIKE ANY OTHER

WRITER, CONRAD ACHIEVES HIS ORIGINALITY IN DEFT PLAGIARY, PERVERTING THE RECEIVED CONVENTIONS OF DIFFERENT TYPES OF STORIES TO SERVE HIS OWN ENDS. MORE REVOLUTIONARY THAN ANY OF HIS CHARACTERS, HE EXPLORES AND EXPLOITS THE INSENSITIVITY OF READERS TO TRITE LITERARY PROPS, THE ARTIFICIAL STAGEMANSHIP OF EVERY FICTION. INSTEAD OF EMPLOYING HIS COMBINED HAT-COLLAR-MOUSTACHE MOTIF TO ENHANCE THE SINISTER ATMO-SPHERE OF HIS TALE, CONRAD RIDICULES ITS CONTRIBUTION TO THE DELINEA-TION OF VILLAINY. THROUGH MIRRORING THE DISTORTIONS OF SUCH PROMPTING SIGNS IN CARICATURAL ILLUSTRATIONS, HIS SCATTERED CATALOG PREDICATES A SUBSTITUTE FOR THE SARDONIC CAPTION. IN THIS PERSPECTIVE EACH OCCUR-RENCE OF THE BOGUS REFERENCE COMMENTS ON THE OTHER. LIKE THE FIRST THAT EVOKES MERELY SPECTRAL FIGURES, THE SECOND ALSO WORKS WITH A SIMILAR METONYMY OF VAGUENESS. THE THIRD LENDS THE CONFIRMING TOUCH TO CONRAD'S INTENTIONAL BURLESQUE OF STOCK APPEARANCES. THE CARD-BOARD CHARACTER CONTINUES TO MIMIC HIMSELF.

CORRESPONDINGLY, OSSIPON APES THE ILLUSIONS OF JOURNALISTIC PRINT. THE ABSTRACTIONS, "ACT OF MADNESS OR DESPAIR," ASSIMILATES ITS CREDENCE FROM FICTION, NOT FACT. IT ACQUIRES ITS AFFECTIVE AND INTELLECTUAL AUTHORITY FROM THE MILLIONS OF CATACHRESTIC WARPINGS OF THE PHRASE IN INVENTED YARNS DOWN THROUGH THE CENTURIES. THE CRIMINAL, AS A GENERAL RULE IN ORDINARY LIFE, ONLY OCCASIONALLY RECEIVES CONDIGN PUNISHMENT AND RARELY SURRENDERS TO REMORSE, CONTRADICTING THE TRAGIC DRAMATISTS, FROM SOPHOCLES TO SHAKESPEARE.

III. TROPOPATHY

[T]he walls without windows, representing scenes of the chase and of outdoor revelry in medieval costumes. Varlets in green jerkins brandished hunting knives and raised on high tankards of foaming beer. (SA, 61)

These fresco paintings undoubtedly contribute to the reputation "of the renowned Silenus Restaurant" (SA, 66), if only by the grotesque contrast of decor and name, not to forget the clientele it attracts. On the other hand, the "varlets in green jerkins" (echoing the vocabulary of one of William Morris' Arthurian romances) act like bacchantes, albeit usurping the roles of their liege knights. Conrad's mock medievalism subsumes a half century of British art and literature, from the Pre-Raphaelite infatua-tion with *Le Morte d'Arthur* to the Beardsleyian perversion of the chivalric tradition. And lurking in the wings of these theatres of nostalgic never-never lands, with an ironical eye cocked on the absurdities of the esthetic movement, George Du Maurier sketches his version of jousting in jest. His *Legend of Camelot* marks a high point in the satirical cartooning of *Punch*. To judge by the caricatural patterns of *A Secret Agent* (a pending topic), Conrad aped the strokes of this virtuoso illustrator.

His jovial purple cheeks bristled with white hairs; and like Virgil's Silenus, who, his face smeared with the juice of berries, discoursed of Olympian

Gods to the innocent Shepherds of Sicily, he talked to Stevie of domestic matters and the affairs of men whose sufferings are great and immortality by no means assured. (SA, 142)

Conrad incarnates Virgil's Silenus (a creation of poetic license like the Galahads and Guiniveres of the Rossetti-Morris-Tennyson tradition) in a drunken cabby. Playing the role of the archetypal Wise Man, the latter lectures Stevie on the art of human and animal brutalization under the extenuating catchword of familial responsibility. Conrad records the imprint of this lesson in humanitarian cruelty on the "purple" name label (SA, 172) that provides Chief Inspector Heat with the identity of the blood and bones of Stevie. The *locus classicus* of the Virgilian allusion hardly wafts the scent of pastoral bliss into the atmosphere of the scene in question.

He was physically a big man [a black native chief whose native country Conrad refuses to designate], too, and (allowing for the difference of color, of course) Chief Inspector Heat's appearance recalled to him the memory of his superior. It was not the eyes nor yet the lips exactly. It was bizarre. But does not Alfred Wallace relate . . . how, amongst the Aru Islanders, he discovered in an old and naked savage with a sooty skin a peculiar resemblance to a dear friend at home? (SA, 105)

The Assistant Commissioner's dissociation in his questioning of Chief Inspector, so precise in the historical documentation of irrelevant matter and so evasive of information pertinent to character development, captures another moment of Conrad's utter contempt for the critic's treasured exaltation of functional detail — that is, if a seriousness of purpose motivates the narration. The digression instead evolves into a parody of genetic science or a jibe at the miscegenation of English colonials. Either way, the retrospect hatches a stillborn piece of hackmanship.

[T]he Assistant Commissioner made to himself the observation that the patrons of the place had lost in the frequentation of fraudulent cookery all their national and private characteristics. And this was strange, since the Italian restaurant is such a peculiarly British institution. But these people were as denationalized as the dishes set before them with every circumstance of unstamped respectability. Neither was their personality stamped in any way, professionally, socially, or racially. They seemed created for the Italian restaurant, unless the Italian restaurant had been perchance created for them. (SA, 129).

The Assistant Commissioner prates about the discrepancy between name and food, a variation on the Silenus-Arthur discordance. His desire to limit rigidly the references of words to things inspires a plunge into a labyrinthine logic that requires more than an Ariadne's thread to follow. An Italian restaurant, failing to serve its claimed nationalized dishes, unaccountably betrays an institution of Great Britain. Though in England, the Assistant Commissioner laments the lack of patronage by Italians. Finally, the Italian restaurant not an Italian restaurant metamorphoses into an Italian restaurant for customers not Italian. Not surprisingly, "he himself had become unplaced" (SA, 129). This exercise in nonsense reduces Humpty Dumpty to a semantic libertarian by comparison with the Assistant Commissioner. But what about the author of this gibberish — Conrad? Plotting against the intelligence of one of his principals, he evolves into the paterfamilias of the anti-novel or perhaps the inventor of self-destroying fiction.

Tendering a coin through the trap door the fare [the Assistant Commissioner] slipped out and away, leaving an effect of uncanny, eccentric ghostliness upon the driver's mind. But the size of the coin was satisfactory to his touch, and his education not being literary, he remained untroubled by the fear of finding it presently turned to a dead leaf in his pocket. (SA, 128)

Though the coin proves real, Conrad's extraneous elaboration of the Assistant Commissioner's stealthiness rings of counterfeiting; if not that, then he takes for granted that the fictionist owns the prerogative to muster his phantoms (the illusions of the word) wherever he chooses. The ghost evoked in the irrelevant analogy borrows its credence from the lies of literature, the imaginary substance of the folk and fairy tale. Conrad mocks his own imagery to establish its underlying absurdity. Yet in the Jamesian sense, the added spice of the supernatural produces "the real real thing," the consummate product of the dupery of language by reflex association.

COMMENT

THE ASSIMILATION OF CULTURAL HISTORY, PAST OR PRESENT, INTO FICTION ALWAYS ENTAILS A PROCESS OF DIGESTION IN WHICH THE FACT CHANGES MEANING WHILE STILL RETAINING ITS NOMINAL IDENTITY. CONRAD'S SILENUS-ARTHUR INCONGRUITY PICKS UP HIS IMPRESSION OF THE TOPSY-TURVY CAREER OF BRITISH ESTHETICISM, AND, MORE OR LESS OBVIOUSLY, IT PASSES A JUDGMENT ON ITS MANIFESTATIONS — MOST LIKELY ON THE QUIXOTIC ACTIVITIES OF WILLIAM MORRIS IN SOCIALIST POLITICS. BUT THE REFERENCE TO ANACHRONIST MEDIEVALISM STILL REMAINS AN INTEGRAL PART OF THE WORD-WORLD OF THE NOVEL, FOR, IN THE COUPLING OF OPPOSING MYTHOLOGIES, CONRAD DELIBERATELY SHORTCIRCUITS THEIR RESPECTIVE FIELDS OF ENERGIZING IMPLICATION. IN SHORT, HE DISAVOWS THE LEGITIMACY OF ALLUSIVE CORRELATION BY DISTORTION, DIVULGING THE IRRATIONALITY OF ANY ATTEMPT TO INTERPRET THE PRESENT IN IMAGINARY INTERPOLATIONS OF THE PAST. THE REINCARNATION OF SILENUS IN THE ALCOHOLIC CABBY MERELY FOOTNOTES THE ARBITRARY ANALOGIES THAT PERVADE FICTION AND POETRY TO EMPHASIZE THE GULF THAT ETERNALLY SEPARATES WORD AND REALITY. CONRAD'S SUBORDINATION OF FICTIONAL TO HISTORICAL FACT IN THE WALLACE EQUIVOCATION

AGAIN ILLUSTRATES THE INCONSISTENT AND AUTOCRATIC CHARACTER OF THE
CREATIVE ACT, AND THUS HE TRANSFORMS THE ARTIST INTO THE LORD OF
WHIMSY. UNLIKE THE LATTER, THE ASSISTANT COMMISSIONER LABORS UNDER
THE DELUSION THAT THE DICTIONARY CONTROLS THE DEFINITION OF RESTAU-
RANTS. HIS IRRITATION, SO MARVELOUSLY CONSTRUED IN THE RHETORICAL
CONFUSION, DRAMATIZES THE INSECURITY THAT GRIPS THE MIND WHEN A
FOSSILIZED TERM SUDDENLY DISINTEGRATES INTO ITS OWN EMPTINESS.

IV. THINGAMY

*But there was also about him an indescribable air which no mechanic
could have acquired in the practice of his handicraft however dishonestly
exercised: the air common to men who live on the vices, the follies, or the
baser fears of mankind; the air of moral nihilism common to keepers of
gambling hells and disorderly houses; to private detectives and inquiry
agents; to drink sellers and, I should say, to the sellers of invigorating
electric belts and to the inventors of patent medicines. But of the last I am
not sure, not having carried my investigation so far into the depths. (SA,
24–25)*

For the first and only time Conrad's narrator intrudes in the first
person to unload a cargo of red herrings. Though he acknowledges the
ineffable aura of Mr. Verloc, he still persists in undertaking its delineation
by addressing the autosuggestive habits of his readers. At the outset he
plays around with the reflex responses associated with stereotypes of
immorality, all of them, inevitably, the products of fiction and the
anathemas of respectability. Poor Verloc hardly stands a chance to vindicate his character under such gratuitous libel. Then with the narrator's
invocation of private detectives and other ferrets, the already tarnished
reputation of Mr. Verloc undergoes still further degradation, if only
because the vocations touch on the secret iniquities of readers. The
reference to drink-sellers abates the speculative calumny somewhat, given
the history of alcoholic indulgence in merry England. Finally in the
uncalled for attack on civilized mankind's preoccupation with health fads,
the narrator betrays the makeshift formulation of his analogies, with
fiction failing to provide the authority for an absolute judgment (a dearth
unfortunately remedied by the impoverished imaginations of modern
writers). Since this depiction of Mr. Verloc's appearance impedes the flow
of narration by its irrelevance, Conrad apparently introduces the nonsensical passage to divulge a clue to his treatment of the action, namely, except
for the joy of manipulating language (and, no doubt, assuring a steady
income) none exists.

*And a peculiarly London sun — against which nothing could be said except
that it looked bloodshot — glorified all this [the panorama of the streets] by
its stare. It hung at moderate elevation above Hyde Park Corner with a air*

of punctual and benign vigilance. The very pavement under Mr. Verloc's feet had an old-gold tinge in the diffused light, in which neither wall, nor tree, nor beast, nor man cast a shadow. (SA, 23).

Though exempt from ridicule, the eye of heaven, red and irritated, excites suspicion in context. Suspended above Hyde Park Corner (with Conrad punning on "hide" and secretly maligning the sun in a burst of soapbox casuistry), it plays tricks with chromatics or with miracles in transforming red into gold. Conrad records this phenomenal dereliction in his string of Peter Schlemihl disshadowings. The personification implicit in "stare," "punctual," and "benign" mimics the arbitrariness of the Greenwich Meridian where nothing (zero) controls everything in the punctilio of human time.

An upright semi-grand piano near the door . . . executed suddenly all by itself a valse tune with aggressive virtuosity. (SA, 62)

Note that Conrad refuses to use the denomination player piano. Persisting in the maintenance of a counterfeit Wonderland atmosphere, he reveals this strategy in the witticism that the din of the piano prompts, for the Professor "emitted calmly what had the sound of a general proposition" (SA, 62). The physics of this relationship represents a formidable challenge to science.

The lonely piano, without as much as a music stool to help it, struck a few chords courageously, and beginning a selection of national airs, played him [the Professor] out at last to the tune of "The Bluebells of Scotland." (SA, 75)

Apparently intimidated by the Professor's Nietzschean nihilism (a running parody), the piano's gentle recessional also reverberates another joke, the sound of the "blue bells." "The painfully detached notes" (SA, 75) register the agonies of the instrument's humanity in the midst of the Professor's dehumanized vision of society. Deprived of even the company of a stool, it laments the estrangment of things from the pity of mankind. Obviously, Conrad here broaches a theory of knowledge too long left unexplored—the politics of inanimateness.

Facing the only gas-lamp yawned the cavern of a second-hand furniture dealer, where, deep in the gloom of a sort of narrow avenue winding through a bizarre forest of wardrobes, with an undergrowth tangle of table legs, a tall pier-glass glimmered like a pool of water in a wood. An unhappy, homeless couch, accompanied by two unrelated chairs, stood in the open. (SA, 78)

The Perfect Anarchist and the Imperfect Chief Inspector meet deep in the heart of things in an alley, with Conrad retrospectively commenting on the sinister enveloping mood of one of his own fictions. What inference to draw, I leave to more temerarious critics. Immediately, the landscape of this scene plunges the reader into *Through the Looking-Glass*. Properly so, all things speak in its environment of play, even as the lonely couch and the orphaned chairs ventriloquize the mechanical associations of their state in the mind of the reader, all of them assimilated from various mediums of fictional representation.

[T]he flanks of the old horse, the steed of apocalyptic misery, smoked upwards in the light of the charitable gas-lamp. (SA, 142)

The besotted cabby's hack (the virtual twin of Yorick's broken-winded jade in *Tristram Shandy* and Don Quixote's Rozinante) offers a revelation far more frightening than the pale horse of biblical prophecy, both admittedly conjured up in the rhetoric of hermeneutic obscurantism. On the one hand, Conrad ironically toys with the rehearsed responses of Victorian pietism, raising Death and Hell out of the haunts of words in fundamentalist theology. On the other, he cruelly burlesques the unrelenting horrors of temporality in the streets of London, improvising a transfiguration with the help this time of a compassionate gas-lamp that charts an ascent into the heavens through the unteleological smoke and mist of the filthy streets. Though groans of pathos run through the recreation, the scene also sounds a horse laugh.

He felt her now clinging round his legs, and his terror reached its culminating point, became a sort of intoxication, entertained delusions, acquired the characteristics of delirium tremens. He positively saw snakes. (SA, 237)

The robust Ossipon, the scientist, succumbs to the ghostly fears of his own verbal conditioning on the symptoms of degeneracy. Conrad stages this accidental entanglement of limbs as a climax to Ossipon's diversion from his pursuit of lustful adventures, and it evolves into one of the great comic scenes in literature (perhaps inspired by a similar incident in "The Fall of the House of Usher"). Conrad adds a religious footnote on the subject of Ossipon's imaginary snakes in Winnie's subsequent comment, "Not unless you crush my head under your heel" (SA, 237) — a grotesque inversion of an iconographic emblem of the Virgin Mary.

COMMENT

OBVIOUSLY, CONRAD DISCLAIMS ANY CONNECTION OF LANGUAGE WITH REALITY (IN LIFE OR FICTION). AS HIS CONSTANT ADDICTION TO ANALOGY AND PERSONIFICATION DISCLOSES, THE VERISIMILITUDE OF THINGS CONSTITUTES NO MORE THAN AN EMPTY PHRASE. THE NAMES OF THE NAMES (OR QUALITIES) OF OBJECTS, HOWEVER FANCIFUL OR NATURALISTIC, OPERATE TO VEIL THE PERCEPTION OF THE ENTITY IN QUESTION. WORDS DESCRIBE ONLY WORDS, ALL THE CREATION OF ARBITRARY CEREBRAL ACTIVITY. TO CIRCUMVENT THE CONFRONTATION OF THIS ILLUSION, SOME INGENIOUS CRITIC INVENTED THE CATEGORY

OF THE UNRELIABLE NARRATOR. HOW RIDICULOUS! THE VOICE OF EVERY VERBAL OPINION, VOCAL OR WRITTEN, ECHOES OUT OF A CHAMBER OF DISTRUST — THE PHYSIOLOGICAL SOURCE OF LANGUAGE THAT INVOLVES THE TRANSFORMATION OF SOUND INTO SYMBOL (LETTER), OF LETTERS INTO SYLLABLES, OF SYLLABLES INTO ROOTS AND AFFIXES, OF THE LATTER INTO WORDS, ETC. ETC. ETC. ETC. ETC. STEP BY STEP IN THIS PROCESS, THE WORD DEGENERATES INTO A WIND, FINALLY REPLICATING ITS VERY ORIGIN.

V. PICTOLALIA

This meritorious official, laying the papers on the table, disclosed a face of pasty complexion and of melancholy ugliness surrounded by a lot of fine, long dark grey hairs, barred heavily by thick and bushy eyebrows. He put on a black-framed pince-nez upon a blunt and shapeless nose, and seemed struck by Mr. Verloc's appearance. Under the enormous eyebrows his weak eyes blinked pathetically through the glasses. (SA, 27)

Privy Councillor Wurmt hardly warrants this verbose description. A stage prop rather than a character, he affords Conrad the opportunity to practice his prose cartooning. Indeed, the latter creates a frame of whiskers for his pictures, inviting, it seems, inquiry on the purpose behind this graphic impulse. At first glance the caricature reflects the influence of the humor magazines, particularly the work of the older illustrators, Cruikshank, Browne (Phiz), and Leech. If so, then Conrad's depiction takes into account the contribution of such etchers to the popularity of a writer like Dickens. As much as his novels themselves, the superb counterpoint of the pictorial art in the middle of the nineteenth-century helped to institutionalize Dickens' gallery of eccentrics. Conrad shows his envy of this stroke of luck and capitalistic enterprise with this pastiche. Put on display with no function except to generate a guffaw of appreciation, it divulges his mastery of simple, concrete language, handled with the bite and stroke of a stylus. By the same token, the stylistic grotesquerie puts into perspective the still ambiguous question of his rhetoric. Too often the glutinous tergiversation of *The Heart of Darkness* crops up as the index of his facility in English. Not so: he uses language in his fiction cunningly for the end of using his reader.

As Wurmt's caricature indicates, Conrad stresses one feature of his face more than any other — the eyebrows, and, by extension, the eyes. Though the embassy official lacks perfect vision, it matters not at all. He sees with his preconceptions, and his image of the physical Verloc reciprocates these prejudices. The phenomenon operates throughout the novel in the game that Conrad plays with his characters' perceptions of one another. They never envisage person or personality. Rather they project and retroject the illusions and delusions of their cultivated word-worlds (even like us ordinary mortals). Yet in the face-to-face verbal duels among the principals (Vladimir and Verloc, the Professor and Ossipon, the

Professor and the Chief Inspector, the Chief Inspector and the Assistant Superintendent, the Assistant Superintendent and the Great Personage, even Verloc and his wife) Conrad constantly emphasizes the gratuitous exercise of the visual faculty.

The man slowly turned his bloated and sodden face of many colours bristling with white hairs. His little red eyes glistened with moisture. His big lips had a violet tint. They remained closed. With the dirty back of his whip-hand he rubbed the stubble sprouting on his enormous chin. (SA, 135)

One of the many descriptions of the cabby during the brief interlude of the trip to the almshouse, this one allows Conrad to experiment in the color drawings so popular among the Victorians. Anyone acquainted with the three volumes of John Leech's *Pictures of Life and Character* (all extracted from illustrations in *Punch*) experiences the sense of a familiar *déja vu* in contemplating the verbal picture. However much Conrad tints his canvas, it still recalls the blubbery visages of Leech's favorite subjects. Obviously, Conrad delights more in his pictorial razzle-dazzle than in maintaining any sustained tempo of action. However, he deserves credit for his ingenuity in removing Winnie's mother from the scene in order to prepare for the great comic scene of Ossipon's belated romance with Mrs. Verloc.

A bush of crinkly yellow hair topped his red, freckled face, with a flattened nose and prominent mouth cast in the rough mould of the negro type. His almond-shaped eyes leered languidly over the high cheek bones. (SA, 48)

The ancestry of Ossipon, based upon his facial characteristics, betrays the stigma of promiscuous miscegenation. As to which racial feature predominates, take your pick. Whatever that happens to be, not the subtlest speculation promises a resolution of Conrad's intention, especially when Ossipon suddenly metamorphoses into a mythic lecher in the last chapter of the novel, "beloved of various humble women of these isles, Apollo-like in the sunniness of his hair" (SA, 251). The latter analogy, like the others of similar irrelevancy, merely calls attention to the swaggering nonsense of Conrad's figurative language. Like the hieroglyphic inscrutability of Ossipon's heredity, it dangles its brightness in a desert of associations. However, if Vladimir's assessment of the role of science in the Western world supplies a clue to the function of the caricature, then Conrad's metonymic tour de force sneers at the attempts of evolutionary theorists to establish the family tree of mankind.

Karl Yundt giggled grimly, with a faint black grimace of a toothless mouth. The terrorist, as he called himself, was old and bald, with a narrow, snow-white wisp of a goatee hanging limply from his chin. An

*extraordinary expression of underhand malevolence survived in his extin-
guished eyes. When he rose painfully the thrusting forward of a skinny
groping hand . . . suggested the effort of a moribund murderer summon-
ing all his remaining strength for a last stab. (SA, 47)*

The epithet "senile sensualist" (SA, 47) with its sib-ilant alliteration
inspires this grotesque. Conrad's coupling of similar nonsensical cacopho-
nies hints at the fabrication of a joke based less on physiological realities
than on humanity's gratuitous debasement of the goat, which, at least,
remains faithful to its own nature in its caprices of lust. The introduction
of imagery plundered from *The Ancient Mariner* occasions no surprise. It
surfaces in notes of similar clangor in *Lord Jim* and *Victory*, no doubt
salting whatever moral concerns hover in the wake of the respective
actions. Here "the last stab" evolves into a hilarious sexual parody, for
Yundt holds "a thick stick" (SA, 47) in one of his trembling hands. No
Freudian profundities, thankfully, reside in the description. Rather, in its
contrived exaggeration, it correlates with Conrad's handling of the gathering of the anarchists in Verloc's parlor. Snarling insults at one another like
bedlamites, the men engage in a logomachic farce in which their ideological and political principles explode in utterance — the inevitable fate of
windbags.

*[The Professor's] flat, large ears departed widely from the sides of his skull
. . . the dome of the forehead seemed to rest on the rim of the spectacles;
the flat cheeks, of a greasy, unhealthy complexion, were merely smudged
by the miserable poverty of a thin dark whisper. (SA, 62)*

What to leave in or what to leave out: the handbooks on the writing
of fiction never tackle that problem. Here Conrad shuns any description of
the nose or the hair on the head of the Professor, apparently too
preoccupied with the sleight-of-hand disposition of the domed forehead.
He models the face on the cut-out, pull-out pictorial playthings so popular
in the latter half of the nineteenth and early part of the twentieth century.
The Lilliputian anarchist, the only character in the novel with the ability
to act in accordance with his volition, towers above the other members of
the cabal in the courage of his madness, hardly deserving this blue-
beardish mutilation of human features. On the other hand, Conrad fits
him neatly into his gallery or menagerie of subhuman monsters.

COMMENT

THE TECHNIQUE OF THESE PEN PORTRAITS, APART FROM THE OBVIOUS
INFLUENCE OF THE ILLUSTRATORS OF THE DAY, REFLECTS CONRAD'S READING OF
FLAUBERT. THE GREAT ADVOCATE OF HATE OF THE MIDDLE CLASS AND EVEN OF
LITERATURE ITSELF, THE FRENCH NOVELIST, HIMSELF LOOKING BACK TO
RABELAIS, POURS HIS FLAYING SCORN ON HIS CHARACTERS IN *MADAME BOVARY*
BY CORRELATING SENSIBILITY WITH ANTHROPOMETRY (THE DIMENSIONS OF THE
BODY). LIMITING HIS LITERARY SCIENCE TO FATNESS AND THINNESS, HE TRACES

THESE CONDITIONS TO THE APPETITE, NOT FOR FOOD AND DRINK LIKE RABELAIS BUT RATHER FOR A STARVING OR FATTENING DIET OF CULTURAL STUPIDITIES. EMMA BOVARY, FOR EXAMPLE, EATS UP ROMANTIC BROMIDES SO VORACIOUSLY THAT SHE CONSTANTLY SUFFERS FROM BOTH MENTAL AND INTESTINAL CONSTIPATION (ALL CLEARLY GRAPHED IN HIS PUNS, WHICH, AMONG THE ENGLISH TRANSLATORS, ONLY ELEANOR M. AVELING ON OCCASIONS NOTES, QUITE CIRCUMSPECTLY). CONRAD EXPLOITS THE SAME METHOD. VERLOC AND MICHAELIS BALLOON OUT IN AN OBESITY DIRECTLY CONNECTED WITH THE COMPLACENCY OF THEIR RELISH FOR IDEOLOGICAL FORMULAS. GLUTTONOUSLY, THEY GOBBLE UP THE STALE OFFERINGS OF POLITICAL THEORIES THAT THEY FAIL TO DIGEST. CONVERSELY, YUNDT AND THE PROFESSOR STARVE THEMSELVES ON ABSTRACT NIHILISTIC PRINCIPLES WITHOUT ANY SUBSTANCE IN MEANING. ON THIS UNNUTRITIOUS FOOD OF THOUGHT THEY DEGENERATE INTO SCARECROW INTELLECTUALS. CONRAD TREATS ALL THE OTHER CHARACTERS IN MORE OR LESS THE SAME FASHION, ALWAYS TRANSLATING STATES OF MIND INTO DISORDERS OF GASTROLOGIA. EVEN THE ALWAYS KNEELING MRS. NEAL, THE DOMESTIC, AND THE HACKMAN CULTIVATE THEIR THIRST FOR SPIRITS ON THE PARCHED SENTIMENTALITIES OF THEIR IGNORANCE. ALMOST FIENDISHLY, CONRAD CONVERTS OSSIPON INTO THE ULTIMATE DUPE OF THE HUNGER FOR THE IMPOVERISHMENTS OF LANGUAGE. THE GENETIC MUTANT STUFFS HIS HEAD WITH JOURNALISTIC SWILL, AND, LIKE A SWINISH MELANCHOLIAC, WALLOWS IN ALCOHOLIC REMORSE: "HE COULD NEITHER THINK, WORK, SLEEP, NOR EAT. BUT HE WAS BEGINNING TO DRINK WITH PLEASURE, WITH ANTICIPATION, WITH HOPE" (SA, 252).

VI. HUMPTY-DUMPTY AMONG THE SPRATS

Vast in bulk and stature, with a long white face, which, broadened at the base by a big double chin, appeared egg-shaped in the fringe of thin grayish whisker, the great personage seemed an expanding man. Unfortunate from a tailoring point of view, the crossfolds in the middle of a buttoned black coat added to the impression, as if the fastenings of the garment were tried to the utmost. (SA, 118)

Alice's first glimpse of Humpty-Dumpty, "the egg only got larger and larger," recapitulates the Assistant Commissioner's impression of the Secretary of State, the proponent for the nationalization of English fisheries.[2] By the same token, Alice's bewilderment at the girth of Humpty-Dumpty inspires Conrad's transformation of the figure into two eggs, the one balanced on top of the other—something possible only behind the looking-glass of fiction. His parody of the nursery rhyme accommodates the situation at hand, for the riddle ("Who is it?") duplicates the Assistant Commissioner's search for the perpetrator of the plan to destroy the Greenwich Meridian Observatory. This sacred edifice of mankind's arbitrary manipulation of time (a reverberation of Humpty-Dumpty's autocratic linguistic practices) emerges in the surrogate of the clock in the great man's office, and then subtly develops into a mockery of the bureaucratic obsession with busyness (the consumption of time, like that of food, reflecting another misrepresentation of hunger). Conrad also introduces Alice's makeshift simile for Humpty-Dumpty's posture, "with his legs crossed like a Turk" (AA, 261), into the dialogue between the Assistant Commissioner and the Secretary of State, adapted of course to suit the circumstances: " 'A Turk would have more decency' " (SA, 120). The feedback loop of the simile warrants a comment here. Probably originating in *The Arabian Nights*, it crops up in Charlotte Bronte's *Jane Eyre*, not surprisingly with the explicit references to the Eastern tales. Lewis Carroll, in turn, plagiarizes the figure verbatim, no doubt fascinated by the heroine's predilection for sitting in a window-seat behind a curtain and dreaming up her thousand-and-one melodramas. It enters *The Secret Agent* incognito, except for the reader thoroughly schooled in the treacheries of Humpty-Dumptyism.

The conference between the officials unfolds in an atmosphere of utter absurdity, for Conrad takes Alice's image of the "stuffed figure" of Humpty-Dumpty for his model of a stuffed shirt, namely, the Secretary, the personification of princely pride (AA, 261). This sin, of course, lies allegorically behind the fall of Humpty-Dumpty and other equally celebrated figures of the runes of Christianity. Though the prototype of vainglory, Humpty-Dumpty sitting hardly offers any competition in the demonstration of this conceit to the Commissioner standing on a rug (perhaps another resonance of *The Arabian Nights*). At any rate, in a series of cartoon caricatures Conrad puts the latter through a burlesque routine. In context the situation merely extends the pattern of dialogic agons that cohere the slender plot. As always, either social, political, or familial rank determines the victor in these wordbaths, at least to the satisfaction of the superior. But regardless of the verbalized communication between and among the characters, its ultimate meaning or meaninglessness undergoes mediation in Conrad's enveloping descriptions of some bodily idiosyncrasy, in this case the Secretary's facial expressions. The first one establishes the imbalance of authority with the implicit threat that failure in the Assistant Commissioner's counterplot against Verloc carries the stigma of disgrace: "From the head, set upward on a thick neck, the eyes, with puffy lower lids, stared with a haughty droop on each side of a hooked, aggressive nose, nobly salient in the vast pale circumference of the face" (SA, 118). Typically, in all such exercises of grotesquerie Conrad drops an oxymoron, "nobly salient," that comically boomerangs against the preceding thrust of statement. Improvising another nonsense anatomical analysis, Conrad endows the nose with the faculty of sight, however tentatively, and then homologizes its nasal modulation of the voice with a nonexistent pipe in an organ: "Sir Ethelred opened a wide mouth, like a cavern, into which the hooked nose seemed anxious to peer; there came from it a subdued rolling sound, as from a distant organ with the scornful indignation stop" (SA, 120). The last prepositional phrase outrageously posits the presence of such a stop in all organs, the "the" instead of an "a" throwing a tremendous burden on a would-be critic of Conrad's rhetoric. Either the editors of the typescript or its typesetters inherit the blame for this grammar, though perhaps neither group of workmen, from the beginning to the end of the novel, stood willing to confess their inability to cope with the monstrous explosions of its dyspeptic prose. The next grimace evolves into a revolutionary subversion of the function of metaphor: "The haughty drooping glance struck crushingly the carpet at the Assistant Commissioner's feet" (SA, 120–21). This relentless assault on figurative language illustrates Conrad's practice of a renovated Humpty-Dumptyism. If not, then no interpreter of *The Secret Agent*, regardless of his approach, dares talk about the substance of the dialogue without taking into consideration its framework of qualifying horseplay. Contrary to this injunction, almost all critics choose to ride their hobbyhorses around this problem.

As if setting up the Commissioner for a mortifying pratfall from pride, Conrad describes a posture that likewise humbles the imagination of the reader or, at least, arouses serious questions about the content of truth in fiction (and of fiction in criticism): "In order to raise his drooping glance to the speaker's face, the personage on the hearthrug had gradually tilted his head farther back, which gave him an aspect of extraordinary haughtiness" (SA, 123). Needless to say, it also gives him the aspect of a pose that perfectly fits into a music-hall routine. One way or the other, it baffles visualization. And when Conrad adds another few degrees to this arc, "and tilting back his head, looked steadily at him" (SA, 124), the suspense mounts, for now the sacred laws of physics come under the insidious attack of the verities of fiction. As they do, it behooves the reader to thank Coleridge for the formulation of the concept, the suspension of disbelief. Turning the screw one more time, Conrad leaves the Secretary suspended in the position of a clown in a circus: "The Personage had tilted his head so far back that, in order to keep the Assistant Commissioner under his observation, he had to nearly close his eyes" (SA, 124). Throughout this performance the Assistant Commissioner never cracks a smile or evinces any astonishment, apparently glutted by the ceaseless follies of vanity. Climactically, Conrad reduces the conference to a cynical judgment on Western man's servitude to his own ingenuity, implying that the destruction of the Greenwich Meridian Observatory offers civilization its only hope of liberation from the hounding abstraction of time: "[The Secretary] turned his big head slowly, and over his shoulder gave a haughty, oblique stare to the ponderous marble timepiece with the sly, feeble tick" (SA, 124). How he manages to synchronize this movement while still in his former backward position remains one of the minor mysteries of *The Secret Agent*. Or perhaps like Humpty-Dumpty, Conrad disdains to reveal the subjective hanky-panky behind these corporeal acrobatics.

The Assistant Commissioner's chat with the great man's aide directly links up with the Humpty-Dumpty episode in *Through the Looking-Glass*. Responding to Toodle's remark, " 'He does it all himself. Seems unable to trust anyone with these Fisheries' " (SA, 125), the police official via Conrad's continuing skullduggery seines a red herring: " 'And yet he's given a whole half hour to the consideration of my small sprat' " (SA, 125–26). "Toodles," a colloquialism for "twaddle" or "nonsense," reverberates the quotation from "Jabberwocky" (AA, 270), and the small herring converts the Assistant Commissioner into a surrogate of the messenger in Humpty-Dumpty's poem on the fish, at the same time echoing the absurd haughtiness of the Secretary:

> But he was very stiff and proud:
> He said: "You needn't shout so loud!"
>
> He was very proud and stiff:
> . . . . (AA, 275)

No one-to-one relationship of details prevails in this parody. As the enveloping language of gesture indicates, Conrad merely invents a situation that corresponds to Alice's meeting with Humpty-Dumpty. Though a ridiculous pastiche, it evolves into the controlling scene of the novel — the revelation of the anarchy of fiction. Elevating Humpty-Dumpty into the muse of inspiration, Conrad violates every rule of conventional narration, like Henry James fully aware that the artist writes for himself and to himself. Whatever amusement or edification the reader derives from the verbalization of imaginary experience depends upon the conditioning of his sensibility. He never reads the words upon a page; rather he interpolates them in the looking glass of his word-world as arbitrarily as Humpty-Dumpty.

THE LAST WORD BY JOSEPH CONRAD: ON THE FICTIONS OF HUMAN THOUGHT

Life knows us not/and we do not know life — we don't know even our own thoughts. Half the words we use have no meaning whatever and of the other half each man understands each word after the fashion of his own folly and conceit. Faith is a myth and beliefs shift like mists on the shore; thoughts vanish; words, once pronounced, die; and the memory of yesterday is as shadowy as the hope of tomorrow.[3]

THE LAST LAST WORD

TURNING LANGUAGE AGAINST LANGUAGE, CONRAD EMPTIES FICTION (AND LIFE) OF INTELLECTUAL MEANING. HIS SEMIOTIC VEHICLES — CORPOREAL, SARTORIAL, CARICATURAL, TROPOLOGICAL, AND THINGUMBOLIC — OPERATE INDEPENDENT OF ONE ANOTHER AND, ADAMANTLY, RESIST CONNECTION WITH

THE ACTION LINE OF THE NOVEL, THE IMAGINARY PATTERN OF A SEGMENT OF HISTORICAL EXISTENCE. AS THEY ENVELOP THE INTERPRETATIONS OF EXPERIENCE BY THE CHARACTERS AND BY CONRAD'S BROMIDIC NARRATOR, THEY CONFIRM THE SUBSTANCE OF THE LETTER TO GRAHAM. EVERYONE LIVES IN THE CAGE OF HIS OWN WORD-WORLD, BARRED FROM THE UNDERSTANDING OF HIS THOUGHT AND THE THOUGHTS OF OTHERS BY THE CONCEIT AND DECEIT OF PRECONCEPTION. IN THIS PERSPECTIVE LINGUISTIC USAGE EXCEEDS THE AUTOCRATIC CONSTRAINTS THAT HUMPTY-DUMPTY IMPOSES UPON SPEECH. HE KNOWS WHAT HE INTENDS A WORD TO MEAN. CONRAD'S CHARACTERS NEVER DO BECAUSE THE AFFECT CONTENT OF THEIR RHETORIC FALLS OUT OF THE PROVINCE OF DICTIONARY DEFINITION. SUCH SUBJECTIVITY DEFIES CODING, LEAVING MAN IN PRECISELY THE CONDITION OF THE LETTER — LOST IN THE LABYRINTHS OF GLOSSOLALIA.

Notes

1. Joseph Conrad, *The Secret Agent* (New York: Doubleday, Anchor Books, 1953), p. 25. All subsequent references to this work, abbreviated SA, are cited in the text.

2. Lewis Carroll, *The Annotated Alice* (New York: Crown, 1960), p. 261. Subsequent references to this work, abbreviated AA, are cited in the text.

3. Joseph Conrad, *Letters to R. B. Cunninghame Graham*, ed. C. T. Watts, (Cambridge: Cambridge University Press, 1969), p. 65.

INDEX